Jamaican Leaders

OUT OF MANY, ONE PEOPLE

by WENDELL BELL

Jamaican Leaders

POLITICAL ATTITUDES IN A NEW NATION

UNIVERSITY OF CALIFORNIA PRESS

Berkeley and Los Angeles, 1964

UNIVERSITY OF CALIFORNIA PRESS
BERKELEY AND LOS ANGELES, CALIFORNIA
CAMBRIDGE UNIVERSITY PRESS, LONDON, ENGLAND
© 1964 BY THE REGENTS OF THE UNIVERSITY OF CALIFORNIA
LIBRARY OF CONGRESS CATALOG CARD NUMBER: 64-19447
PRINTED IN THE UNITED STATES OF AMERICA

To LORA-LEE, SHARON,
and DAVID

PREFACE

ALTHOUGH ITS ROOTS can be traced deep into the past, nationalism, as we know it today, did not emerge until the middle of the eighteenth century when it appeared in Northwestern Europe and its American settlements. During the nineteenth century, it became a general movement throughout Europe. However, if one considers the dominance and geographical spread of political organizations based upon the priority of the nation-state, the "age of nationalism" has not reached fruition until now, during the second half of the twentieth century. The final stages of the global spread of nationalism began at the end of World War II with the dismantlement of the empires of European nations and the simultaneous creation of new and independent nation-states out of the former colonial areas, a process that is just now nearing completion. Today, on every continent, the characteristic form of political organization is the nation-state.

This book constitutes a case study in the sociology of nationhood. It is about one new nation, the island of Jamaica in the Caribbean Sea, during the final stages of its transition from colonial dependence to full political independence, and it focuses on the exploration and discovery of the causes of nationalism, those factors that produce nationalist attitudes, that underlie a person's desire and drive for political independence, and those that in others result conversely in preferences for colonial status and opposition to the formation of the new independent nation-state.

Additionally, this is a study of attitudes toward some of the important decisions that any new nation must make—or have made for it. Social scientists are often so busy describing and understanding the present and the past that they neglect the possibilities for the future. They describe, among other things, existing and once-existing social structures, past and present forms of government, contemporary external political alignments and their histories—often highlighting present limitations for future developments, if future change is considered at all. But today more than ever before the conscious, volitional aspects of political, economic, and social life are obvious and important, and they lead men to try still harder to bend the future to their collective will. Perhaps in the new nations more than anywhere else, despite the practical difficulties they face, the future is something to be selected from a number of possibilities; the future is planned and controlled as far as possible. Directed change is the order of the day, although it is not always accomplished with complete success nor without unanticipated consequences. Thus, my concerns in this book include an interest in certain ideological commitments that shape one's image of the future, and that determine the most desirable future of the many that may be possible.

Thus, in addition to asking about the present and past nature of Jamaican polity, economy, and society, I have asked about its future: "Should Jamaica be politically independent?" "What kind of social structure should Jamaica have?" "Should Jamaica have a democratic political system?" "What should Jamaica's social and cultural history be?" "What should Jamaica's global alignments be?" A sense of *becoming* may be more appropriate to a developing nation than a sense of *being,* and I have tried to convey it.

The answers to the "should" in each of the above questions, however, were not found by appealing to my personal values; rather they were constructed from my analysis of data describing Jamaican people and society, especially from a survey of attitudes of Jamaican leaders. As might be expected, unanimity of opinion concerning answers to the "big decisions of nationhood" was not always found among Jamaican leaders. In fact, differences in such opinions among elites reflected basic cleavages in Jamaican society, represented sharp conflicts concerning different images of Jamaica's future, and revealed one aspect of the internal struggle to control that future. Thus, this is also a study of elites, primarily of their attitudes, but also of how they changed in social composition and power as a result of the political transition to nationhood.

Nationalism is a subject about which much has been written. But some writers have been more nationalists (or antinationalists) than scholars and their works are often unreliable, biased, and propagandistic. Some historians and others have provided precise, scholarly studies that have given us brilliant insights, much organized data, and useful interpretations, but there are limits to the historical reconstruction of certain aspects of social situations, and many important questions are left unanswered. In the past, writers who made on-the-spot observations were not trained social scientists, empirical social research having become an important part of scholarship only in recent years. Thus, using today's emergent nations as laboratories for the study of nationalism, we can in some sense transcend time and space and bring modern methods of empirical social research to bear on some questions that men have been asking since before the French Revolution. By so doing, we learn not only about the new nations, but also gain insights about the old; and we understand more about the process of nationalism itself, a phenomenon that must be ranked with urbanization and technological change in transforming and shaping the lives of modern men. This book is part of the growing, but still short, list of works that apply methods of modern social research to the study of the creation of new nations.

One of the strengths of this book, compared to most other studies of nationalism, is that it is based upon the systematic collection, analysis, and presentation of a questionnaire survey (among the first of its kind ever carried out in Jamaica) and other data with explicit statements of all procedures used. This is, of course, standard practice in modern social research. It permits the reader to evaluate the validity of my data, to assess my interpretations of them, and—if he feels so inclined—to reinterpret them for himself. Such frankness is a strength to be sure, but it also reveals—even underscores—the weaknesses. The questionnaire survey reported here, which was completed in 1958, resulted in a disappointingly low response rate; the meaning I attach to the answers to some questions may be debatable; in the analysis, confounding variables often cannot be controlled; the discrepancy between the concrete data and the general abstractions they are supposed to represent is too often glaringly clear—quite apart from the question of alternative meanings; the data are uneven, covering some topics less well than others; and my interpretations are for the most part *ex post facto,* representing plausible and reasonable explanations that appear consistent with the data but that were formulated after I had begun the analysis of the data. Thus, I cannot claim, however much I wish I could, that this book contains a set of propositions that were formulated prior to the data collection and verified by the data analysis. Instead the conclusions of the questionnaire survey are hypotheses, although they are my best estimates of the truth.

Also, they are in my opinion *the* best estimates available at the present time. My interpretations have been influenced by repeated discussions with informants and lengthy interviews with many persons, including Jamaican leaders (both with respondents and nonrespondents to the questionnaires). These discussions and interviews took place in Jamaica during 1956, 1958, 1960, 1961, and 1962, and in the more recent years sometimes included a discussion of the results of the questionnaire survey itself. Additionally, the findings of this book are giving direction to research now in progress, not just in Jamaica but in other West Indian territories as well, and preliminary findings from these new studies generally support the conclusions which I reach here. Thus, I am convinced that with few exceptions the questionnaire data reported here accurately represent the beliefs and attitudes of Jamaican leaders, and that my interpretations of them are substantially correct. Nonetheless, since this book does not deal with many aspects of nationalism, it must be regarded as only one step—a preliminary and exploratory one at that—toward a fuller and more certain understanding of the rise of nationalism in Jamaica.

Los Angeles, California   WENDELL BELL
February 6, 1963

ACKNOWLEDGMENTS

THE MAJOR FINANCIAL support for this study came from the Social Science Research Council, New York City, and I wish to thank them for awarding me a Faculty Research Fellowship which I held half-time during 1956–59. For grants-in-aid at different times, I am also indebted to the Penrose Fund, American Philosophical Society, Philadelphia; the Graduate School, Northwestern University, Evanston, Illinois; the Research Institute for the Study of Man, New York City; and the Research Committee, University of California, Los Angeles.

Without the good offices of Dr. H. D. Huggins, Director of the Institute of Social and Economic Research, University of the West Indies, Mona, Jamaica, this research would have been much more difficult, if not impossible, to carry out and our field trips would not have been the pleasant and enjoyable experiences they turned out to be. I am grateful to Dr. Huggins and members of his staff—especially Lloyd Braithwaite, George E. Cumper, David T. Edwards, and M. G. Smith (now at UCLA)—for encouragement, coöperation, general assistance, and intellectual guidance that far exceeded the usual standards of academic courtesy. Other persons at the University of the West Indies were very helpful also, including the Registrar, Dr. Hugh W. Springer, and the present Vice-Chancellor, Dr. Philip M. Sherlock.

During various phases of the research, I was assisted by a number of persons whose efforts have contributed to this book. I thank Lora-Lee Bell, Hyacinth M. Cummins, Donna Gold, Charles C. Moskos, Jr., Andrew P. Phillips, Harry E. Ransford, and Emily Smith Reed.

Since 1960, I have been Director of a large-scale study of elites and nationalism in the West Indies financed by a grant from the Carnegie Corporation of New York. This grant made it possible for me to continue research in Jamaica, and to initiate it elsewhere in the West Indies, and has helped me to complete the research reported here. Additionally, under the Carnegie grant, I led a research team of UCLA graduate students to the

West Indies in 1961–1962 where we did field work in Antigua, Barbados, British Guiana, Dominica, Grenada, Jamaica, and Trinidad. Working with these students as they designed and carried out their research, I learned a great deal and inevitably I have been influenced by them. My intellectual debt to James T. Duke, James A. Mau, Charles C. Moskos, Jr., Andrew P. Phillips, and Ivar Oxaal is hereby gratefully acknowledged.

To Professors Scott Greer and Richard C. Snyder, with whom I discussed my work many times, I owe thanks for numerous helpful suggestions. Also, three of my former teachers should be mentioned for I am obliged to them, above all others, for my general intellectual interests out of which this book has developed. They are Professors Earl Lyon, Leonard Broom, and Eshref Shevky.

Finally, I thank the many Jamaican leaders who coöperated in the survey and who often gave me many hours of their time despite their busy schedules. I am especially indebted to Vernon L. Arnett, member of the new Parliament of Jamaica.

Earlier versions of several of the chapters presented here have been published before. I thank the following publishers and editors for their permission to rewrite and reprint these materials in this book:

"Attitudes of Elites Toward Independence in a New Nation," in Raymond J. Murphy and E. Gartley Jaco (editors), *Social Change: A Reader in Theory and Research,* New York: Thomas Y. Crowell Co., 1964.

"Attitudes of Jamaican Elites Toward the West Indies Federation," in *Annals of the New York Academy of Sciences,* 83 (January 18, 1960), pp. 862–879.

"Equality and Attitudes of Elites in Jamaica," *Social and Economic Studies,* 11 (December, 1962), pp. 409–432.

"Images of the United States and the Soviet Union Held by Jamaican Elite Groups," *World Politics,* 12 (January, 1960), pp. 225–248.

Additional acknowledgments of quoted materials are made elsewhere throughout the book.

CONTENTS

West Indies

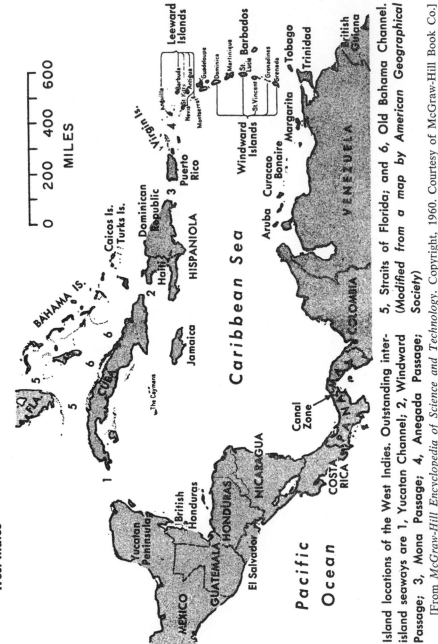

Island locations of the West Indies. Outstanding inter-island seaways are 1, Yucatan Channel; 2, Windward Passage; 3, Mona Passage; 4, Anegada Passage; 5, Straits of Florida; and 6, Old Bahama Channel. (Modified from a map by American Geographical Society)

[From *McGraw-Hill Encyclopedia of Science and Technology*. Copyright, 1960. Courtesy of McGraw-Hill Book Co.]

Chapter I

Jamaica: Past and Present

ON AUGUST 6, 1962, Jamaica shook off the last remnants of colonial dependence and donned the new garb of a politically independent nation-state within the British Commonwealth of nations, becoming the first new nation in the western hemisphere since Panama in 1903. Jamaica is a small country of only 1.6 million people fairly densely settled on a mountainous island about 146 miles long and at most 50 miles across. It is located in the Caribbean Sea just 100 miles west of the dictatorial and stagnant Republic of Haiti and 90 miles south of Communist Cuba. Jamaica faced independence with high hopes for a better life—for economic development, distributional and social reforms, and other fruits of the new freedom. But Jamaica also faced independence with realistic appraisals of the difficulties standing in the way of progress, difficulties inherent in a social structure that had developed through long years of slavery and colonial neglect. Economic deprivation, social inequality, and political dependence made up the heritage of the Jamaican people, but so did the struggle for economic progress, equality, and freedom.

Discovery

Columbus landed on Jamaica on May 5, 1494, during his second voyage to America. He found it inhabited by sixty to seventy-five thousand people of the polished stone-age period—although they were people whose ceramics were more highly developed than the polished stone-age people of the Old World. They were the Tainos, a branch of the Arawaks. Fragmentary evidence reveals that they were apparently somewhat less advanced than were the Arawaks in the other islands of the Greater Antilles, and that they had a small-scale society based on ascriptive relations defined largely

1

by age and sex differences, kinship connections, and village communities. They had the dibble with hard-burnt point and stone axes for clearing the soil. They cultivated a variety of plants, and supplemented their dibble-agriculture by some hunting, fishing, and gathering. At the head of their political organizations were hereditary town-chiefs or caciques who may have been loosely integrated on a larger scale and may have owed allegiance to an over-cacique or king. In addition to political functions, the caciques performed religious and economic functions as well. Below the caciques was a class of persons who fulfilled certain directive functions in the community, a kind of nobility who had the right to vote and to take part in the town council. Then came the common people who apparently had no say in the government, and at the lowest level were the *naborias,* who constituted a servant class whose work assignments were usually confined to the limits of the towns. There was no writing and little specialized knowledge, myths and geneologies being transmitted orally. Their religion included ancestor worship and belief in local spirits, magic, and witchcraft.[1]

The Arawaks of Jamaica, as elsewhere in the Greater Antilles, perished under the rule of the Spanish, were transported elsewhere, or fled in their canoes to Yucatan. A few members of the indigenous population must have been absorbed into the groups of African slaves who escaped from the Spanish and who were known as Maroons, after the mountains in which they lived. Escape to join them represented a risky alternative to slavery both under the Spanish and British. When the latter occupied Jamaica, the slaves of the Spanish joined with the Maroons in the mountains, and the Maroons still exist in Jamaica as identifiable social groups claiming a small part of their descendance from the Arawaks.

The Spanish Period, 1509–1655

The colonization of Jamaica began in 1509. Diego Columbus, who was then Governor General of Hispaniola, had power over adjacent territory and sent Juan de Esquivel with seventy men to establish a town called Sevilla Nueva on the northern coast of Jamaica. The Arawaks were set to digging mines for gold, but only a small amount of gold was ever obtained from Jamaica, and the idea was given up. Instead, Jamaica became an agricultural and grazing country, and herds of horses, cattle, and hogs were developed in a relatively short time.

Sevilla Nueva was left in 1534, and a new town and capital was founded on the south side of the island called St. Jago de la Vega; this the English were later to rename "Spanish Town," a name it retains today.

By about 1545, the Caribbean islands lost much of their original importance for Spain. On the mainland the richest native civilizations had been conquered and the stream of wealth from them to Spain had begun. A few ports in the islands remained of some importance as places where Spanish shipping congregated, such as Havana, Santo Domingo, Puerto Bello, Nombre de Dios, Cartagena, and Santa Marta, but on the whole ". . . the islands themselves were of slight and decreasing interest to the Spanish government and to colonists." [2]

Many of the colonists on the islands left for the mainland to take part in the looting of Mexico and Peru. The islands were generally unpopular compared to the mainland at this time, and Jamaica was additionally unpopular due to the fact that in 1536 it had been given to Don Luis, the grandson of Columbus, as his personal estate. He was to govern it as a fief under the Crown, and he and his heirs were to have the title of Marquis of Jamaica in addition to the title of Duke of Veragua (a province of Panama). However, Don Luis never came to Jamaica, nor did any of his successors, although he and his successors received small revenues from customs duties. "This state of affairs made Jamaica the least attractive place in the region for the colonists. They could not feel that their holdings were secure. Who could tell when some Columbus would appear and reduce them all to the level of serfs? Consequently Jamaica languished." [3]

There were a few planters and herders. Cassava bread was exported; sugar cane was introduced; tobacco, cotton, citrus, and pineapple were cultivated; and pimento, a spice unknown elsewhere, grew wild. There were feuds between the clergy and the officials, and occasional piratical raids by the French, English, and Dutch. However, Jamaica was not prosperous enough to be very tempting, although ". . . it lay close to the routes followed by the Spanish treasure ships, and the bays on its neglected northern coast were ideal lurking places for marauders." [4] The white population probably never reached five thousand persons.

By 1502 the first African slaves were brought into the Caribbean, and by 1506 there were many Negroes working the mines of Hispaniola. In Jamaica, Esquivel was allowed on his appointment in 1509 to import three Negro slaves into the island with the proviso that they had to be Christians. They arrived sometime before 1517, at which time there were Negroes in Puerto Rico, Cuba, and in the first mainland settlements of Darien as well. In 1510 royal orders were issued to the *Casa de Contratación* for shipment of 250 Negroes to be sold to the colonists of Hispaniola for work in the gold mines. A direct and organized trade was opened between Africa and the West Indies in 1518 when King Charles gave the privilege of importation of slaves to a favorite who disposed of the licenses for the highest prices he could get. "The grant conferred the sole right of transporting negroes to the West Indies up to the number of 4000 without paying any duty or tax." [5] Thus began the flow of the enslaved black men from Africa into the new world which was to continue for nearly 370 years until the abolition of slavery in Brazil, and which was to have profound effects upon Jamaica and the other new societies that were to emerge there.

The sporadic settlement of Jamaica during the Spanish period called for relatively few slaves, yet by 1611 about 44 per cent of the population were of African origin while the Arawaks had been reduced to less than 5 per cent. The population in 1611 as given by Cundall and Pietersz [6] is as follows:

Adult Spaniards	523
Children	173
Free Negroes	107
Native Indians	74
Slaves	558
Foreigners	75
TOTAL POPULATION	1,510

The extermination of the Indians in the West Indies generally, as well as in Jamaica, was by this time far along in spite of the fact that there had been considerable opposition to the gross mistreatment of the Indians both from Church and state. As early as 1494, the Queen had commissioned a committee of jurists and theologians to determine if the Indians could or should be reduced to slavery, reflecting the early Spanish concern with the legal problems of justice and Christian principles as they applied or didn't apply to the Indians. The committee declared them free, but this was to be only a single occurrence in a long-lasting debate. The debate centered on the status and rights of this new species of man—if in fact the Indians really were men and not some sort of inferior animal as some persons claimed. Actual and virtual slavery of the Indians was the rule in the new world. The rights of the Spanish to continue the exploitation of the Indians were upheld in the Laws of Burgos in 1512, although the humane treatment of the Indians with respect to housing, food, religious instruction, and so on, was also enunciated. Later, the Dominican missionary and converted conqueror and new world settler, Las Casas, was appointed Protector of the Indians. He continued his fight for Indian rights, which he had begun by enumerating the horrifying atrocities committed by the Spaniards in their dealings with the Indians while he was in Hispaniola. Twenty-three of the fifty-four articles in the New Laws of 1542 dealt with the status and treatment of the Indians. Their status as free persons was clearly specified and Indian slavery was abolished. However, these laws were seldom properly enforced and were in part suspended so that a modified version of the *encomienda* system continued. Eventually, efforts to protect the Indian had some effect on the mainland, but they were too late to save the Indian in Jamaica and elsewhere in the West Indies.[7]

Those persons fighting for Indian liberty generally saw nothing inconsistent in Negro slavery.

. . . to the sixteenth-century mind the two cases were in all respects widely different. The objections to the enslavement of Indians were primarily on legal grounds. The Indians were the subjects of the King of Castile and were entitled to protection. Africans, on the other hand, were the subjects of independent kings. Europeans visited West Africa as traders, not as overlords. If the local rulers made war among themselves and sold their prisoners to slave dealers, that was not the fault of the King of Spain. The enslavement of prisoners of war was a normal proceeding in most parts of the world. In the Moorish wars and the constant fighting against the corsair towns on the Barbary coast prisoners were regularly enslaved on both sides, and all the naval powers of the Mediterranean employed slaves to row their galleys. . . . The slave trade was carried on under Crown license, and although some Dominicans had misgivings about it there was no serious opposition from missionaries in general. . . .[8]

Little remains today of the 146 years of Spanish rule in Jamaica. A few sites and decaying buildings are left; probably none of Jamaica's present population can trace its ancestry to the pre-1655 population, despite the fanciful claims of the Maroons. Linguistically, place names have remained; ". . . headlands, bays, rivers, mountains and the *hatos* are through their names Jamaica's strongest link with its Spanish past. Many of the mileposts on the Moneague road still give the distance to *St. Jago de la Vega*. . . ."[9] In addition, there are a few everyday terms that are left from the Spanish period, although most of the Spanish terms in present day use have been brought back from Cuba and Panama by migrant laborers during the last eighty years.

English Rule and Tutelage, 1655–1962

The English captured Jamaica in May, 1655. It was a military conquest to be sure, but in the nature of a consolation prize after General Venables and Admiral Penn bungled their attempt to take Hispaniola from the Spanish. When the English had occupied Spanish Town, the Spanish removed their women and children to the north side of Jamaica and from there to Cuba. The able-bodied men and many of their Negro slaves stayed to carry on what perhaps is most accurately described as guerilla warfare against the English. During 1658, the English finally defeated the Spanish guerillas and captured the whole of Jamaica, but their hold over the island was precarious for many decades of conflict, and the Maroons and their descendants troubled the English for the next two hundred years.

PEOPLE AND SOCIETY.—From Barbados and the Leewards in the Eastern Caribbean some whites, probably mostly Irishmen and west-of-England men, came to Jamaica. They were joined by ". . . a small but steady stream of indentured servants, mainly from the west of England and London; reprieved felons and political prisoners from England, and a few independent planter and merchant adventurers from both England and North America." [10] Later, in addition to English, Irish, and others, the population of Jamaica gained Welsh, Scottish, French, Portuguese, German, East Indian, Chinese, and Lebanese immigrants. But the total numbers of all these groups were small compared to the number of slaves brought to Jamaica across the Atlantic from Africa. For it was Africans who for the most part supplied the labor for the labor-intensive production of sugar in Jamaica. One can almost say that the people of Jamaica were imported from Africa, although the dominant ideas and institutions came from England.

From 1655 to 1808, between 736,000 and 759,000 slaves from Africa were imported into Jamaica in excess of those exported. They came from Senegambia and Sierra Leone, the Windward Coast, the Gold Coast, and Wydah; from the Bight of Benin, the Congo, and Angola; from Bonny and the Calabars, with slaves from the Gold Coast overrepresented because of the preference for them in Jamaica.[11]

From as far north as the Senegal River, just north of Cape Verde, to the Congo River country, six degrees south of the equator, the slave-traders from England, France, Holland, Portugal, North America, and even Sweden, Denmark, and Brandenburg plied their trade. From the African traders, the Europeans got slaves, ivory, gold, dye woods, wax, and provisions for the middle passage such as wood, water, rice, fowls, goats, hogs, Indian wheat, yams, bananas, and plantain. A variety of European goods was traded in return. For example, an English slaver out of London, Bristol, or Liverpool might bring goods from Manchester, Yorkshire, Birmingham, Sheffield, and elsewhere. Woolen and cotton goods, gunpowder, bars of iron, basins and tankards, muskets, hatchets, cutlasses, knives, pistols, beads and other trinkets made up their cargoes. In Jamaica and elsewhere in the new world, the slaves were sold, and sugar, rum, and spice were bought for shipping back to London, Bristol, or Liverpool, where the triangular route from Europe to Africa to America to Europe was completed. As is well known, the trade and the wealth from the new world were important to the economies of the European nations, and in England, for example, King Charles II at an early period in the trade had ordered the minting of a new gold coin, equal to twenty-one shillings, to be called a *guinea* in honor of the lucrative trade with the Guinea Coast. The African slave trade and the wealth of the West Indies itself, which was largely the product of African labor, were among the financial supports of the British Empire and the sources of capital that financed the industrial revolution in England. Jamaica was an important part of this trade and wealth.[12]

By 1673, black and brown persons constituted over half of the 17,200 people of Jamaica, and by 1696 they accounted for more than 80 per cent of nearly 50,000 (see Table 1). The numerically small, but socially, politically, and economically dominant, whites were alarmed about the small proportion of whites to Negro slaves, and the Jamaican Assembly in 1703 passed an act setting the proportion of white to Negro labor to be followed by employers under penalty of fine. Additional acts were passed in 1736, 1738, 1743, and 1749 to stimulate the immigration of whites, but none was very effective. There were relatively small numbers of migrants from Ireland, and larger numbers from Scotland. Later attempts to stimulate the immigration of white labor also were generally unsuccessful. Three shiploads of German peasants and artisans arrived in 1835. Some stayed, but those who could afford to left for the United States when they learned what work was expected of them in Jamaica. Probably, hardly more than four thousand white indentured laborers came to Jamaica as a result of these schemes.

European sailors and soldiers and their children have made up a small part of the Jamaican population. Lawyers, doctors, and members of the clergy have also contributed a small, but steady, stream of white immigrants to the island. In 1792, a number of Frenchmen arrived in the island from Haiti in order to escape the consequences of the revolutionary war there; a small number of loyalists apparently arrived from the North American colonies during the American Revolutionary War; and a few Portuguese peasants arrived just after emancipation.

In the latter half of the nineteenth and the first half of the twentieth centuries, small numbers of whites, mostly from the British Isles or Canada or the United States, came to Jamaica. Many were in government service, with the army, or with foreign-owned business concerns as representatives, managers, or technical personnel.

But the white immigrants were more than offset by the drain of whites off the island. There was no absolute increase in the number of

TABLE 1. *Percentage Distribution of the Population of Jamaica by Race, 1673–1960* *

Year	Black and Colored		White	Chinese †	East Indian †	Others	Total no. (in 000's)
1673	55		45	—	—	—	17.2
1696	84		21	—	—	—	(47.4) ‡
1736	85		8	—	—	—	(94.2)
1775	95		6	—	—	—	(209.6)
1788	88		6	—	—	—	(291.4)
1793	90		10	—	—	—	291.4
	Black	*Colored*					
1844	77.7	18.1	4.2	—	—	—	377.4
1861	78.5	18.4	3.1	—	—	−0.1	441.3
1871	77.6	19.8	2.6	—	—	—	506.2
1881	76.5	18.9	2.4	−0.1	1.9	0.2	580.8
1891	76.4	19.1	2.3	0.1	1.6	0.6	639.5
1911	75.8	19.6	1.9	0.3	2.1	0.3	831.4
1921	77.0	18.3	1.7	0.4	2.2	0.4	858.1
1943	78.1	17.5	1.1	1.0	2.1	0.2	1,237.1
1960	76.8	14.6	0.9	1.2	3.4	3.1	1,609.8

* The percentages given from 1673 through 1793 are from data compiled by Leonard Broom, "The Social Differentiation of Jamaica," *American Sociological Review,* 19 (April, 1954), p. 116; those given from 1844 through 1943 are from George W. Roberts, *The Population of Jamaica,* Cambridge: University Press, 1957, p. 65; those given for 1960 are from *West Indies Population Census,* 1960 (provisional), Bulletin No. 20 (Jamaica), Kingston, Jamaica, W.I.: Department of Statistics, 1962, p. 1.

† In 1943 and 1960 the Afro-Chinese and the Afro–East Indians, who might have been earlier included among the Colored are counted among the Chinese and East Indian respectively.

‡ Numbers in parentheses are census estimates which do not equal the sum of the racial components.

whites since 1844 when there were 15,800 white residents on the island (excluding tourists). A variety of factors accounted for a stream of whites off the island throughout the history of Jamaica, including the wealthy whites' view of England as the home to which they returned to spend their Jamaican fortunes or to consolidate their losses and where they sent their children to be educated. Also, the heavily masculine sex ratio and the practice of concubinage with Negro women reduced the natural increase of whites, and the low life expectancy of the poorer white immigrants, bookkeepers, mechanics, clerks, overseers, and others, further depleted the white population. By 1844, they represented only 4.2 per cent of the population, and they generally declined proportionately over the years since, representing in 1960 less than 1 per cent of the total population.

After emancipation, attempts to acquire labor included efforts to recruit nonwhite as well as white labor. Workers from Africa, India, and China were recruited. Perhaps as many as ten thousand free Africans came to Jamaica from 1838 to 1867, some to return again to Africa. Many of them were freed slaves from Sierra Leone and St. Helena, who had been brought to these places from captured slavers by the British navy after 1808. By 1865, this immigration had virtually ended.

Although the immigration of indentured laborers from India contributed consequential numbers of persons to the populations of British Guiana and Trinidad, probably no more than about 14,000 East Indians stayed in Jamaica out of the estimated 36,400 brought in between 1845, when they first arrived, and 1917. Considerable miscegenation took place with this group and the group expanded in absolute numbers. By 1960, 1.7 per cent of the Jamaican population was classified as East Indian with another 1.7 per cent classified as Afro–East Indian. East Indians were assimilated racially to a considerable extent, and they became fairly well assimilated socially and culturally into the particular social classes of which they were part.

The effort to bring in indentured Chinese laborers resulted in only about 1,400 being brought in totally in 1853–1854, perhaps in 1864, and in 1884. Starting in the 1890's, however, further immigrants from China were obtained not as sugar workers but as traders, and they came as free persons. A small immigration of Chinese continued, and by 1943 the Chinese owned a considerable percentage of the grocery businesses in Jamaica. Men generally outnumbered women among the Chinese immigrants, and there was a considerable amount of intermarriage between the Chinese and other groups, especially the Negro. For example, in 1960 the Afro-Chinese population was as large (0.6 per cent of the total population) as the pure Chinese population. Nonetheless, the Chinese remained largely behind their ethnic wall and were clearly differentiated as a separate cultural group. Although generally fluent in the Jamaican dialect, many of them, including children, were still fluent in Chinese.[13]

Additionally, small, but socially significant, proportions of Syrians, Jews, and Portuguese were differentiated.

Thus, most of the people of newly independent Jamaica were descendants of slaves brought from Africa, the racial composition had changed little since 1844, and racially the population was relatively homogeneous—91.4 per cent of the people being colored or black (not including the Afro–

East Indian and Afro-Chinese). Also since 1844, the percentage of native-born persons was high, and in 1960 reached 98.6 per cent.[14] Thus, many years before political independence, Jamaica had a relatively homogeneous population in racial and "nationality" terms. No great tides of immigrants with varying nationality backgrounds swept into Jamaica in recent years, such as the ones that flowed into the United States; and compared to Jamaica, the United Kingdom itself was more heterogeneous according to racial and nationality criteria. The English, Irish, Scottish, and Welsh still have distinct "nationalities" in the cultural sense (e.g., many hours of Welsh language programs are broadcast each week over London television), there has been a recent influx of continental Europeans, and before the Commonwealth Immigrants Act, which went into effect in 1962, a flood of immigrants from existing and former colonies—including several hundreds of thousands of Negroes from Jamaica and elsewhere in the West Indies—had arrived in the United Kingdom.[15]

This is not to say, however, that Jamaica was not a stratified society nor that the social differentiation of Jamaica was not an obstacle to social unity. In fact, a serious problem in the society, although not as serious as in other places even as nearby as Trinidad and British Guiana, stemmed from the correlated cleavages of social class, race, and subculture.

Afro-Europeans (coloreds or browns) were being differentiated from the blacks as early as the eighteenth century when they began achieving middle-class status. Broom gives a rough approximation of the status ladder as it appeared in the first quarter of the nineteenth century:

(1) The invisible man, the absentee landlord; the executive; the resident creole planters and the top representatives of overseas companies—all whites.
(2) Estate attorneys and agents and well-to-do Scottish and Jewish merchants; some professionals—all whites.
(3) Other merchants and urban specialists, including some colored; a few colored planters and professionals.
(4) Colored artisans, tradesmen and semi-professionals.
(5) Brown slaves not in field labor.
(6) Black slaves working in the fields.[16]

During the period of transition to independence, Jamaica was divided in gross terms, according to Smith, into three broad social classes: [17] lower-class blacks, middle-class browns, and upper-class whites. There were blacks, browns, and whites in each of the major classes, but whites were greatly overrepresented in the upper, browns in the middle, and blacks in the lower, thus the color-class linkage in the terminology. For example, a rough indicator of the correlation between socioeconomic and

racial differentiation in 1943 can be seen from the occupational distributions of male wage earners and unpaid workers by color given below: [18]

Occupation	Black	Brown	White
Managers and officials	0.1%	1.9%	20.4%
Professionals	0.6	2.6	13.8
Clerical and sales	2.1	14.9	31.5
Skilled manual and skilled service	15.6	27.3	20.2
Unskilled manual and unskilled service	81.6	53.3	14.1
Total	100.0%	100.0%	100.0%
Number of cases	(162,554)	(31,225)	(2,495)

Had employers and "own account" workers been included the correlation
would have been higher still.

Similar relationships existed between color and such variables as income,
literacy, education, family life, speech patterns, and religion.

For the most part, African-style political institutions, judicial systems,
economic organizations, and family structures did not survive the plantation system of slavery. The dominant institutions of Jamaica came from
the English. Nevertheless, behavior patterns among the lower classes were
reminiscent of West Africa even at the time independence was achieved—
especially in religion and magic, dancing and singing, folklore, women's
hair styles, and the like. Additionally, slavery itself left its mark in more
or less subtle ways on the social differentiation of Jamaica and on the
ways in which the different social classes think about and relate to each
other. At best, this heritage from slavery took the form of dependent-
patron relationships that were degrading to the lower-class persons and
onerous to the middle- or upper-class persons, and at worse it was manifested in sullen, resentful attitudes that widened the social gulf between
the black lower classes on the one hand and the brown middle and white
upper classes on the other.

At independence the culture of the small upper class was that of mid-
twentieth century West European society—particularly English—mixed to
some extent with patterns from the United States. The middle-class was not
only biologically, but also culturally, the most variable, practicing a general mixture of social and cultural patterns from the higher and the lower
classes.[19]

After specifying such characteristics of the three major social classes in
Jamaica at the time of independence, one must add the obvious observation that, although they are useful abstractions in thinking about Jamaican
social structure, such a formulation is nevertheless an oversimplification.

As we shall see in Chapter III, the middle and upper classes can be further divided into various institutional sectors, and although the data show that the correlation between class and color still remained in 1958, it appeared to be getting less among certain specified groups. Similarly, the lower classes were differentiated among themselves; for example, there were common laborers, fishermen, small cultivators, vendors, revival leaders, prostitutes, domestic servants, farmers, artisans, and many others. Although there were hardly any white persons in such groups, there was much blurring of the color lines between them so far as black and brown persons were concerned.

POLITY.—Unlike many other new world colonies, there was no proprietary period in Jamaica under the English. After the capture of Spanish Town in 1655, the chief concern of government was to prevent anarchy and to consolidate English control over the island, and Jamaica was ruled by military commissioners under military law until 1661.

The period from 1661 to 1865 was characterized by a political structure dominated by a Governor and a Council (that formed an upper house) appointed by the King, and an Assembly that formed a lower house. Additionally, there were a number of administrative posts that at first were granted by the Crown to persons residing in England who in turn farmed or rented them to deputies and subdeputies acting in Jamaica.

This period has been called the "old representative system," because the Assembly was elected. But quite apart from the common abuses of bribery, corruption, and bogus voting, the system was not representative of the population in any modern sense of the term. The electorate was very small, consisting primarily of land-owning whites, and the Assembly came to represent primarily the planting and land-owning interests, although near the end of the period some professional and mercantile interests were represented as well. For example, in 1864, out of a total population of about half a million, there were only 1,903 persons listed on the registries as being qualified to vote, and only 1,457 actual voters who elected 47 Assemblymen. "In the county of Cornwall, containing five large parishes, and a third of the entire population of the island, there were only 246 voters, 162 of whom returned ten members to the assembly." [20] Additionally, in England the absentee land-owners from Jamaica and elsewhere in the West Indies formed a powerful and wealthy interest group exercising considerable influence through both King and Parliament.

The chief political development during this period was the continual assertiveness of the Assembly in financial matters, which resulted in the limitation of the powers and discretion of the Governor and Council. "It was in Jamaica that the most thorough and ingenuous system of executive control was devised by the Assembly. . . . Three months was the usual period for which to vote supplies, so that the power of the purse could be used very rapidly if the Governor misbehaved." [21]

"The Council was generally under the thorough control of the Governor. Although he did not appoint the members himself, he was able to keep the Crown appointments under his influence, and by his power of suspension prevent any embarrassing show of independence. It was intended that the counsellors should be the most substantial men in the colony." [22] However, the Governor was in continuous conflict between imperial interests, as defined in his instructions, and local administration, which he had to supervise. Local and imperial interests clashed almost without intermission. "His position was such that it was hardly possible for him to avoid trouble either with the colonists or with the Home Government." [23]

During the more than two hundred years of the "old representative system," the slave trade and the plantation system of slavery reached their peak. The West Indian islands—including Jamaica— prospered and declined, and finally slavery was abolished. As early as 1776, a resolution to the effect that "the slave-trade is contrary to the laws of God and the rights of men" was lost in the English Parliament. It is significant not that the resolution was lost, but that it was introduced at all, because it was based upon radical ideas concerning the rights and status of subordinate races and classes. In 1787, about the time that a slave could be purchased on the African coast for £22 and sold in the West Indies for £65, the powerful Society for Effecting the Abolition of the Slave Trade was formed in England, and in 1789, although they lost, no less than 12 resolutions condemning the slave trade were presented by Wilberforce to Parliament. Denmark was the first European nation to forbid the slave trade to her subjects, which she did with an act passed in 1792 to go into effect in 1802. An act was revived in 1804 which prohibited the introduction of any more slaves into the United States, although despite this slaves were brought to U.S. ports as late as 1860. A bill was passed in England in 1807, and strengthened in 1811, which abolished the slave trade; and in 1814, the Dutch prohibited the slave trade as did the Swedes a year later. France agreed in principle at the Congress of Vienna that the slave trade should be abolished. Great Britain paid Spain £400,000 in 1820, and Portugal £300,000 in addition to canceling a debt of £600,000 in 1836, in order to get these two countries to prevent the slave trade.[24]

By 1833 the British West Indian planters

. . . were politically stranded; they had rejected the advice of the group of absentee planters and merchants in London; they offered no marketing prospects to the newly represented interests in the House of Commons; they sold expensive sugar compared with Mauritius, Cuba, Brazil and India, and they had challenged the authority of the Imperial Government. Throughout these developments the abolitionists were urging action.[25]

An English reform Parliament passed the Emancipation Act in August, 1833. It stipulated that, although there was to be an apprenticeship period of six years for field laborers and four years for domestic workers, slavery was to be abolished August 1, 1834. The Parliament paid £20,000,000 to the slave owners for the loss of their slaves, of which more than £6,000,000 was appropriated to Jamaica.

The political implications of emancipation created the conditions for the eventual elimination, some thirty years later, of the so-called old representative system in Jamaica. So long as slaves were property, one could argue that the Assembly was perhaps representative enough, since, like other forms of property, slaves were represented by their owners. But with the abolition of slavery about three hundred thousand human beings in Jamaica

. . . were tranferred from the category of property to the category of citizenship. . . . The defects of the old system of government were clear enough, but, so long as slaves were property, in theory the West Indian colonies were communities of white people, and therefore as much or as little fitted for self government as the North American colonies. When the slave became a citizen the social revolution involved made any form of representative government next to impossible. . . .[26]

The powers of the Jamaican Assembly just after emancipation were controlled by a small and prejudiced minority of all the English citizens in Jamaica—including the freed slaves, who had the right, theoretically, to share in basic civil and political equalities.

From emancipation to 1864, the Jamaican Assembly stubbornly refused to accept the new conditions, and failed to pass any of the legislation necessary to ameliorate the conditions of the mass of the people, the lower socio-economic-racial groups. In 1838, the Assembly went so far as to go on strike and refused to perform any of their duties whatever with the exception of those necessary to maintain public credit. By 1864, the island contained a handful of white oligarchs, a smaller number of colored leaders, and a huge black population in a state of nearly complete political inertia.

The British Parliament for some time had been trying to change the

Jamaican constitution, but it took an act of violence to bring this about. The Morant Bay Rebellion took place in 1865—and marked an end to a period. It is called a rebellion, but the rebellious acts were on a relatively small scale and generally unorganized. It was typical of violent acts of protest against a repressive system which take place under similar social circumstances. The reaction was itself far more violent than the original action of the rebels. Apparently only a dozen white men were killed by the insurgents—certainly no more than thirty persons of all colors—but over five hundred "rebels" were killed—some executed by hanging—and six hundred were flogged.[27]

Fear of continued disorder combined with the prophecy that eventually the freed blacks might demand their political rights and come to dominate the Assembly led the Assembly to give up its heretofore jealously guarded prerogatives of self-government. On the British Parliament's part, a colonial administration dedicated to the welfare of all socio-economic-racial groups on the island could be established, and social reforms which at that time never would have been adopted by the oligarchical Jamaican Assembly could be introduced.

From 1866 to 1884, Jamaica had "pure" crown colony government, which was characterized by a Legislative Council that was entirely non-elective. The Governor had great power, and acted effectively with his new and coöperative legislature to accomplish many needed reforms. In fact, it was not until the early years of the crown colony period that some of the benefits of emancipation were first made available to the vast majority of Jamaican Negroes, and most of the public services in Jamaica had their beginning. In effect, this was a time of benevolent despotism during which the welfare of the common people was often considered more important than the planters.

In 1884, a constitutional change was made permitting the unofficial members of the Legislative Council to be elected, although the electorate was still restricted by financial qualifications (38,376 names were on the register in 1896 out of a population of well over 600,000) [28] and the elected members were granted very little power. Only minor changes in the governmental structure took place between 1884 and 1944. Among other things, female suffrage on a restricted basis was introduced in 1919, and the financial qualifications of voters were reduced still further. However, these were but minor moves in the direction of more self-government and somewhat more democratic participation. The Governor was still the chief ruling authority, although advised by the official and nominated members of the Legislative Council; and the elected councilmen generally constituted a vocal, but irresponsible and largely ineffectual opposition.

But the adequacy of the political system in fact declined markedly, not so much in absolute terms perhaps, but relative to the changing value systems and conditions of the larger society—not only in Jamaica itself, but in England and other Western societies. Within Jamaica, new ideas about civil, political, economic, and social equality spread, political skills became more widely distributed, and local politicians appeared who articulated the interests of the mass of Jamaicans (for example, in 1910 there were five brown members and one black member of the Legislative Council out of the total of fourteen elected members).[29] At the same time, liaisons had developed between the more established and conservative members of the society and King's House; new changes and reforms continuing the promise for improvements shown under the early crown colony governors were no longer being made. And finally, two of the major conflicts of interest between imperial policy and local interests—the mercantile system and the emancipation of slaves (and the early treatment of former slaves by the embittered local oligarchs)—which had contributed to the metropolitan power's opposition to self-government virtually disappeared.[30]

Although proposals for constitutional changes to grant political advancement toward self-government were being made frequently in the early 1920's, recent political changes may conveniently be viewed as having their immediate origins during 1937–1938. At that time poverty and unemployment were widespread; discontent, work stoppages, and disturbances increased throughout the island and came to a head during May of 1938 in Kingston. Starting among a crowd of striking dock laborers and banana loaders on the waterfront, the riots and disorders spread throughout the entire city. A few days later the rural areas were also struck by disorder. "Mobs of strikers and unemployed, carrying sticks and cutlasses, roamed the roads and estates, forcing those at work to stop, entering houses and demanding food and money, assaulting residents and pedestrians, burning crops and buildings, stopping cars and trucks, interfering generally with traffic and public services, blocking roads and damaging bridges, intimidating the communities, and requiring the dispatch of police and volunteer constables." [31] Amazing as it seems, such a widespread upheaval resulted in relatively little cost in human lives. "The final count of casualties over the period was 8 persons killed, 32 wounded by gunshot, and 139 otherwise injured. Of 745 persons prosecuted, 265 were found not guilty, while 480 were convicted and varying punishments imposed." [32]

The legitimate political elites, the Governor and Council, were now faced with the necessity of dealing with a new set of leaders, who were legitimated not by any formal offices that they held, but by their hold over the

1. Kingston and Newcastle in Old Jamaica. Courtesy of *Spotlight*.

2. Kingston Parade in Old Jamaica. Courtesy of Jamaican Information Service.

3. The Georgian Square in Spanish Town. Courtesy of Jamaican Information Service.

4. John Canoe was a stock character among the slaves in Jamaica during Christmas holidays when they were encouraged to get up carnival acts and dances. Courtesy of *Spotlight*.

5. A scene from *Hamlet* during the Arts Festival for Independence. *Gleaner* photograph.

6. Coaching in cricket. Courtesy of Jamaican Information Service.

7. Miss Chinese Jamaica, 1960. Courtesy of *Newday*.

8. Lady Hailes, wife of the Governor-General of the short-lived West Indies Federation, presents certificates to nurses at a graduation ceremony. Courtesy of Jamaican Information Service.

9. A kindergarten in the parish of St. Catherine. Courtesy of Jamaican Information Service.

10, 11, 12, 13. A lower-class neighborhood in West Kingston. Photographs by John W. Evans.

14. Members of the Ras Tafari Brethren bring their complaints to the Minister of Health. Courtesy of Jamaican Information Service.

15. Most Rastafarians, some of whom make their headquarters here, wish to leave Jamaica and "return" to Africa. Photograph by John W. Evans.

16. A lower-class man in Kingston.
Photograph by John W. Evans.

17. Bust of Jamaican Marcus Garvey in
Kingston. Well known as an international
Negro leader, Garvey helped pave the way
for the national movement in Jamaica.
Courtesy of *Spotlight*.

18. The governments of Jamaica and the United States coöperate
on a housing project in West Kingston. Photograph by John W.
Evans.

19. A middle-class neighborhood in the outskirts of Kingston. Courtesy of Jamaican Information Service.

20. Sir Arthur Richards, Governor of Jamaica, and Manley during the early days of Jamaica's modern political development. Courtesy of *Spotlight*.

21. Bustamante leading a march in 1946. Courtesy of *Spotlight*.

22. Manley and Bustamante sign Jamaica's Independence agreement in London. Courtesy of British Information Services, Jamaica.

23. Bustamante with a poster showing some of Jamaica's new national symbols: the flag, the national pledge, the coat of arms, the national prayer, the national anthem, and the national song. Courtesy of Jamaican Information Service.

24. Sir Clifford Campbell, the first Jamaican Governor of Independent Jamaica. *Gleaner* photograph.

25. Sir Kenneth Blackburne, the last British Governor of colonial Jamaica. Courtesy of Jamaican Information Service.

26. A new session of the Legislature is opened during the tutelary democracy period in 1959 in the old mansion where the Legislature sat before Gordon House was erected. Courtesy of Jamaican Information Service.

27. Sir Kenneth Blackburne reads the throne speech and opens the first Parliament of Independent Jamaica in Gordon House, which is named after the once-traitor and now national hero, George William Gordon. *Gleaner* photograph.

28. The People's National Party Cabinet after the elections of 1959. From left to right: the Hon. Jonathan Grant, Minister of Labour; the Hon. Dr. Ivan S. Lloyd, Minister of Health; the Hon. A. G. S. Coombs,

Minister of Communications and Works; the Hon. Wills O. Isaacs, Minister of Trade and Industry; the Hon. Dr. Glendon Logan, Minister of Housing and Social Welfare; the Hon. Norman Manley, Q.C., Premier and Minister of Development; the Hon. William Seivright, Minister of Home Affairs; the Hon. Vernon Arnett, Minister of Finance; the Hon. Douglas Fletcher, Minister without Portfolio; the Hon. Florizel Glasspole, Minister of Education; the Hon. Rudolph Burke, Minister without Portfolio; and the Hon. Keble Munn, Minister of Agriculture and Lands. Courtesy of Jamaican Information Service.

29. The Jamaica Labour Party Cabinet after the elections of 1962 with Sir Kenneth Blackburne (fourth from left front). Front row, left to right: the Hon. E. L. Allen, Minister of Education; the Hon. R. C. Lightbourne, Minister

of Trade and Industry; the Hon. D. B. Sangster, Minister of Finance; Sir Alexander Bustamante, Kt., Premier; the Hon. D. C. Tavares, Minister of Housing; the Hon. K. A. N. Jones, Minister of Communications and Works. Back row, left to right: the Hon. R. A. McNeil, Minister of Home Affairs; the Hon. H. L. Shearer, Minister without Portfolio; the Hon. Wilton O. Hill, Minister without Portfolio; the Hon. J. P. Gyles, Minister of Agriculture and Lands; the Hon. N. N. Ashenheim, C.B.E., Minister without Portfolio; the Hon. Dr. H. W. Eldermire, Minister of Health; the Hon. E. P. G. Seaga, Minister of Development and Welfare; and the Hon. L. G. Newland, Minister of Labour. Courtesy of Jamaican Information Service.

30. Bustamante addresses supporters of the Jamaica Labour Party and the Bustamante Industrial Trade Union at a Labour Day march in Kingston. *Gleaner* photograph.

31. Millard Johnson, leader of the People's Progressive Party, campaigns with little success in the 1962 elections. *Spotlight*, by W. Errol Bowen.

32. Bustamante escorts Princess Margaret at a dinner at King's House in Jamaica during the Independence celebrations. Courtesy of Jamaican Information Service.

33. The United Nations General Assembly opened its seventeenth regular session on September 18, 1962, and admitted Jamaica and three other new states to membership. The Jamaican delegation is seated at desk in center. United Nations photograph.

34. PNP leaders campaign for election. *Spotlight,* by W. Errol Bowen.

35. Excavating bauxite in Jamaica. Courtesy of Jamaican Information Service.

36. A straw-goods sidewalk vendor helps a tourist put on a hat made of Jamaican straw. Courtesy of Jamaican Tourist Board.

37. Tourists enjoy Jamaican rum on one of the island's beaches. Courtesy of Jamaica Tourist Board.

38. Fishing canoes on Jamaica's north coast. Courtesy of Jamaica Tourist Board.

39. A small farmer reaps cocoa. Courtesy of Jamaican Information Service.

40. A sugar-cane cutter. Courtesy of Jamaican Information Service.

41. Pushcarts haul a variety of goods in Kingston. Jamaican market women, called higglers, gather 'round. *Gleaner* photograph.

42. In addition to being an export crop, Jamaican bananas are important in the local markets. Here they are brought to Kingston where they are unloaded in front of a market clerk. *Gleaner* photograph.

people and by their claim that they spoke for the majority of Jamaicans, leaders who could restore order and send the workers back to work without force and further bloodshed. Of these new leaders, two emerged outstandingly. The first was Alexander Bustamante (later knighted). He became a charismatic leader after the events of May, 1938. His

. . . magnetic appeal to the masses flowed from his impressive physical stature, his use of oratorical pyrotechnics to arouse his listeners to a pitch of emotional frenzy, his earthiness which seemed but a larger projection of his followers, his physical courage in times of stress and his shrewdness in sensing and mastering a particular political tide. There was, too, his overweening self-confidence in manipulating his followers, expressed in the boast that they 'would vote for a dog,' if he so directed.[33]

. . . Bustamante was the Messiah of the unenfranchised, the unemployed, the underemployed and the underpaid. His followers were the great majority of the Jamaican people who before then had only known representative leadership and organization in the apocalypse of Bedward or the tragic escapism of Marcus Garvey's United Negro Improvement Association, with its programme of social withdrawal and return to Africa. In 1938, for the first time in their history, the mass of the Jamaican people united behind a leader who directed their energies against immediate material conditions and thereby against the current social order itself. . . . The leaderless had for long looked for their leader; but whereas Bedward had offered to lead them to Heaven via August Town, and Marcus Garvey had offered to take them to Africa via Harlem, Bustamente led them along the streets of Kingston and through the sugar estates, and his offer was their demand, a better life, here and now, in a country of which they formed the majority, but from whose society they had hitherto been actively excluded.[34]

The second outstanding leader was Norman Washington Manley, whose background was in sharp contrast to Bustamante's.

He attended Oxford and earned high honours at Gray's Inn in London immediately after the first World War. His reputation in the legal profession, quickly established in Jamaica, was extended to England, when in a famous case he successfully defended a Jamaican charged with murder. . . . To Jamaican politics in 1938 Manley brought a first-rate mind, a comprehensive diagnosis and remedy for Jamaica's ills based on Fabian Socialist postulates. . . .[35]

During the years that followed, these two leaders came to dominate over all other political personalities. Manley gained strength among the lower-class blacks just as Bustamante's charisma wore somewhat thin. Both have a clear claim on the title "father of the nation," but each one must always share it to some extent with the other.

Manley was instrumental in forming the People's National Party (PNP)

as a Socialist party affiliated with the British Labour Party. The PNP program in 1940 contained three basic goals: self-government, political democracy based on universal adult suffrage, and economic and social reforms including as one means the public ownership of the island's major resources.[36] Bustamante formed the Bustamante Industrial Trade Union (BITU) with himself as "Founder and Life President." Bustamante was interned for sedition, during which time a working alliance developed between the BITU and the PNP, but with his return he dissolved it as an impediment to his sole and total authority. Relations worsened between Manley and Bustamante.

To him [Bustamante] the P.N.P. objective of self-government would mean 'brown man rule' or coloured middle-class government for Jamaica, scarcely a palatable prospect for the heavily black membership of the B.I.T.U. . . . He deplored the mild socialism adopted by the P.N.P. in 1940. The essential atmosphere of a P.N.P. meeting, serious middle-class intellectuals self-consciously striving to introduce a rationalist political movement in Jamaica, could hardly be congenial to Bustamante. His natural preference was for spur-of-the-moment improvisation and skilful mass manipulation to achieve his narrower trade-unionist objectives.[37]

As a result of the riots, strikes, and other disturbances, a Royal Commission was appointed to investigate social and economic conditions and related matters in Jamaica and elsewhere in the British Caribbean. Although the report was in draft by the outbreak of World War II, the bulk of its contents was not made available until 1945 because of possible ill effects on the war effort. But the recommendations for sweeping reforms were published, and the Moyne Report, as the Commission's report is known, became, though not a blueprint since self-government was not recommended and industrial development was underemphasized, at least a point of departure for further political, economic, and social change in Jamaica.[38]

In November, 1944, a new constitution came into effect establishing a political democracy based on universal adult suffrage under British tutelage, and inaugurating limited self-government. On the eve of Jamaica's first general elections under the new constitution, Bustamante founded the Jamaica Labour Party (JLP) which gave him an instrument for the political expression of the workers' mobilization he had achieved with the BITU. Thus, the stage was set for what developed into a genuine two-party system in Jamaica with the leadership of government and opposition swinging back and forth from Bustamante to Manley with little chance for an effective third party to devlop. Manley's campaign efforts were no match for

Bustamante's charisma in the first general election of December, 1944, and the JLP received 41.4 per cent of the 389,109 votes cast (663,069 persons were eligible) for twenty-two of the thirty-two seats available in the House of Representatives. The PNP secured 23.5 per cent of the votes for five seats, but Manley lost in his own constituency. The five remaining seats were won by independent candidates, and the total proportion of votes cast for candidates who were not members of the JLP or the PNP was the highest that it ever has been since.[39]

In 1949 when 65.2 per cent of the 732,217 eligible voters went to the polls, the PNP got 43.5 per cent of the total votes to the JLP's 42.7 per cent, but owing to the distribution by constituencies the JLP still controlled the House with seventeen seats. The PNP created its own labor union linkage with the establishment of the National Workers Union in 1952, and deliberate efforts were made to enhance Manley's popular appeal largely by the manipulation of his public image. Dissatisfaction with the JLP government grew, the PNP opposition was active in the House, and throughout the island the PNP engaged in an organizational campaign. In 1955, the PNP swept into office with 50.5 per cent of a popular vote of 495,680, which resulted in eighteen PNP seats. The JLP with 39 per cent of the popular vote won fourteen seats.[40]

Constitutional changes providing for more and more self-government, and less and less British tutelage, took place in 1949, 1953, 1956, 1957, and 1959. During 1958, Jamaica became part of the West Indies Federation along with other British territories in the Caribbean: Antigua, Barbados, Dominica, Grenada, Montserrat, St. Kitts–Nevis-Anguilla, St. Lucia, St. Vincent, and Trinidad. The PNP, then in power in Jamaica, suffered a severe setback in the first federal elections in 1958 with the Democratic Labour Party (the federal equivalent of the JLP) securing most of the Jamaican seats in the new federal Parliament. However, in the Jamaican general elections of 1959, the PNP surged back to gain 54.8 per cent of the total votes to the JLP's 44.3 per cent for twenty-nine of the newly enlarged forty-five seat House of Representatives. Thus, with Manley as Premier the PNP continued preparations to lead Jamaica into independence as part of the Federation.

Yet many Jamaican leaders were never much in favor of federating, and many lower-class persons understood little or nothing about it. Souring on the idea of federation, Bustamante and the JLP opposition made federation a party issue and began fighting actively for a separate, independent Jamaica. Manley, falsely secure in his belief that Jamaicans would stick by him in his stand for independence within the West Indies Federation, called a referendum on the issue, which was held in September,

1961. The largely antifederation rural vote outweighed the urban pro-federationists, and of 473,580 total votes 45.9 per cent were for federation while 54.1 per cent were against. Thus, the voters had decided that Jamaica would "go it alone." [41] Personally saddened, Manley had little choice but to begin negotiations for Jamaica's separate independence, which he began at once with a bipartisan committee, and to call another general election so that the country would have the party of its choice to lead it into full nationhood.

Although nearly eighty years old, Bustamante campaigned vigorously, surrounded by a revitalized JLP leadership which included a group of fresh, young, well-educated persons. The usual battle between Bustamante and the JLP on the one hand and Manley and the PNP on the other was complicated by the emergence of a third party, the People's Political Party (PPP), which claimed some of the credit for the defeat of federation in the referendum and which put candidates against the PNP and the JLP throughout most of the island. This was done despite the fact that in the general election of 1959 the JLP and the PNP together accounted for 99.1 per cent of the total votes.

Millard Johnson, the leader of the PPP, was dark brown in color compared to Bustamante's near white and Manley's light brown complexion, and his political appeal included a clear racist theme. With African robes, stories and movies of Africa, slogans in African dialects, Johnson and his party leaders preached directly or by implication against white and brown men. Even though examination of the PPP proposals revealed little startlingly different from either the PNP plan or the JLP program—except perhaps a greater emphasis upon equality—the racist overtones and style in a Jamaica becoming prideful of its racial equality led to considerable attention being given to the PPP. However, in the general election held in April, 1962, the PPP obtained less than 1 per cent of the more than half-a-million total votes, the PNP and the JLP together getting 98.6 per cent. To add insult to injury, a white Syrian and Harvard University graduate in Sociology running against a medium-brown candidate who called himself "Burning Spear" (although a PNP not a PPP candidate) won a seat in an urban slum composed mostly of unemployed and underemployed blacks where the racists' appeal should not have fallen upon deaf ears unless racial factors were of considerably less importance than economic factors to the depressed classes of Jamaica. But the PNP government fell, capturing but nineteen seats to the JLP's twenty-six. Jailed for sedition about a quarter of a century before, Sir William Alexander Bustamante became the first Prime Minister of independent Jamaica.[42]

When Jamaica became independent on August 6, 1962, the new constitution provided for a system modeled after the British parliamentary structure: an appointed upper chamber to be called the Senate (formerly the Legislative Council) with limited powers, and an elected lower chamber, the House of Representatives, from whose members the Cabinet was selected.

ECONOMY.—Jamaica stepped into the new role of independent nation-state at the end of more than a decade of rapid economic growth. Based in part upon the exploitation of bauxite resources and an expanding tourist trade, Jamaica's recent economic growth was nearly as spectacular as were Japan's and Puerto Rico's earlier. Thus, the transition to independence was accompanied by a drive toward economic development, and as throughout Jamaica's history, economic and political factors were inextricably interwoven in the realities of Jamaican life.

The Jamaican economic historian, Douglas Hall, has succinctly summarized the economy of Jamaica under the British up to the end of slavery:

From the late seventeenth century onwards the island rapidly grew in importance as the largest British colonial producer of cane-sugar, and by the mid-eighteenth century it was the most prized possession of the British Crown, far exceeding in importance and value any of the other British Caribbean or American mainland colonies.

The sugar estates and other properties were worked by slaves imported from Africa and their local-born descendants. Although other crops, such as coffee, cotton, and pimento, were exported, the economy of the island was founded on slave-labour, sugar, and the protection given to colonial producers in the British home market. Within the compass of the British acts regulating colonial trade an important commerce was carried on with the American mainland colonies, whence the Jamaica planters imported foodstuffs, lumber, and certain other estate supplies.

Soon after the mid-eighteenth century, however, the fortunes of the island began to decline. The declaration and winning of American independence reduced the direct American trade (since the United States was barred from direct British colonial trade) and increased the cost of American supplies. Increasing sugar production in the French and Spanish islands (especially French San Domingo before 1791 and Spanish Cuba afterwards) by planters in North and South America (chiefly Louisiana and Brazil) and by other British producers (in Mauritius and the Far East) tended to depress sugar prices, while the costs of production tended to increase. The expenses of planting were affected by much more than the new scarcity and dearness of American supplies. Planters were faced with soil deterioration on their estates; rising prices for slaves, as sugar producers throughout the Caribbean increased their production; and increasing costs of shipping and marketing their sugar in Britain.

The long period of almost unbroken war between England and France between 1793 and 1815 temporarily arrested the decline, but even so, new problems were introduced by such events as the ending of the British slave trade in 1807 and the beginning in France of the manufacture of sugar from beetroot (though the full effects of this new source of competition were not felt before the 1870's and 1880's).

After 1815 the sugar industry and trade suffered by the long post-war depression of the 1820's and 1830's, during which the reformed British Parliament voted the emancipation of the slaves.

Between 1834 and 1838 labour in nearly all the British Caribbean territories was organised on an 'apprenticeship system' by which the slaves (now called 'apprentices') were required to give about forty hours of unpaid labour a week to their owners but were allowed to demand wages for any time worked in excess of this maximum. For many reasons apprenticeship did not succeed: it was a misconceived attempt at compromise that pleased neither planters nor apprentices, and it was therefore terminated before the appointed date.[43]

In 1846, the Sugar Duties Act was passed by the English Parliament. It called for a gradual withdrawal of the preferential duties for sugar from the British colonies, and resulted further in shattering the confidence of the sugar planters in Jamaica, many of whom were well on their way to adjusting to the new conditions of the labor market created by the abolition of slavery. By 1852, the British sugar colonies had to compete in the British market without any preferential price assistance. Rising labor costs, falling prices, and lack of capital, the latter, being drawn into expanding industries in Britain as well as into new developing overseas territories brought about a decline among the Jamaican sugar estates.

Gradually, the sugar industry in Jamaica again adapted to the new conditions. Estates were amalgamated, the use of tools and machinery was increased and improved, and wages were reduced where possible. These things combined with a rapid expansion in the world demand for sugar slowed the decline and gave new life to the industry, and for a brief period financial prosperity appeared possible. But the expansion of the sugar beet industry in Europe combined with the increase in slave-grown sugar cane in non-British areas depressed the price of sugar (which in 1896 was only about one half what it was in 1881), and the troubles of the planters throughout the West Indies were aggravated by droughts, hurricanes, and an outbreak of a serious cane disease in the nineties.[44]

Captain Lorenzo Baker took the first shipment of bananas from Jamaica to New York in 1870. In 1899, he co-founded the United Fruit Company which, ". . . by its control of markets and ships . . . controlled the Jamaica banana industry for thirty years, until in 1929, six thousand small holders formed the Jamaica Banana Producers' Association to transport and sell their fruit in the United States and Europe." [45] The association succeeded, and bananas grew in importance as an export crop, although banana cultivation was generally a small farming operation. "There was moderate prosperity between the eighteen-nineties and the nineteen-twenties for the small man who had his land planted in bananas. . . ." [46] In 1912, bananas accounted for about 55 per cent of the total value of exports, while sugar and rum combined had been reduced to about eight per cent.[47]

The Brussels convention of 1903 abolishing the system of beet sugar subsidies and protections in Europe did relatively little to help the Jamaican sugar manufacturers, but they struggled along, usually in debt, until World War I, when rising world prices created a boom with high profits reminiscent of the properous days of the eighteenth century. But the boom was shortlived, and prices fell suddenly in 1920. The economic crisis was heightened by the fact that three "safety-valve" channels of emigration had ceased. From 1904 to 1914, thousands of Jamaicans had gone to help build the Panama canal; between 1911 and 1921, Jamaicans went to Cuba to work in the cane fields; and up until 1924, when the United States began its restrictive immigration policy, there had been a general movement of Jamaicans to the United States. (In fact, expatriate Jamaicans in New York City gave expression to an independence movement as early as 1936 when they formed the Jamaica Progressive League.) An imperial preference on sugar was granted, but nonetheless a serious crisis arose in 1929. Jamaican sugar producers were saved from ruin when the preference was increased in 1934 and Britain agreed ". . . to buy a certain quota annually from each colony, so that a market was now guaranteed." [48]

The Moyne Commission's report was an indictment of crown colony government. In general, the Commissioners described the economic and social plight of the people as distressingly abject. They found ". . . no longer a mere blind protest against a worsening of conditions, but a positive demand for the creation of new conditions that will render possible a better and less restricted life. It is the co-existence of this new demand for better conditions with the unfavourable economic trend that is the crux of the West Indian problem of the present-day period." [49] Long before this the crown colony system had failed to continue the reforming impetus of its early years after 1865. Instead, its revenue over the years had barely been adequate to maintain the continuing costs of earlier reforms under the pressure of population increases, much less to inaugurate new ones. By 1937–1938, there was wide-spread malnutrition; inadequate housing; few educational opportunities for the average Jamaican; widespread poverty and unemployment; and spreading resentment, discontent, and agitation among the Jamaican masses as well as among some middle-class Jamaican intellectuals.

crown colony government had become an obstacle to further progress.

In addition to other things, the Moyne Commission recommended reforms in education, the establishment of ". . . health services, housing and slum clearance, the creation of labour departments, social welfare facilities and encouragement for land settlement. . . ." [50]

After the 1937–1938 period, the Jamaican economy began to grow and distributional reforms were introduced, although more growth and more reforms are still needed if poverty, unemployment, and other deprivations are to be reduced further. The outbreak of World War II in 1939 immediately increased the demand for West Indian sugar. "After the war the British Government promised to buy all the sugar produced in the five years after 1944, and renewed the offer in 1948. Consequently, since 1939 the sugar industry has returned to relative prosperity." [51] Later, under the Commonwealth Sugar Agreement of 1951, the United Kingdom agreed to buy a set quota of sugar for a price to be negotiated annually.

Funds made available to Jamaica under the Colonial Development and Welfare Act of 1940 also have contributed to Jamaica's development. For example, from 1951 to 1960 such grants when combined with imperial grants-in-aid totaled about seven million pounds sterling.[52]

Jamaica's bauxite deposits may be the largest in the world, and they began to be exploited in 1952 with considerable expansion taking place in 1956 and 1957 resulting in a tremendous boost to the Jamaican economy. The bauxite and alumina industry did not employ a large number of people compared to other industries—about five thousand with a wage and salary bill of over £3 million in 1960, but in that same year its contribution to the revenue of the Jamaican Government reached nearly £6 million, almost 20 per cent of the total tax receipts, and its export receipts reached almost 50 per cent of the value of total domestic exports.[53]

Similarly, the tourist industry by exploiting the natural beauty and subtropical climate of Jamaica expanded to be the major source of U.S. dollars. By 1960, the number of tourists coming to Jamaica exceeded a quarter of a million, and in 1961 tourists spent an estimated £13.5 million in hotels and shops, on inland transportation and sightseeing, entertainment, and other local services.[54]

With the help of the "invisible export" of tourism and the bauxite and alumina industry, Jamaica moved out of the category of "underdeveloped country" and became, economically speaking, a "developing country." It is estimated that gross fixed capital investment in terms of the Gross National Product (GNP) increased from about 10 per cent in 1950 to more than 20 per cent in 1956, where it remained through 1961. Impressively, domestic sources represented 8 per cent in 1950 and 12 per cent in 1959.

As can be seen from Table 2, the most rapid growth in the GNP took place between 1953 and 1957 inclusive. During 1958, a slump occurred, but economic recovery came relatively quickly—although the annual rates of growth did not reach the formerly high levels. In 1953, the value of the GNP was £114.6 million; and in 1961, it had increased to £256.4 million.

TABLE 2. *Annual Increases in Gross National Product, 1953– 1961*

Year	Gross national product *	Annual increase *	Annual percentage increase
1953	114.6	—	—
1954	127.7	13.2	11.5
1955	145.3	17.6	13.7
1956	166.7	21.4	14.8
1957	199.6	32.9	19.7
1958	207.0	7.4	3.7
1959	221.2	14.2	6.8
1960	240.8	19.6	8.8
1961	256.4	15.6	6.5

SOURCE: *Economic Survey, Jamaica, 1961,* Central Planning Unit, Government of Jamaica, 1962, p. 28.
* Current values in millions of pounds.

This high rate of economic growth was only partly offset by population increases, which threaten Jamaica's development program as they do those of other developing and less developed areas. Disease control and rising minimums of health and welfare services reduced the crude death rate, which leveled off under 10, while the crude birth rate actually increased slightly to 41 in 1961. However, a natural increase of somewhat over 3 per cent a year was partly compensated for by the emigration of Jamaicans to Britain. From 1957 to 1961 inclusive, nearly one hundred thousand Jamaicans entered the United Kingdom in excess of those returning from the U.K. to Jamaica, so that in 1961 the net annual population increase was only about 1 per cent. Per capita income rose during the transition to full self-government and reached £131 in 1961, hitting about the middle of the world scale.

The 1962 restriction placed upon immigration from Commonwealth countries by Britain may pose a serious threat to Jamaican economic development and a dreadful challenge to Jamaican leaders. How much of the flow of Jamaicans to the U.K. will be cut off is not now known, but considerable reduction can be anticipated. By herculean efforts, unemployment was reduced from an estimated 120,000 in 1957 to about 82,000 in 1960, but further reductions are desired. Assuming that migration ceases, the Central Planning Unit has estimated that 182,000 new jobs must be created between 1960 and 1970 even if the rate of unemployment remains as high (about 13 per cent of the labor force) as in 1960.[55] Of course, if the United States places Jamaica on a par with the other independent states of the Americas, which enjoy nonquota immigration rights into the U.S., then much of the flow of emigration from Jamaica, which formerly went to Britain, may come to the United States.

However, it is easy to overstress the negative effects of population increases on economic growth. The logical plausibility underlying the notion of the ultimate need for population control and stability on limited land dims our vision of the immediate, though possibly short-term, positive contributions. Cumper reminds us that population growth does stimulate economic development through the demand for housing and other facilities:

Housing has been one of the bases of Jamaican development since the war; it is a field in which levels of consumption seem to be well below aspirations, it is the form of investment for which financial facilities are best established and it has the advantage that it involves a high proportion of local outlay, on labour and on such materials as cement, so that the multiplier effect is marked. Unless the economy has reached the point of zero or negative marginal returns to the application of extra labour, it should also be true that population growth increases the demand for goods of many other types, and so is a precondition for the establishment of industries which need a sizeable minimum market for profitable operation. This is not to say that development cannot proceed without rapid population growth; but the historical evidence for association between the two processes is significant.[56]

In 1960, about one-half of the labor force was employed in agricultural pursuits, yet agriculture, forestry, and fishing contributed only 13 per cent to the Gross Domestic Product (from Table 3). Both the distribution and manufacturing sectors surpassed the agricultural sector in total contributions, and all other sectors had higher per capita outputs.

Incomes varied according to industrial sector as well as by particular occupations with the higher incomes going to the industries of higher productivity. A 1954 sample survey in Kingston showed that 30 per cent of all households had weekly incomes of less than £2 a week while 15 per cent had £15 a week and over. More recently, rates for unskilled male labor ranged from about 10 shillings to £1 per day; a carpenter may earn nearly £2 per day, a welder still more.

TABLE 3. *Percentage Contribution of Industrial Sectors to Gross Domestic Product at Factor Cost, 1961*

Industrial sectors	Per cent
Agriculture, forestry, and fishing	13.0
Mining	8.9
Manufacturing	13.4
Construction and installation	11.5
Public utilities	1.1
Transportation, communication, and storage	6.5
Wholesale and retail distribution	15.9
Banking, insurance, and real estate	6.1
Ownership of dwellings	3.0
Central and local government	7.8
Miscellaneous services	12.8
Total	100.0
Total in millions of £	(241.2)

SOURCE: From *Economic Survey, Jamaica, 1961,* Central Planning Unit, Government of Jamaica, 1962, pp. 30–31.

In the case of the white-collar occupations, the differential in rates tends to be reinforced by a difference in regularity of employment, and incomes are high. For the occupations demanding professional qualifications, indeed, they are becoming increasingly influenced by the need to keep incomes competitive with those to be secured in similar occupations overseas. Incomes among qualified clerical workers are also relatively high; among the lower grades of sales workers, however, both rates and regularity of employment are often below the skilled level. . . .[57]

Exports to Dollar Countries, chiefly the United States and Canada, increased in the last decade relative to exports to Sterling Countries, mainly the United Kingdom, and by 1961 exports to the former were valued at £35.4 million compared to £18.0 for the latter. Imports from the Sterling Area, valued at £31.7 million in 1961, however, still exceeded imports valued at £28.7 million from the Dollar Area.

The total value of domestic exports in 1961 was £60.9 million (compared to £32.4 million in 1955), to which bauxite and alumina contributed 49.9 per cent; sugar, rum, and molasses, 27.1 per cent; bananas, whose relative contribution was declining, 7.7 per cent; citrus, cocoa, coffee, pimento, ginger, and their products altogether, 7.4 per cent; and other products, 7.9 per cent. As in other primary producing countries, the balance of trade, comparing the value of imports with the value of visible exports, was moving against Jamaica, although there was some improvement over recent years in 1961 when imports were £13,235 above visible exports. This unfavorable balance was compensated for in part, however, by sheer increases in the volume of exports and by invisible exports such as tourism.[58]

Land distribution in Jamaica was very unequal. For example, in 1954 there were 42,911 farms of under one acre in size accounting for only 0.9 per cent of the total farm acreage; 95,851 farms between one and five acres accounting for 12.1 per cent of the total; 34,849 farms between five and 10 acres accounting for 12.4 per cent of the total; 18,474 farms between 10 and 25 acres accounting for 13.8 per cent of the total; 5,575 farms between 25 and 100 acres accounting for 12.1 per cent of the total; and only 1,308 farms of 100 acres or more accounting for fully 48.6 per cent of the total farm acreage.[59]

One of the big decisions of nationhood concerns how large a role the government should play in the affairs of the society—especially in the economy. Such a decision, of course, is subject to constant review with an eye to an alteration of policy, and it is often the subject of class conflict within a society, frequently being expressed through political action by clashes between class-linked political parties. As Jamaica approached independence, it was clear that the decision had been taken, in part because of the importance of foreign trade and foreign capital from the Western bloc, that the Jamaican government should not generally play the role of owner and employer, but rather should be a regulator and stimulator of the economy and a provider of welfare where necessary on the margins. The PNP had backed away from its socialistic program and differed little from the JLP on the subject of private ownership and free enterprise.

By 1958 about 15 per cent of the national income passed through the hands of the Jamaican government—a relatively small percentage.[60] There was little demand to nationalize the major industries, such as sugar or bauxite, and the telephones, electric power, radio, and major bus services were operated by private companies.

Government, however, played a large role as an influencer of economic activities. Agricultural marketing was regulated in a variety of ways including price negotiation and control, compulsory grading of products, and quotas. "The economic thinking . . . is oriented toward supplying agricultural products for export and to protecting the farmers and wage earners who grow these exports. Entrepreneurs who operate public utilities, factories, or services (except shipping) may do more or less as they please." [61] However, private investment and productivity were stimulated after World War II by a series of incentive measures, such as farm improvement schemes designed to aid small farmers, and pioneer industries programs in manufacturing industries and the tourist business. The Industrial Development Corporation was created by government to ". . . advertise the island's suitability for factory development, to create industrial estates, to build factories for renting, to lend debenture capital, and otherwise to assist industrialists." [62] The role of government as described by a former Director of the Central Planning Unit included: (1) the formulation of a comprehensive plan of development; (2) a survey of the private sector to find out what it can be expected to do *vis-à-vis* government's plan; (3) direction of the private sector, where necessary to achieve government's plan, by various incentive measures considerably short of out-and-out government control; and finally (4) government action to fill the gaps in the plan left by the private sector. "I think the correct view is that we are trying to get private enterprise or the private sector to fit into a programme which the government itself has drafted and we must use various indirect influences to do this." [63]

In conclusion, the years of transition to self-government from 1944 to 1962 were relatively prosperous with structural changes in the economy taking place as part of the development process. Cumper concludes his discussion of economic development in the West Indies by saying that:

. . . the possibilities of further changes in the same direction are far from being exhausted and . . . failing very unfavourable external events there is no reason why the area should not maintain a rate of economic growth sufficient to support an increasing population at a rising level of living for many years to come. Successful development will of course involve many problems of economic and social policy and of public finance. . . . The recognition that these problems are in principle soluble and that long-term development is a real possibility would appear to be a new and itself important factor in the history of the West Indian economy.[64]

Chapter II

Generalizing Jamaica's Development: Increases in Scale and the Spread of Equality

EACH GENERATION in a sense writes its own version of history. It is not simply that new discoveries are made and new facts uncovered, but that new interpretations are formulated, interpretations that explain people to themselves and to others and that give people's lives new and different meanings. Nations, too, face the task of interpreting themselves, their place in the world, and their relations with other nations. After World War II, the newly formed nations faced the task of writing their own histories from their own points of view, and discarding, when necessary, the histories that had been provided for them often by Europeans writing from the point of view of the colonial powers or by the European-descendant upper-class minority within their boundaries writing from the point of view of a narrow sectional interest. In fact, another of the big decisions of nationhood concerns this very question: "What should the social and cultural history of the new nation be?"

Perhaps few people outside of those in the intellectual classes realize that the question is formulated so explicitly, but it frequently is. It is an important part of what several writers, in discussing nascent nations, have referred to as "the search for identity." Furthermore, the answer to the question cannot be found simply by looking at the facts—if by "facts" we mean some notion about the nature of reality which contains nothing but perception. Facts do contain perceptual elements, but they also contain inferences as to meaning the very second we state what the fact is, no matter how low the level of abstraction. A fact has been defined as "a complex of sense data organized with respect to a prior frame of reference." What that prior frame of reference is determines, out of many possible percepts, which ones are to be considered relevant, and it determines what inferences we as observers, even objective observers, add to the percepts to give them meaning.

However, as the British historian E. H. Carr points out:

> It does not follow that, because a mountain appears to take on different shapes from different angles of vision, it has objectively either no shape at all or an infinity of shapes. It does not follow that, because interpretation plays a necessary part in establishing the facts of history, and because no existing interpretation is wholly objective, one interpretation is as good as another, and the facts of history are in principle not amenable to objective interpretation.[1]

Thus, to say that facts alone cannot answer the question, "What shall the social and cultural history of the new nation be?" is not to say that facts are not important, nor that one man's history is as good as the next man's. It is merely to say that something else is needed. This something else, I think, is the conception of the future and the past as interpenetrating each other—the explicit recognition of the interdependent relationship between the directions of past change and the aspirations for future developments. As Carr says further, a coherent relation between past and future is necessary to give meaning and objectivity to history. And a society that doesn't believe in its progress in the past may quickly lose its belief in its capacity to progress in the future.[2]

Like the people of other nations, the people of Jamaica draw on their conceptions of their own history for some understanding of themselves, for what they and their nation mean and stand for. Such interpretations do not wait on the years of historical research necessary for definitive evaluations, if indeed we could ever have definitive evaluations. Interpretations of the past are made, and they function with immediate consequences for the future of the society. It is true that scholars are at work, and as they dig deeper into the archives, they will discredit some interpretations, reformulate others, and make still others more plausible than they were before, if free inquiry is permitted. But with or without recourse to solid grounding in historical materials, the struggle to control the image of the society through control of the interpretation of its history goes on, and it is part of the struggle to control the future character of the society itself.

There have been many histories of Jamaica and the Caribbean territories. Interpretations changed from one writer to another and from one period to another depending on the different purposes of the historians, differences in stated or unstated assumptions, variations in the dominant cultural and social milieu of the times and places within which the histories were conceived and written, and so forth. The history of the Caribbean area has been, through differential emphasis of one chronicler or another, the sea battles of European navies, European adventurers seeking their fortunes to spend in Europe, a hell of torture and pain for mistreated Indians, ships and trade, the derring-do of buccaneers, the production of sugar and rum, the exploitation of indentured servants and Negro slaves, and the imperial rape of colonies, among many other things.

With respect to the status of the lower socio-economic-racial groups in Jamaica, we can identify at least four major lines of interpretation. Elsa Goveia in her excellent historiography of the British West Indies specifies three of them. She shows how interpretations shifted from (1) the ideas of human equality and natural liberty of the humanism of the early historical interpretations, through (2) the myths of racial inferiority and authoritarian principles of the proslavery period, to (3) the humanitarian interpretations of the postemancipation writers.[3] Additionally, there was a new period of interpretation just emerging during the political transformation to independence which reflected the new issues, the aspirations of an independent Jamaica, and the political, economic, and social problems which it then faced. Although this too may be essentially a humanitarian interpretation, it appeared to differ in important respects from that of the post-emancipation writers.

This chapter contains a general interpretation of Jamaican history organized around three themes: the increase in the scale of society,[4] the spread of equality, and resolutions of problems of legitimacy. My chief purpose is to give broader meaning than would otherwise be possible to the results of the empirical study of elites and nationalism which follow in the remaining chapters by building a bridge between the past and the future, between the direction of past political, economic, and social change, and aspirations for future developments. Also, I hope to show that Jamaican nationalism and the drive to political independence were not unique events unrelated to other changes, but that they were simply additional steps along a road that Jamaicans have been traveling for centuries.

I have tried to generalize Jamaican history by applying some formulations of other writers which have been put forward to explain social change at other times and places, selecting the ones that I felt were most appropriate and modifying them where necessary. The following outline of trends seems more than reasonably plausible in the light of present knowledge of Jamaican history. Incidentally, it is consistent with the way

Jamaican intellectuals were beginning to conceive of Jamaican history during the final stages of transition to political independence (and probably with the way some of them will end up writing it after additional historical research has been done), and it is in harmony with the nationalists' hopes for Jamaica's future to which the achievement of independence gave force. The latter fact meets the criterion of an interpretation that attempts to view the past and the future as inextricably linked together.

Increases in Scale

My thesis is that change in Jamaica can best be understood as a set of interrelated long-term trends toward increases in the scale of society, that is toward increases in the range of social relations, in the scope of social interaction and dependency. In spite of social cataclysms and obvious cases of discontinuous interruptions, of temporary reactions and setbacks, there have been certain continuities and trends that suggest developmental changes. The idea of increasing scale is not suggested, however, as a cosmic principle nor a mystical determinant, but as a theory of political, economic, and social change which can be usefully applied to different times and places.[5]

Jamaica represents, at least since discovery and probably before that, a society that has been expanding in people, in degree of organization and complexity, in total power and wealth, in equality and internal inclusiveness, in space, and in time. This is not to say that there have never been contractions in scale in the course of Jamaican history. There have. But the long-term nonrepetitive movements of the time series—the *trends* rather than the cycles or apparently random fluctuations—have been toward the increase in the scale of society.

At the end of the fifteenth century, the peoples of the then-unifying nation-states of Western Europe looked upon the exploits of Columbus as the "discovery of a new world." Of course, the "new world" was previously unknown to them, but it was, after all, inhabited by a variety of peoples with a diversity of cultures and social structures. What Columbus and his crew did was to initiate social contacts that were to enlarge the scale of society—for Amerindians (as they were to be called), for the Europeans, and for the Africans, Asians and others who were to be drawn into trade relations and who were to constitute much of the labor force on the "new" lands—by increasing the geographical spread of social interaction. "Columbus did not discover a new world; he established contact between two worlds, both already old." [6] His discovery was part of a long-term process of the emergence of societies that were to encompass "worlds" that had been unknown to each other. Larger numbers of people, more lands, and more resources were brought under a new network of political, economic, and social relations that were to promote the elimination of isolation, the bringing together of groups with diverse cultures, and the development of larger worlds, for example, empires, voluntary regional associations, and international organizations, conscious of their unity and the interrelatedness of their parts.

Jamaica was part of this trend and increasingly was drawn into a network of relations that were expanding territorily. Although the densities of communication vary with different parts of the world, Jamaica became part of global society. With independence, the links of economics and government necessarily binding Jamaica to the metropolitan power were no longer enforced by colonial domination. Jamaica was then free to establish wider territorial ties, both economically and politically, through agreements, treaties, and alliances.

Jamaican society expanded through time by the spread of literacy, increasing education, and most recently an increasing emphasis upon a Jamaican (or West Indian) perspective to Jamaican history. Not only were more contemporary Jamaicans increasingly "in touch" with more of their own past, but their thoughts and actions were increasingly informed by the accumulated knowledge of Western civilization and by other civilizations as well.

As Jamaican society increased in scale, it increased in complexity and became organized into manifold hierarchical levels of skill, income, and prestige. The organization of human effort became more intricate, while managerial and supervisory personnel both in and out of government, occupying positions of coördination, control, and direction, increased in importance. Differentiation of function, specialization, rationality, and impersonality increased.

Jamaican society increased in total power. I am not merely referring here to technological advance although it is related, but to *social power*. The ability of the Jamaican people to achieve their collective goals increased immeasurably. This was partly owing to technological advance, but it was also owing to increasing differentiation of function, increasingly complex organization of effort, and increasing social mobilization. The application of a zero-sum concept of power—the notion that power is limited and a scarce commodity—is simply inadequate to describe the *changing* total power of Jamaican society and probably of other developing societies as well. However useful the zero-sum concept of power may be to describe the competition over the distribution of power *at any given time,* it is more accurate to view power as a resource that can be developed when describing *changes in total power through time.* Power per capita, wealth per capita, and energy per capita increased.

Belief in ancestors and local spirits, in magic and witchcraft declined greatly and became, by the time of independence, of little practical importance. There was a spread of universal religions with membership in world organizations. The aboriginal culture was wiped out; although obeah men still existed as retentions of the African heritage, their influence and their clientele declined greatly.

An increasing consciousness of the widening relations and dependence on past and contemporaneous groups among more and more Jamaicans followed the increase in the scale of society.

Although social differentiation increased as Jamaican society increased in scale, there was a reduction of hereditary privilege. As will be pointed out in detail in Chapter III, the circulation of elites increased, and the elite expanded in relative size and became less exclusive. Elites were recruited from a wider range of social origins than before—although they may eventually become more homogeneous in origin with respect to one characteristic, country of birth; and recruitment of elites was increasingly based upon universalistic criteria of achieved skills. Elites became more accessible to the masses, and the masses became more accessible to the elites.

As Jamaican society increased in scale, an increasing diversity occurred with the resulting isolation of subgroups that were functionally significant for the total society. Jamaican society was a heterogeneous aggregation of individuals of diverse origins resulting from migration—by choice and by force. Yet the contacts between diverse groups resulting from increasing heterogeneity were also preconditions for the reduction of that heterogeneity, for an increase in the *internal inclusiveness of the society.* This process had not yet run its course, but the trend was in the direction of the reduction of ascriptive barriers that in the past prevented the association of some persons with other persons in the society and the institutionalization of equal opportunities for mutual access to facilities and services. It is the process of repeated redefinitions of society to include more and more people within it on a more equal basis, in some respects, in relation to the formerly more favored members of the society. In part, this is an aspect of increasing mobility in that the size of the group within which any Jamaican may move freely increased in social as well as in geographical distance.

In one sense, of course, this trend seems to be contradicted by the dismantlement of empires and the creation of new nations. The resulting new "nationality" became a new ascriptive barrier, sometimes where little national identification existed before, between the peoples of the different new nations and the peoples of other nations, both old and new. The rise of modern nationalism, however, served to reduce many ascriptive barriers that used to stand between various social groups within the territory of the new nations, and was a basis for a new and more thoroughgoing internal unity. In Jamaica, even the new national motto reveals this integrative hope: "Out of Many, One People." Also, the transfer of highest loyalty and allegiance from small traditional or sectional groups to the national level set the stage, as others have pointed out, for a further step in which political and other organizations may be developed which transcend the nation-state in the priority of its claim on the individual and which are larger in geographical scale than presently existing nation-states. Among the older nations of Europe, this trend is already apparent. There, the growth of supra-national organizations and the consequent decline of some degree and aspects of national sovereignty can be clearly seen today.

There is interaction between scale in space, in time, and in internal inclusiveness. An increase or decrease can occur in one type and not in the others. Instability may result, however. For example, an increase in territorial scale can occur with very little internal inclusiveness. As a result, the integrative institutions of the new unit may be inadequate to maintain the geographical scope of the society and contraction in territorial scale may take place—or as happened often in Jamaican history, territorial scale may be maintained by brute force. As the internal inclusiveness of Jamaican society increased, however, there was a decreasing reliance on brute force for the maintenance of social cohesion and an increase in social integration based upon consensus. This process had not yet run its course either. In fact, a serious problem of social disunity and the need for still more social integration faced Jamaica at independence, but again the trends were clear. Consent had increased and naked power had decreased in importance.[7]

The trends toward increasing mobility and circulation, more equal opportunities, and the reduction of ascriptive barriers occurred *pari passu* with the trends toward increasing social differentiation. The spread of equality, to be discussed more fully below, and increased differentiation are sometimes viewed by writers, when one or the other is not simply ignored, as a dilemma in that the two trends seem opposed to one another. But they both can contribute to an increase in the ability of members of a society to achieve their collective and individual goals and in this sense, at a higher level of abstraction than before, they appear, not opposed, but alike in their consequences. Increased differentiation *can* contribute added power, more effective organization of effort, and higher levels of social mobilization. And the trend toward equality *can* result in more people being more committed to the society, in more people being more highly motivated to achieve, in a greater overall development of human resources, and in a more effective distribution of talent and skills in the most important positions in the society.

The Spread of Equality

The spread of equality in Jamaica can be identified by the extension of rising minimums of human rights, universally applied to an increasing proportion of persons in Jamaica. Following the United Nations' usage, I subsume civil, political, economic, social, and cultural rights under the term human rights, as defined as follows:

Civil rights—freedoms from torture and slavery; freedoms of religion, expression, and assembly; the right to security of person, equality before courts and tribunals, a fair and public hearing by competent and impartial tribunals established by law, presumption of innocence until proved guilty, and the right of everyone to be considered a person before the law, among other such rights.

Political rights—freedom to take part in the conduct of public affairs, voting, and equal access to public service as well as others that define the people's rights to participate in the political system on the basis of equality.

Economic rights—the right to fair wages and equal remuneration for work of equal value; safe and healthy working conditions; equal opportunity to be promoted subject only to considerations of seniority and competence; rest and leisure; reasonable limitation of working hours and periodic holidays with pay; ownership of property either alone or in association with others; the right to form and join a trade union for the promotion and protection of one's economic interests, and the right to strike; among others.

Social and cultural rights—the right to marry and establish a family, to the free choice of a marriage partner; to enjoy the highest attainable standard of physical and mental health; to free primary education and equal access to secondary and higher education; to an adequate standard of living including adequate food, clothing, and housing; and the right to take part in the cultural life of the nation; among others.

From the point of view of the historical extension of these rights, it is accurate to describe much of the social history of Jamaica in terms of the changing, that is *rising,* minimums of rights—especially as they were applied to the lower classes whether white, brown, or black, or whether slaves, indentured bond servants, agricultural laborers, urban workers, unemployed poor people, or whatever—depending on the period of Jamaican history one is discussing. The Jamaican lower classes emerged as participants in the society on the basis of more equality than they had in the past enjoyed. The gradual extension of civil, political, economic, social, and cultural rights—*rights* that were embedded in law, not simply benefits deriving from benevolent paternalism which were granted in exchange for personal subservience and submissive gratitude—to the lower classes in Jamaica can be easily documented.

This is not to say that gross inequalities of status and opportunities did not exist in Jamaica at the time of independence. Although there was equality of civil and political rights, as these were expressed in law, such equality was partly irrelevant and partly only nominal when actual practice is considered. The laws against obeah (black magic) and the use of *ganja* (marihuana), for example, applied *equally* to the upper and middle classes, who generally considered these practices to be foreign, and to the lower classes, for whom such practices were in some cases still part of accepted cultural patterns. Furthermore, the high costs of legal advice, differential unfamiliarity with the law, and differential participation in legal administration reduced the power of the lower classes, as in other countries, to implement and realize their nominal rights fully.

Since 1944, equality of political rights was undoubtedly more fully achieved in fact than equality of civil rights. Nevertheless, the inequalities of social and economic stratification in Jamaica resulted in some reduction of real equality in the political arena. Money bought election propaganda and thus influenced the election outcome, the conferral of prestige coöpted some elected political leaders to some degree, and the differential distribution of skills by classes tended to restrict the formulation and administration of governmental policies to members of the middle and upper classes.

Economic and social inequalities in Jamaica were even greater than civil and political inequalities. As social facts rather than as legal statements, economic and social equality and equality of opportunity did not exist. In his analysis of Jamaican social structure, M. G. Smith accurately highlights inequalities in Jamaica in recent years. The white upper classes, the brown middle classes, and the black lower classes were grossly unequal, with economic and social advantages accruing most to the upper and least to the lower classes.[8]

However, the inequalities with respect to civil, political, economic, social, and cultural rights had a past during which the inequalities were far greater; and the long-term trends in these rights were toward increasing equality, toward rising minimums applied to more and more people. The new constitution of Jamaica reached a new peak and a comprehensive set of human rights to apply equally to all Jamaicans was entrenched in it.

Much of the story of the spread of equality in Jamaica is the story of the Negroes brought from Africa as slave laborers and of their descendants. Literally, they began their journey into their new lives with no rights at all—a circumstance generally different from that even of the slaves within the African societies themselves. It is true, as Herskovits says, that a plantation system of slavery resembling the conditions of labor that the slaves were to encounter in the new world existed at least in the kingdom of Dahomey, before the European slave trade, but on the whole slaveholding in Africa had been of the household variety.[9] Some slaves had been family or hereditary slaves and they were usually considered members of the master's family, sometimes eating with him from the same dish, sharing his enjoyments, intermarrying with his children, acquiring property of their own, and in exceptional cases even rising to wealth exceeding that of the master. There were many other slaves, however, either purchased or pawns who were pledged by relatives, masters, or themselves for repayment of debt, and they were often made to work hard and sometimes were treated with great cruelty.[10] Slaves were also sacrificed in worship to the ancestors of members of African royal families, and a few of them were exported in the trans-Saharan slave trade.

The existence of slavery in Africa naturally had a bearing on the development of the Atlantic slave trade in that the European traders were not repulsed when they asked for slaves in return for goods. Dominant ideologies and social institutions in neither Africa nor Europe at the time were committed to the rights and dignity of all human beings, so there seemed nothing unnatural or wrong with the Africans selling men and women nor with the Europeans buying them. Slavery, however, was part of the whole fabric of social life in Africa and some, if not many, of the slaves had, either by custom or by law, civil, economic, social, cultural, and in a few cases even political rights as well as duties. The slaves purchased by the Europeans, branded with a hot iron on breast or shoulder, had, at first, no rights as human beings at all, but had to depend for what fair treatment they received on their value as property in which their owners had invested for a profit of one kind or another.

M. G. Smith has contrasted the structural aspects of slavery in Jamaica with those among the Hausa of Zaria. He explains how the Hausa slave was assimilated while the slaves in Jamaica were socially and culturally differentiated by their slave status.

Among the Hausa, master and slave participated in the following identical institutions; religion, marriage, kinship and family, marketing, education, and government. They also spoke the same language, shared the same technology,

and took part in common economic processes. Both groups had a common
lore, a common classical language, Arabic, in which the daily prayers were
recited, common conventions, etiquette, and value systems. Law provided
further links between master and slave, such as participation in common courts,
and the code of land tenure, which restricted rights in land to usufruct, placed
both the slave and his master on a similar footing.

Among the Jamaicans on the other hand, masters and slaves practised and
professed different forms of the following institutions; religion, marriage, kinship, family, marketing, education, and government. They spoke different lan-
guages, operated different technologies, and took part in different economic
processes. They were further differentiated as sections in terms of lore, conventions, etiquette, and value systems. . . . Law defined differences of master and
slave sharply, underlining the latter's classification as a chattel, by his exclusion
from the same courts as his master, thereby providing conditions favourable to
the development of tribunals among the slaves to settle their internal differences,
and of conspiracy or rebellion to settle accounts with their masters. Whereas
it was forbidden for a slave to bear arms in Jamaica, the soldiery and command
of Zaria included slaves in all ranks. Yet whereas the period 1804–1900, for
which the history of Zaria is known in detail, contains no instance of slave
rebellion, the Caribbean colonists lived in a perpetual state of siege of their
own manufacture, with somewhat uneasy periods of truce between slave
revolts.[11]

Herskovits says that the hypothesis that the slave trade was selective
so as to result in the least desirable persons or social groups being brought
from Africa to the new world is not borne out by the evidence. For example, members of the ruling classes were sometimes sold as slaves as a
consequence of dynastic disputes between brothers, between brothers and
uncles, and so on. Intertribal warfare often resulted in the least compliant
priests of the defeated tribe being sold into slavery. Captives from other
tribes, criminals who couldn't pay their fines and others whose punishment
was banishment, debtors who refused or couldn't pay their debts, and children who were sold by parents in order to relieve their poverty contributed
to the slave populations. Debtors and criminals were apparently only a
small proportion of those slaves sold to the Europeans if one considers
the whole period of the slave trade. And the chief means of attaining slaves,
warfare and kidnaping, contributed all social levels to the ranks of the
slaves. Selective factors were introduced, however, by the European traders
themselves who preferred, with an eye on prices in the American slave
market, a larger number of men to women, young adults to the very young
or the very old, and physically fit to debilitated persons.[12]

It is a mistake to think that the slaves accepted their status and their
lack of rights with docility and compliance. The element of force cannot

be overemphasized, nor can the fact that the Negroes often resisted it even when their chance of overpowering their captors and masters or of escaping were slim. Many preferred death to slavery. They were herded like cattle aboard ship. During the Atlantic passage, they were whipped, clubbed, handcuffed, shackled with leg irons and chains, so that order was maintained. If necessary, they were forced to eat with the *speculum oris*—a device that forced the jaws apart after being jammed in the mouth, or by having glowing hot coals on a shovel placed so near their lips that they were scorched and burned. If they still persisted in their refusal, they might be forced to swallow the coals as an example to others. At least one captain poured melted lead on the Negroes who obstinately refused to eat. Forced into overcrowded spaces on board ship, they lay in blood and mucus and human excrement, sometimes on bare planks where the skin and flesh rubbed off the prominent parts of their shoulders, elbows, and hips until the bones were bare. Some jumped overboard, some died in despair, some rebelled and fought, some were killed, and some survived to be resold in new lands.

Some differentiation in the status of the Negroes, and in their rights and duties, took place even during the Atlantic crossing, and was most apparent among those given authority to oversee the others. Sometimes they would be specially purchased Negroes from a tribe or region different from that of most of the slaves being transported, and their jobs included sleeping among the other Negroes in order to prevent quarreling, to discover and report plotting, and to oversee generally the mass of slaves. A badge of their office and authority was sometimes given to them—in some instances it was the cat-o'-nine-tails.[13]

When a slave ship arrived in Jamaica or elsewhere in the West Indies, the slaves were sold—sometimes at a tavern, on the wharf, on the ship itself, or in a company's yard. Sometimes the slaves were lined up so that the buyers could examine them and then a public auction was held. At other times, a method known as "scramble" was used during which all the Negroes "scrambled for" bore an equal price: the Negroes were brought together at one place and at the agreed upon hour the purchasers rushed in and claimed as many Negroes as they could conveniently lay their hands upon. The sale itself was often disorganizing and frightening to the slaves. But sometimes the slaves were eager to be sold, being weary and often sick from the Atlantic crossing, and were cheerful and coöperative before potential buyers.

The planter's first concern after completing his purchases was to issue a suit of coarse osnaburg, a cheap linen, to the slaves who had arrived naked. They were also given a knife, a hat and handkerchiefs before being taken to the plantation. For the first few months the slaves were seasoned, that is, left to adjust to the change of climate and the new country. This was often done by distributing new slaves among those already on the plantation and letting the old hands look after them.[14]

The English proprietors who settled in Jamaica after 1655 simply adopted slavery, it being their belief and experience that slavery was essential for proper cultivation of the island. Even though the legal position of slavery was shaky, the Negroes sold in the early days were in the complete control of their masters. Absolute obedience on the part of the slaves was demanded. They were property, and if the master wanted to destroy his own property there was at first no one to stop him.

Opponents of slavery attacked the legality or constitutionality of slavery, and in 1772 and 1778 gained legal decisions in England and Scotland abolishing slavery in Great Britain. However, the Chief Justice made it clear that these decisions did not apply to the West Indies and that slavery could be abolished there only by positive law.

Gradually, over the years, the slaves received protections both in law and in actual practice. Of course, acutal practice often violated the rights of slaves as legally defined, while sometimes actual practice was less severe than the legal codes implied. Some tightening up and increasing severity of laws resulted in a restriction of rights, and this usually occurred when legal extension of more rights was being pressed most vigorously by reformers or just after slave rebellions or insurrections, which were the constant worries of the white dominant minority. An examination of the legal rights of the slaves is instructive, for it clearly shows first, the codification of the existing harsh realities of slavery, and second, a trend toward rising minimums of rights and protections for the slaves.

The improvement of the status and rights of the slaves is revealed by a series of legal acts, mostly by the Jamaican Assembly but also by the British Parliament, that provided for (in chronological order): a fine of £50 payable to the owner and three months' imprisonment for killing a slave "out of wilfulness, wantonness or bloudy mindedness"; a slave court of two justices and three freeholders to try criminal offenses by slaves; instruction of slaves in the principles of the Christian religion; minimum food supplies and clothing for slaves; slave holidays at Christmas, Easter, and Whitsuntide; the right of slaves to meet together for purposes of innocent amusement; prevention of the master under fine of £100 from dismembering a slave; the right of slaves to hire themselves out to work if they had a certificate notarized by a Justice of the Peace stating the particular work they could perform and for how long a time they were at liberty to hire themselves; the right of the fourth generation removed from a Negro to be declared free; the freedom of the Maroons (the first "Jamaicans" of African origin to gain their collective freedom); the admission of the evidence of slaves against liberated blacks; an increase in the penalty for killing a slave up to one year of imprisonment in addition to burning of the hand; protection of aging slaves from being thrown on their own resources; repeal of previous legislation on surveillance of slaves; the additional penalty of imprisonment of up to one year for mutilating and dismembering a slave; a prohibition on the whipping, beating, bruising, or confining of any other owner's slave without sufficient reason; an increase in the punishment for killing a slave from a fine and twelve months imprisonment to the death penalty; a provision equal to the value of two shillings and six pence per week to each slave for whom no land was available; the master or overseer to swear an oath once a year that their slaves were maintained and clothed properly; the protection of slaves from their own masters as well as others; a limit of thirty-nine lashes at one time or for any one offense; a prohibition on a judge to sentence a slave to be mutilated or maimed for any offense whatsoever; the establishment of a petit jury of nine for slave courts; one free day each fortnight for slaves for cultivation of their own gardens; a maximum work day for slaves of eleven and a half hours; a prohibition against a white to maltreat a slave or load him with chains, irons, or weights, or to place him in iron collars; a limitation on the court to limit confinement to hard labor to two years instead of life; the courts to substitute transportation off the island for the death penalty in some cases; an exemption from hard labor for any mother of six living children and the requirement that the owner must provide her with an easy and comfortable maintenance; a prohibition of the slave trade; an increase in the minimum food allowances for slaves not furnished with provision grounds from two shillings and six pence to three shillings and four pence; a guaranteed daily food ration for slaves; an increase in the penalty for owners convicted of abandoning old, worn-out, or diseased slaves; the freedom of slaves wantonly mistreated by their owners; a full jury of twelve men in the slave court; a special investigation of runaway slaves to make certain of their status, that they were not free, before sentence was pronounced; freedom to be conferred by simple will, such as to dispose of any personal property; the exemption of slaves from estate labor on Sunday; the right of appeal for slaves sentenced to be executed and the power for the Governor to commute all death sentences upon slaves except those tried for rebellion; the notification of the coroner whenever a slave died (so that concealment of slave murders was more difficult); a prohibition on creditors, so that they could not apprehend slaves found outside their owner's property on Saturday, thus giving the slaves a day of grace in addition to Sunday to go off the estate; the right of slaves to receive bequests of money or other personal property, and the repeal of previous legislation requiring the sanction of persons inheriting an estate before a slave could claim his legacy; the death penalty for the crime of rape upon a slave; the removal of the limit upon the amount of money which could be left as a bequest to faithful slaves; the admission of slave evidence even in cases where a white person or person of free condition was charged with a capital crime (but no free person could be convicted of any crime unless more than one slave gave evidence of the same fact or circumstance); the delegation of a public defender to take the defense of any slave on trial for a capital offense to present his case to the jury; the recognition of personal property rights of slaves; the extension of the curfew on slaves, from ten to twelve o'clock, and the permission to owners to grant their slaves three successive holidays instead of only two; the extension of all the rights, privileges, and immunities of whites to free Negroes and mulattoes; the easier manumission of slaves; the discharge from jail any slave detained in custody for six months and still not indicted; a total of twenty-six days throughout the year exclusive of Sundays and holidays to be given the slaves to work their own provision grounds and to provide for their personal wants; and specific definitions of punishments thereby limiting the discretion of magistrates regarding what punishments they could inflict.[15]

Throughout the legal acts leading up to the abolition of slavery, there is ample evidence not only of the extension of rights to slaves, but also of the legal restrictions under which slaves suffered at any given time. Also, the planters' fears of violence at the hands of the slaves are documented.

Emancipation was a significant event in the spread of equality, so significant in fact that we can legitimately call it a revolution.

Revolutions are frequently summarized in one outstanding document which proclaims the intentions of the revolutionaries. For the American Revolution there is the Declaration of Independence; for the French, the Declaration of the Rights of Man and the Citizen. There is also a document for the Jamaican Revolution of the 1830's—'An Act for the Abolition of Slavery throughout the British Colonies; for promoting the Industry of the Manumitted Slaves; and for compensating the persons hitherto entitled to the Services of Such Slaves,' 3 and 4 Wm. Iv, c. 73. This document, however, was more than an epitome of the Jamaican Revolution. In one very real sense it *was* the revolution—an act of the Imperial Parliament overthrowing the old social order in the West Indian colonies and laying the basis for a new one. It forced drastic social change on

Jamaica, and it forced this change through the power of the imperial government rather than through a revolutionary party within the colony.[16]

As dramatic and significant, and as symbolically important for the extension of human rights, as was the passing of the Emancipation Act in 1833, it did not sweep away all the inequalities of civil and political rights, nor did it alone bring about significant changes immediately in the economic, social, and cultural well-being of the lower socio-economic-racial groups—mostly composed of the freed slaves. Nevertheless, it was the most impressive step ever taken up to that time in the progress toward greater equality.

There was more progress in the extension of human rights even during the bitter period leading up to the Morant Bay Riot in 1865, still more progress just after the crown colony system was established in 1866, and then, after some static years, an increasing tempo of change toward more equality since 1938 with the creation of mass political parties and trade unions, and the beginning of universal adult suffrage, tutelary democracy, and internal self-government. Full political independence in 1962 gave to all Jamaicans citizenship in their own country and placed Jamaica on an equality of status with the other independent nations of the world. It transferred power into the hands of the representatives of the Jamaican people, and it was, by its constitutional guarantees, another step in the direction of civil and political equality, and in rising minimums of economic, social, and cultural rights. This link is symbolized by the fact that August 1 had long been celebrated in Jamaica as Emancipation Day, and that August 6 was selected as the day of independence. In the future, the first Monday in August will be celebrated for both events, Emancipation and Independence being the two most significant events leading from a past of deprivation and despair to a future of hope, from inequality to equality, from bondage to freedom.

As the social and cultural history of Jamaica is rewritten, it will undoubtedly emphasize the role of Africa and slavery more than colonial and European histories of Jamaica have done, probably along the lines that I have sketched so briefly here. This is in part because most Jamaicans are the descendants of slaves and have African ancestors. Also, slavery is becoming important because the emergent society is including to an increasing degree the lower socioeconomic groups and their history *is* in large part the history of Negro slavery. Additionally, the recent emergence of African nationalism and the formation of new African nations out of former colonies are similar to and dramatize the recent political transfor-

mation of Jamaica into an independent nation-state. Jamaica is closer to
Africa and Asia in its recent political experience than it is to Latin America, and it is closer to Africa than to Asia in its racial norm.[17]

At the time of independence, some Jamaicans were reluctant to accept
the growing emphasis upon African origins and slavery in the interpretation of Jamaica's past, therefore they rejected these same elements as being an important aspect of Jamaicans' collective character, and they rejected the resultant implications for Jamaica's future. This was so despite
the facts of Jamaica's historical links to Africa and to Negro slavery. Such
reluctance generally flowed from attitudes that were opposed to the trend
toward equality and reflected either the rejection of identification with
Negro racial stock, however flimsy the evidence might be to support such
a rejection, or the principle, subscribed to by some Jamaicans of all colors,
that the symbols of the (primitive) African origins and slavery were somehow degrading.

At the same time, other Jamaicans, in an emotional and often extremely
negative reaction to the European or dominant-sectional biases that have
characterized much of the writing of Jamaican history, were overstressing
these same symbols in their interpretations. The facts certainly support the
story of the rise of the enslaved black men from Africa as being an important part of Jamaican history, but if it is permitted to become *the* history
of Jamaica, then results that will flow from such a decision also may be
inimical to the continuation of the trend toward equality. For example,
some Jamaicans, perhaps all those who are not fairly dark-skinned Negroes, might be excluded from sharing in the new Jamaican history, perhaps from the new Jamaican society itself. This did not appear very likely
when this study was done, but it did seem to be a possible, even if remote,
danger.

Still other Jamaicans realized, however, that there was a more universalistic story to tell than that of Negro slavery, a story closer to the truth
and closer to their own humanitarian hopes for a more inclusive society
in Jamaica in the future. It is the story of the rise of the underprivileged
groups of *all* descriptions—subordinate classes, races, religions, nationalities, even sex and age groups—to a position of more equality than they
had in the past enjoyed. And it is the story of the members of the more
privileged groups whose actions contributed toward raising the minimums
of human rights. Thus, a part of Jamaican history, among some Jamaicans,
was beginning to be interpreted as the increasing internal inclusiveness of
society for *all* members of Jamaican society, not just for the Negroes. Thus,
they said that the meaning and character of the new nation of Jamaica
should transcend even the African and slave origins, as important as they

were, and should be sought in the more universal conception of the extension of equal rights to all men. The facts of history seem to be amenable to such an interpretation.

As pointed out in Chapter I, indentured servants from England, Scotland, Ireland, Wales, India, China, Germany, France, Syria, and elsewhere were brought to Jamaica and shared with the Negroes both the lack of human rights and the struggle for equality. Frequently, the conditions of the bond servants' "slavery" were far worse than those of the Negro slaves. A bond servant was to get his freedom after so many years of labor, and many an employer squeezed the last ounce of energy from him during the time of his contract, not caring whether the bond servant lived or died after his contract was fulfilled.

Similarly, even the sailors on the ships bringing the slaves from Africa were harshly treated. For example, even though the slaves had no legal claim to any rights on board the slaving ships while the sailors did, the conditions of the sailors were often little better than those of the slaves, and their rights were often violated in practice. It was standard operating procedure to fill out the complement of a ship's company by kidnapping, and many a man from the slums of Liverpool and Bristol awoke one morning to find himself on board a slaver on a voyage to Africa and then the West Indies—perhaps to jump ship in Jamaica to escape the hardships on board. The sailors signed articles, but sometimes were not permitted to read the clauses—even if they could read. Often, the sailors were short of water and provisions, had to sleep on deck where they were exposed to the weather during the middle passage, and were brutally treated by the captain and other officers. In addition, many of the slaves were on the alert for a chance to escape or revolt, and the sailors were in danger of violence or death at their hands. Through death or desertion, barely three-fourths and sometimes not even one-third of a crew would return to the European port from which it sailed.

The bond servants and other paying passengers on the ships of the time coming to Jamaica and elsewhere had a legal claim to certain rights as did the sailors, but the conditions of their passage and their treatment by the ship's officers and men were frequently little better than the way in which slaves were treated on some ships. Of course, treatment varied from ship to ship and captain to captain, but the captains usually had no further financial interest in the regular passengers after they had paid for their passages. In fact, if regular passengers died enroute, the captain could sometimes make a small financial gain from the saving on the unused portion of their provisions, while the avarice of the slaving-ship captains sometimes kept the slaves alive—since a dead slave could not be sold.

The following account of an Irish emigrant ship headed for Boston in 1802 shows some of the conditions faced by regular, paying passengers.

The packet ship *Polly,* of Waterford, must have been as bad as any slaver that ever skulked the "Middle Passage" with battened-down hatches. She was 202 tons burden and carried 450 odd steerage passengers. They were so thick between decks that the air became putrid and whenever her sick squads were ordered up the gangways, one or more was sure to die with the first gulp of fresh air. The steerage became pestilential before our voyage was half over, for the emigrants' beds were never cleaned and whole families literally wallowed in poisonous filth. The bodies of men and women, and their tattered garments, were incrusted and impregnated with the most offensive matter. Typhus fever and dysentery soon broke out and then the mortality raged fearfully.

The *Polly's* crew, when she left Ireland, consisted of but ten men and four died of dysentery before we were half way across the Atlantic. One day when I had crawled to the deck and lay on a coil of chain near the capstan, I counted thirty corpses that were hauled up during the morning and thrown overboard. Most of the bodies were women with their long hair tangled in their filthy garments.

The ship's provisions began to run short after a time and were doled out in the most niggardly way until the dysentery thinned out the passengers, when there was enough and to spare of oatmeal and damaged rice. But water grew scantier every day. Foul weather set in and the *Polly* was driven from her course into the hot latitudes and when we made the first light, off Cape Ann, we had 186 left out of 450 odd passengers and some of these died before landing.[18]

In Jamaica, the Negro slaves had no monopoly on subordination, deprivation, brutal treatment, and lack of freedom. Indentured servants were generally mistreated as well and could in effect be bought and sold. Just as in the case of the slaves, their masters' right to their time was absolute; and little distinction was made between the white indentured servants and the Negro slaves. Also, white clerks, accountants, and others were sometimes little better off than the Negroes. Additionally, not just slaves, but all depressed groups shared in the spread of equality and in the transformation of Jamaica from an exclusive to a more inclusive society. With independence, the descendants of all such groups—whether African, European, or Asian—became equally full citizens in the new nation.

The trend toward rising minimums of human rights for more and more people over the long course of Jamaican history seems well enough established, but a word of caution should be reiterated. To identify such a trend is not to say that there have never been decreases in minimums of rights. Cycles and random fluctuations have occurred, but the long-range nonrepetitive changes are clear. Also, there has been interaction between demand for and achievement of civil, political, economic, and social rights. Although the long-term trends show that the direction of change has been toward the application of an equal set of rights to all adults in the society, at certain times there was a "substitution rate" of one type of right for others. That is, certain rights were gained at the expense of others. For example, with emancipation, new civil rights were obtained, but certain traditional economic rights were lost. The former masters of the former slaves no longer were obligated to prevent economic deprivation among their workers, although with modern developments new and more thoroughgoing economic rights are enjoyed by all Jamaicans.

Of course, the identification of a long-term trend toward equality, toward the rising minimums of human rights for an increasingly large number of persons, does not mean that the continuation of the trend is inevitable, nor that it will continue automatically without definite actions being taken. Mathematically speaking, one can write a number of different formulas that would adequately fit the known past trend but that would extrapolate the trend in different directions; that is, each would predict a different future from the same past. Also, the trend toward equality did not always occur without agitation and violence, and it may not continue without further disorder. Thus, future developments toward further extensions of human rights in Jamaica may be problematical, but the analysis of social trends suggests that the trend toward equality of rights was no accident and may reflect some underlying principle of change. If so, then causal analysis can replace simple extrapolation.

The Resolution of Problems of Legitimacy

How did the trend toward equality of rights come about? What was the dynamic mechanism underlying the changes in the nature and application of human rights in Jamaica? Tentatively, the answer seems to be the *resolution of problems of legitimacy*. Changes in human rights occurred as a result of resolutions of anomalies between structures and practices on the one hand and ideas about what was legitimate on the other. There was a demonstrable interplay between ideas and institutions throughout the history of Jamaica. Institutions fostered certain ideas about what was right or wrong, what should or should not be; and ideas, often exogenous to Jamaica itself originally, led to organized social action that often resulted in changing, eliminating, or creating institutions. For example, ideas about the social inferiority of Negroes were fostered in and diffused from Jamaica and elsewhere in the West Indies during one period of history when a justification of an important institution, slavery, was needed. The currency and spread of these ideas were in some sense "caused" by the institution and functioned as legitimations of it. On the other hand, ideas emerging in Europe raised questions of legitimacy concerning slavery, and social action based on these ideas eventually resulted in the disappearance of an institution: the slave trade was abolished and the slaves were freed.[19] From this viewpoint, social change in Jamaica, to be understood more fully, should be set against the background of developments that took place in Europe and in the United States. The breakdown of feudalism; the rise of the modern state in Europe; the formation of a national citizenry (which implied equality for all adults in some respects); the American and French revolutions, the industrial revolution in England; the trade union movement; the formulation of new ideologies—political, economic, and social; the spread of mass education; and the growth of the welfare state were all relevant to political, economic, and social changes in Jamaica. Available evidence supports the contention that ideas, usually imported from Europe—particularly England—and to some extent from the United States, over the course of Jamaican history led to social action that resulted in the reduction of anomalies between such ideas and institutions. Usually, the result was structural change toward more equality, and it also was usually what might be considered "progress"; that is, more equality was created by giving more people more rights. (But not always. One of the more interesting examples occurred in 1865 when the white ruling oligarchs, who feared domination by the numerous former slaves, created more equality by giving away some of their own political rights because it was no longer agreed that it was legitimate, after emancipation, for one section of the citizenry to have such rights without the newly created citizens, the former slaves, having the same rights too.)

Ideas regarding human rights of various kinds often were expressed in lower-class demands, discontents, disaffection, and alienation. Before 1944 when universal adult suffrage was begun, lower-class collective protests in Jamaica took the form, as Reinhard Bendix says of Europe before the formation of the modern political community, ". . . of millenarian movements, social banditry, and direct outbursts of violence, which ranged from an inchoate venting of accumulated grievances to a cunning or righteous insistence upon the customary rights even of the most subordinate groups." [20] Such patterns of protest remained in Jamaica in August, 1962, but their frequency and significance were greatly diminished owing to the fact that in recent years major protests were expressed by participation of the lower classes in the new national political community. Legitimate political action and legal trade union activity accounted for the expression of many modern demands.

The elites, of course, played a crucial role throughout the whole process of circular causation between ideas and institutions. Their actions or inactions, their ideologies, attitudes, and beliefs contributed toward expansion or contraction of internal inclusiveness or helped maintain existing barriers of exclusiveness. On some occasions, they boldly led change toward increasing scale and more equality, and on others they, as Tawney points out in a similar connection, walked reluctantly backward into the future, as other European governments did after the leveling doctrines of France, doing from above what is sometimes accomplished by revolution in spite of their contrary ideologies and attitudes, but because of their belief that, if they did not, something far worse than a change toward equality might befall them.[21]

There was ample evidence of lower-class discontents, disaffection, and alienation as Jamaica approached independence. Many lower-class persons were saying that their interests were not being served. They were raising questions about the civil service ("a middle-class preserve"); the new office buildings for the Ministries ("Why not more housing?" "The brown men take care of themselves!"); they were seeing new factories and a new air terminal, but they saw their own circumstances improved less than they expected. Some members of the new Jamaican elite realized that, although Jamaica had experienced considerable economic growth on the basis of conventional criteria, not enough of Jamaica's increased wealth had yet reached the mass of the population. They hoped to spread available resources wider than in the recent past. But some of them also realized that the lower-class Jamaican could be a recalcitrant tool of action, usually uneducated and perhaps illiterate, suspicious of change, often actively resisting efforts of field workers to change his ways, short-tempered in his expectations for government to do something for him, being only half a citizen in that his duties and obligations were not clear to him while his rights were increasingly in his consciousness, and increasingly alienated if his expectations were not met and if his obligations were pointed out to him.

During the transition to independence, Jamaica had reached another stage of development where an anomaly developed between ideas concerning human rights and some elites' ability or willingness to provide for them. The realities of change toward more equality were catching up with and passing by the images of the future held by some elites. Such elites began to wonder how much more the lower socio-economic-racial groups would want before they would be satisfied, and they sometimes found themselves in the position of resisting the rising minimums of rights rather than struggling to achieve them. Thus, new problems of legitimacy were arising, and new solutions were being sought—the formulation and implementation of such solutions remaining an important part of elite functions whether an existing elite likes it or not.

However, with the political developments that led to an independent Jamaica—especially since 1938—the social composition of elites was changing, a new leadership group was emerging. The decisions that were molding the future of Jamaica, that were determining the fate of the hope for more equality, were being placed in the hands of this new Jamaican elite. Who were these new elites? What were their social backgrounds and their positions in the social structure? What were their beliefs and attitudes? To what ideologies were they committed? Did they believe in equality, and democracy, and the Western world? The answers to these questions will reveal much about the kind of society that Jamaica was becoming and will become. The following chapters are attempts to answer these questions.

Chapter III

Who Are Jamaica's Leaders?

THE ELITES in any society have an importance far exceeding their numbers. In a preface to the Stanford University comparative study of elites, it was stated:

The ways of a society are largely fixed by the myths and doctrines of a ruling few. Democracy differs from oligarchy not in the presence or absence of an elite who wield most influence, but in the closed or open, representative or unrepresentative, responsible or irresponsible character of the elite. Who these elites are, how they live, what training they get, how they circulate, are among the most significant facts of the history of a society.[1]

In the new and developing nation-states, by their sheer scarcity elites may assume even more importance than in the older and more developed countries. Even though few in numbers it is they who lead and facilitate change, or oppose and hinder new developments. Their talents and initiative are crucial in getting new ideas accepted in the society, yet they function also to maintain a continuity with the past and to preserve social integration. They are mediators and communicators, interested articulators and aggregators, creators and disseminators of culture, preservers of values, change leaders, and standard makers for the general population. Thus, with the transformation of former political dependencies into new nations, the development of indigenous leaders having adequate training and experience becomes of great significance. Political change formally transfers political power from an old colonial elite, often intertwined with an indigenous traditional elite, to an emergent national elite, and at the same time planned economic and social changes place a premium on new skills and talents and demand new personnel possessing them.[2]

The social composition of elites is of course inextricably linked to political, economic, and social developments in the emerging nations. Increased governmental functions, the development of responsible self-government, new patterns of elite recruitment and socialization, the changing modes of interest articulation and aggregation, economic advancement, increased social welfare and educational opportunities, the spread of national citizenship, and other developments are changing the social characteristics of elites as well as changing the nature of elite positions themselves and their interrelationships. In turn, the changes in elites affect the direction, tempo, and content of future political, economic, and social changes.

The purpose of this chapter is to understand some of the changes in the social composition of Jamaican leaders during the transition from colonial status to political independence, and to describe the social backgrounds of the elites who were leading Jamaica into independence. We know a good deal about the polity and economy of the new nations, but we know considerably less about related *social* changes within them. Thus, this chapter is addressed to the following questions: As progress toward political independence and economic advancement was made, how did the elites change? What were the social characteristics of the emergent elites when compared to the elites of the late colonial period? What distinctions developed between the occupants of different types of elite positions? Was the social base from which elites were recruited changing? If so, in what ways? Did shifts in the locus of political power change the superordinate-subordinate relationships between different types of elites? What positions in social institutions were held by the most influential persons?

Top Governmental Leaders, 1939–1954

In 1939, Jamaica had a modified crown colony government little changed since 1884 and faced five more years before the beginning of tutelary democracy. Although there were elected members in the Legislative Council, the electorate was limited and generally uninterested in politics. For the most part, the elected members played the role of an irresponsible opposition, but they had special powers over finance that often made governance difficult. The Governor had great powers that included the reserved right to override the elected members in case of necessity. In addition to the Governor, the Legislative Council contained a number of *ex officio* and nominated members equal to the number of elected members.[3]

In contrast, Jamaica had been ten years on the road to self-government by 1954, the most recent political change at the time being the introduction of the ministerial system in 1953. The Legislative Council then was composed of only official and nominated members and its powers had been reduced with a few exceptions to the consideration of legislation passed by the new House of Representatives. The latter body then consisted of thirty-two members elected on the basis of universal adult suffrage from the thirty-two constituencies into which Jamaica had been divided. The Executive Council was the principal policy-making body and had become a kind of quasi Cabinet (and a schoolroom for full-fledged Cabinet members-to-be). Thus, it included eight elected members from the House of Representatives, who were Ministers with responsibility over the work of the government departments, in addition to the official and nominated members. Although the element of tutelage was still present in the Governor's reserved legislative power, which could be exercised without the consent of the Executive Council, there was considerable responsible self-government regarding internal affairs under the 1953 Order in Council. In fact, political power had shifted significantly, although not completely, into the hands of the elected representatives of the Jamaican people.[4]

Table 4 shows some of the changes in the social characteristics of the top governmental leaders during this transition period. Included among "top governmental leaders" for each year are members of the executive and legislative branches of the government, the directors, permanent secretaries, and other important civil servants of all governmental departments (and in 1954 of the new Ministries as well), and the *custos* (nominated persons) of each parish. In other words, elected political leaders, higher civil servants, top officials, and occupants of certain nominated positions were included among the top governmental elites. As far as possible, persons occupying functionally equivalent positions were selected for both times, although this was not a simple thing to determine because of the proliferation and change in governmental positions between 1939 and 1954. The data are based upon information on such persons available in the *Handbook of Jamaica* and in *Who's Who, Jamaica* for 1939 and 1954.[5]

Note in Table 4 that about half of the top governmental leaders of 1939 were Jamaican-born, but by 1954 the percentage had increased to 75. Thus, from the point of view of Jamaicans, the top governmental leadership positions were less exclusive in 1954 than they were in 1939, with Jamaicans having a greater chance of occupying such positions in 1954.[6] There was a relative reduction of non-Jamaicans (mostly English) in these roles. During the period under consideration, this was accomplished in part by the replacement of Englishmen by Jamaicans in given leadership roles, and also by the creation of new roles (e.g., an increase in elected political leaders from 14 to 32) that were filled by Jamaicans for the most part. This process of increasing the total number of leadership roles in government continued after 1954 as the functions and services of government expanded, and the replacement of foreign personnel in existing roles since 1954 increasingly contributed to an increased access to such leadership positions on the part of Jamaicans. Still more new roles for Jamaicans were created in defense and foreign affairs with the coming of complete independence.

The top governmental elites are subdivided further in Table 5. For each type of elite the trend is the same—an increase in the percentage of Jamaican-born persons from 1939 to 1954. The smallest increase was for the elected political leaders, but for 1954 the percentage of Jamaicans among them was fully 93 per cent. The largest increase was in the case of the higher civil servants, yet in 1954 about a third of such persons were still non-Jamaicans. This large increase for the civil servants reflects the results of a deliberate policy to "West Indianize" the civil service [7] and the steps that had been taken to promote opportunities for Jamaicans (and some other West Indians) to receive formal, technical, administrative, professional, and other specialized training. It also reflects the facts that comparatively few Jamaicans possessed the necessary skills and experience to perform top civil service roles expertly in 1939 and that, although the increase in Jamaicans in these positions continued since 1954, Jamaica, as other new nations, may be in part dependent for some years on the distribution of specialized and differentiated skills available in technologically more advanced societies. Officials and nominated persons (for convenience designated "appointees") increased from 54 to 70 per cent Jamaican-born.

Of the elites born in Jamaica, 29 per cent were urban-born (in Kingston, Spanish Town, or Montego Bay) in 1939 compared with 34 per cent in 1954 (see Table 4). Thus, the 1954 top governmental elites were slightly more urban with respect to place of birth than the 1939 elites. The elites were more likely to be urban-born than the entire Jamaican-born population. In 1943 about 12 to 14 per cent of the population was urban-born.[8]

The general trend on urban birth is somewhat misleading, however, since the different types of elites did not change in the same way. The elected political leaders increased in percentage of urban-born from 0 to 20 per cent, while the appointees and the higher civil servants had reductions in the percentage of urban-born (from Table 5). In 1939, the differences between the three types of elites were greater than in 1954, with the civil servants most urban, the appointees next, and the elected political leaders least urban. The rank order was the same in 1954 as in 1939, but the differential changes resulted in the different types of elites being more alike in 1954 than in 1939 in this respect.

TABLE 4. *Percentage of Top Governmental Leaders Having Selected Social Characteristics, 1939 and 1954*

	Leaders having selected characteristic:	
	1939 (N = 63) *	1954 (N = 126) *
Selected social characteristics	Per cent	Per cent
Jamaican-born	53	75
Urban-born (Jamaican-born only) * .	29	34
Holds at least one nongovernmental elite position	62	41
Elementary education or less	20	12
Secondary school education	44	54
Some university or more	36	34
Upwardly mobile	70	71
Age 55 or older	40	34

SOURCE: *Who's Who, Jamaica,* 1939 and 1954.

* The number of cases is only approximate because of a few instances in which no information was available for some of the variables. The percentages of urban-born persons are based upon the Jamaican-born leaders only and the number of cases is 31 for 1939 and 90 for 1954.

The study of governmental leaders becomes increasingly meaningful as the relationships between such elites and other institutional sectors of the society are specified. One such relationship is revealed by an examination of the relative number of top governmental elites concurrently holding elite positions in other institutional structures. The simultaneous occupancy of elite positions in different institutions creates networks or circles of communication and influence which transcend particular institutions, and the number of nongovernmental elite positions held by top governmental elites is one indicator of the range of their influence in the larger society. For example, top governmental elites who also occupy an elite position in the private economic sector are able to extend their influence into the economic life of the nation in ways that would be impossible if they occupied only their governmental roles. Also, governmental elites who are simultaneously economic elites may have their performance in their governmental roles affected by economic interests in ways that would otherwise be impossible.

The percentage of top governmental leaders who hold at least one elite position in an institution other than government (mostly in economic institutions) is given in Table 4. From 1939 to 1954, the percentage of top

TABLE 5. *Percentage of Top Governmental Leaders Having Selected Social Characteristics by Type of Elite Position, 1939 and 1954*

	Type of elite position *					
	Elected political leaders		Appointees		Higher civil servants	
Selected social characteristics	1939 (N=14) † Per cent	1954 (N=32) † Per cent	1939 (N=27) † Per cent	1954 (N=29) † Per cent	1939 (N=22) † Per cent	1954 (N=64) † Per cent
Jamaican-born	85	93	54	70	32	68
Urban-born (Jamaican-born only) .	0	20	38	26	57	48
Holds at least one nongovernmental elite position	100	45	63	83	36	20
Elementary education or less	29	36	13	3	23	3
Secondary school education	57	46	35	54	46	58
Some university or more	14	18	52	43	31	39
Upwardly mobile	83	93	58	35	79	76
Age 55 or older	27	23	63	63	23	26

SOURCE: *Who's Who, Jamaica,* 1939 and 1954.

* The percentages represent the relative number of persons in each type of elite position having a particular social characteristic.

† The number of cases on which the percentages are based is given for each type of elite. It is approximate for some variables since a few cases did not have full information. The urban-born percentages are based upon the subuniverse of Jamaican-born only. These N's are: elected political leaders 11 (1939) and 29 (1954); appointed officials 13 (1939) and 19 (1954); and higher civil servants 7 (1939) and 42 (1954).

governmental elites holding at least one nongovernmental elite position declined from 62 to 41 per cent.

Table 5 shows, however, that the different types of elites did not change in the same way. Consistent with the general trend, the higher civil servants were less likely to hold nongovernmental elite positions in 1954 than in 1939, the percentage decreasing from 36 to 20. At both time periods, the civil servants were most likely, compared to elected political leaders and appointees, to have their authority confined to their governmental roles. This finding is consistent with the fact that the civil service was increasingly professionalized while the governmental bureaucracy increased in size and functions.

Also consistent with the general trend is the change in elected political leaders. Changing more than any other type of top governmental elite, the elected political leaders had 100 per cent who occupied at least one non-governmental elite position in 1939 but only 45 per cent in 1954. Thus, although the elected political leaders had much more formal responsibility and authority in 1954 than in 1939 as a result of constitutional changes that redefined their governmental positions, their authority was more confined to purely *governmental and political* roles at the later time.

A bifurcation—or at least a partial bifurcation—of power is reflected in this trend. As the economic and social elites lost direct control over the elected political positions, representatives and spokesmen of the laboring classes gained. Both major political parties in Jamaica—the People's National Party (PNP) and the Jamaica Labour Party (JLP)—are in a sense labor parties. As pointed out in Chapter I, each is linked to a particular trade union, and although each has middle and upper class supporters, each must depend upon the lower socioeconomic groups for the bulk of its support at the polls. Increasingly committed to economic and social development, the new Jamaican popular government has taken an increasingly larger part in shaping, although indirectly, economic and social life. Thus, whatever decline in the total power of the elected political leaders may be indicated by the increasing confinement of their authority to purely governmental and political roles may be somewhat offset by the increase in the authority of such roles themselves over certain aspects of the Jamaican economy and society.

Contrary to the general trend is the change in appointees. The dual occupancy of governmental and nongovernmental roles increased among them from 63 to 83 per cent from 1939 to 1954. Thus, while constitutional changes reduced the formal responsibilities and authority of the role of the appointees, the occupants of these roles in fact were more likely to be persons who had a wide range of influence due to interlocking elite positions in governmental and other institutional sectors. In other words, the established economic and social elites grasped more firmly the diminishing powers of the nominated positions during the period under consideration.

Returning to Table 4, fewer of the 1954 elites had only an elementary school education compared to the 1939 elites, and more of them had a secondary school education. There was little difference, however, between the two groups with respect to the percentage who had some university education or more. The elected political leaders were the least educated of all the top governmental elites at both time periods (from Table 5). Also, unlike both the appointees and the higher civil servants, they had a larger percentage of their number who had received no more than an elementary school education in 1954 than in 1939. Since educational levels are rising generally in Jamaica, one cannot expect this particular change to reflect a future trend. Also, many educated persons were somewhat reluctant to risk their positions in society by standing for elected office before a generally black, lower-class, and poorly educated electorate —especially in the years of limited self-government when the element of tutelage still restricted to some extent both the authority and prestige of elected positions and when many members of the highly educated groups were still suspicious and uncertain about domination by what they thought of as "mob-rule." With full self-government and complete independence and with the chance of becoming an honorable member of the Cabinet, elected political office should be somewhat more enticing to members of the educated groups.[9]

The elected political leaders, with 36 per cent of their number having no more than an elementary school education in 1954, became more like the general population in level of education than they were earlier. Also, they were more like the general population in this respect than either the appointees or the higher civil servants. Yet they were still considerably better educated than the average person in Jamaica. In 1943, fully 95 per cent of the Jamaican population over age 25 had received no more than an elementary school education, and in 1960 the provisional figure was 92.5 per cent.[10]

The higher civil servants were more highly educated in 1954 than in 1939, and they were more highly educated on the average than the elected political leaders at both times, especially in 1954. After the ministerial system was introduced in 1953, this fact (and correlated differences in outlook and behavior) apparently resulted in friction between some members of the two types of elites in their day-to-day working relationships, the higher civil servants sometimes chafing under the rule of a less-educated politician and a politician in turn sometimes overly asserting himself in an effort to validate himself in his new role as head of a ministry. Of this problem, one informant told me the following:

The political leader is looked upon as a real leader of the country. At public functions he is the top man. He has dominated the scene from a power point of view in the public mind. At the same time, the civil servants in the governmental bureaucracy in some senses have become the real rulers and they have assumed too much importance in the actual making of policy. Take a politician who has power that derives from the formal position that he occupies, but he is surrounded by high-powered civil servants who have benefited from higher education, special courses of various kinds, etc. This government has, by the way, done a great deal, has invested a great deal, in giving civil servants and others the opportunity to receive high-powered technical training. The politician represents the will of the people since he was elected by them. And yet, the technical advice he gets tends somehow to submerge the will of the people. As you know, technical people can do great damage in the policy-making process. Policies may have no relation to the ordinary conditions of the life of people of the country if the technical people play too much of a role in either formulating a policy or in a nonsupervised implementation of it. . . . Sometimes a Minister is so intimidated by his civil servants, by what he assumes is their superior technical skill and higher education, that he may seek refuge in Cabinet to turn down his own recommendation. That is, he was afraid to tell his civil servants that he didn't want to recommend something because he couldn't think of the definitive reasons for his action. But he could go back to the civil servants in his ministry and say that Cabinet had turned it down and that was that.

But the same informant pointed out later in the interview that the civil servants had legitimate complaints too. What appeared to be correct policies to them in terms of the economic and social development of Jamaica were sometimes not adopted by the politicians for "political reasons," that is, because the politicians had to be concerned with the public reaction to their policy. Perhaps this would have been acceptable to the civil servants if the "public reaction" involved were the responses of the general public, but it was often some special group, especially some articulate and already favored minority.

This conflict between politicians and civil servants, however, should not be overemphasized, and it should be noted that few other new nations were in as enviable a position as Jamaica. One of the distinctive features of Jamaica's transition to independence was early and sustained efforts to develop a governmental bureaucracy containing an increasingly large number of qualified Jamaicans at all levels. A competent and experienced bureaucracy composed of Jamaicans gave Jamaica considerable advantage over some of the other new nations in achieving stability and effectiveness in efforts to attain the national goals of a newly independent country. England was, perhaps, the most enlightened of the colonial powers in the dismantlement of its empire, and Jamaica may be the best example of adequate preparation for independence among the former British colonies, although the collapse of the West Indies Federation had deleterious consequences for the smaller islands.

As expected, the appointees were the most highly educated type of governmental elites at both time periods, although the higher civil servants were almost as well educated on the average in 1954. The percentage of appointees having no more than an elementary school education decreased from 1939 to 1954, and so did the percentage having a university education.

One might expect the governmental elites to have been more upwardly mobile in 1954 than in 1939, since the constitutional changes opened up new routes to power and influence and included the participation of the lower socioeconomic classes in the political process. No such trend is apparent from Table 4, however. At both times the elites were highly mobile with respect to upward occupational mobility—70 and 71 per cent respectively were upwardly mobile.[11]

The percentages for upward mobility in Table 4 are of course averages of differential changes for the different types of elite groups. As one would expect, the elected political elites were more upwardly mobile in 1954 (93 per cent) than they were in 1939 (83 per cent), and they were the most upwardly mobile of the three types of elites (from Table 5). The higher civil servants had about the same rate of upward mobility at both times, 79 and 76 per cent in 1939 and 1954 respectively. The appointees were the least upwardly mobile group at both times, and contrary to the change for elected political leaders, they were considerably less likely to be upwardly mobile in 1954 (35 per cent) than in 1939 (58 per cent). Considering the fact that these persons are elites, one can conclude that about 65 per cent of the appointees in 1954 had elite backgrounds.

Thus, while the predominantly black lower classes were obtaining representation through their elected leaders and the elected political positions were becoming somewhat more accessible to the average Jamaican, the predominantly light or white persons representing the established interests were increasing their hold over the nominated positions. This is consistent with the findings concerning joint occupancy of governmental and nongovernmental positions discussed earlier. Since 1954, however, changes increasing the participation of the leaders of the political parties, while decreasing the discretion of the Governor, in making nominations to these offices, resulted in a decrease in the exclusiveness of this group. In the new constitution for an independent Jamaica, the Legislative Council was replaced by a Senate all members of which were to be appointed on the recommendations of the Prime Minister and the Leader of the Opposition. Thus, the appointees to the new Senate can be expected increasingly to approximate the social characteristics of the elected political elites. Of course, differential campaign contributions and other favors to the political parties, the need for social unity, and the differential distribution of skills by social classes may continue to result in the representation of some members of the highest socioeconomic groups among the Senators.

From Table 4, note that the 1954 elites were slightly younger than the 1939 elites, 34 and 40 per cent respectively being age 55 or older. None of the types of elites, however, actually changed in age even as much as 6 per cent. Rather, this average reduction of 6 per cent was due to changes in the differential proportions each type of elite represented at the two times. That is, at both time periods the elected political leaders and the higher civil servants were much younger on the average than the appointees (see Table 5), and there were relatively more of them compared to the appointees in 1954 than in 1939. In fact, none of the three types of elites changed much in percentage age 55 or over, the appointees being exactly the same with 63 per cent.

The appointees were much older than the average adult in Jamaican society, but the elected political leaders and higher civil servants were much nearer in age to the general population. Of all Jamaicans age 25 and over, 20 per cent were age 55 and over in 1943. In 1960, the percentage was 23 per cent.[12]

Comparison of Different Types of Elites, 1958

A more complete description and analysis of the social characteristics of Jamaican elites requires a more inclusive definition of elites than that so far employed. Persons occupying the "command posts" in institutions other than government need to be considered. Leaders in business, religion, education, law, medicine, and other institutional sectors also exert influence on public affairs in Jamaica and perform a variety of elite functions. Additionally, the transition to independence continued beyond 1954, with more self-government and less tutelage in 1956 and again in 1957. By the summer of 1958, Jamaica had nearly achieved full internal self-government.

A sample of all Jamaican leaders was selected and their social characteristics determined by reference to *Who's Who, Jamaica* (see Appendix II). The social characteristics of this sample of elites are given by type of elite position in Table 6. The categories of "elected political leaders," "appointees," and "civil servants" are not strictly comparable to those same categories in Tables 4 and 5, but are somewhat more inclusive. Elected members of the then new Federal Parliament, mayors, and some parish councilors were added to the elected political leaders. Also, the then newly appointed Senators to the federal government were included among the appointees. And the civil servants in Table 6, although excluding judges, doctors, and teachers who were categorized separately, include some fairly low ranks in the civil service in addition to the higher civil servants considered earlier. Thus, one must be cautious about attributing trends to these data in comparison with the 1939 and 1954 top governmental elites. By logical elimination of alternatives, however, the reader may note that most trends revealed earlier are borne out by the 1958 data.

Since many elites held more than one elite position simultaneously, it would have been possible to categorize them more than once in Table 6. However, a given individual was classified only once, as before. Arbitrarily, governmental elites who held other elite positions were classified only by their governmental positions. That is, governmental positions were given priority over other types of elite positions, the only exceptions being among civil servants who were professionals. For nongovernmental elites, an attempt to determine their major activity was made, and they were thus classified.

COUNTRY OF BIRTH.—There was a wide range of differences between the various types of elites with respect to country of birth in 1958. Nearly three-fourths of the religious leaders were foreign-born. They continued in the tradition of the missionaries of the nineteenth century who did much to spread humanitarian values in Jamaica as elsewhere throughout the world. Their relative role in Jamaica in recent years was in many ways greatly reduced and was far less militant compared to the role that their predecessors played in spreading ideas of equality and freedom. They were, by 1958, in part displaced by change-leading national elites, especially elected political leaders and higher civil servants who occupied the policy-making and administrative positions of a growing welfare state. Aso, the religious leaders had to make room for a growing number of other professionals and voluntary workers who began promoting economic and social development through secular organizations.

Social welfare elites (workers and administrators) were more likely to be Jamaican-born than religious leaders, but over half were still foreign-born in 1958. These foreign-born persons originated from technologically more advanced societies—in this case primarily from England and the United States.

TABLE 6. Percentage of Jamaican Leaders Having Selected Social Characteristics by Type of Elite Position, 1958

Selected social characteristic	Type of elite position									
	Elected political leaders (N = 52)	Appointees (N = 34)	Civil servants (N = 185)	Economic elites (N = 269)	Religious leaders (N = 33)	Educational leaders (N = 35)	Judges (N = 9)	Medical elites (N = 71)	Barristers and solicitors (N = 36)	Social welfare elites (N = 7)
Jamaican-born	98	91	82	69	28	71	63	76	94	43
Residing in metropolitan Kingston–St. Andrew	23	47	87	66	64	63	78	75	81	71
With highest occupational rating	94	100	45	73	94	29	100	93	100	57
Upwardly mobile	83	31	79	62	57	51	56	35	52	57
Male	100	94	96	96	100	66	100	87	97	43
Median age (in years)	50	61	46	49	50	48	53	46	46	50
Anglican	38	73	58	47	25	55	57	53	57	29
Protestant	49	19	30	23	44	34	29	25	17	72
Roman Catholic	9	8	9	20	28	3	14	18	13	0
Jewish	0	0	1	8	3	0	0	2	3	0
Atheist, Agnostic, or Independent	4	0	2	1	0	7	0	3	3	0
Elementary education or less	27	0	2	13	0	0	0	0	0	0
Secondary school education	42	61	52	64	6	31	22	0	58	43
Some university or more	31	39	47	23	94	69	78	100	42	57
Of those elites with some university training, the % whose university was located in:*										
Jamaica	7	0	4	0	3	4	0	3	0	0
British Isles	53	92	69	40	53	78	86	59	93	75
Canada	0	0	12	23	3	13	14	11	0	0
United States	40	8	11	30	40	4	0	20	0	25

SOURCE: *Who's Who, Jamaica, 1957.*

* Does not always add up to 100 per cent, because of a few leaders educated in countries other than those shown.

Sixty-three per cent of the judges were born in Jamaica, and fully 94 per cent of the barristers and solicitors were. Of course, the foreign-born among the judges were mainly English. Related to this is the fact that one of the highest percentages of foreign-born among any type of civil servant was among the higher officers of the police. Also, there were in 1958 only a few top military officers in Jamaica, but expatriates controlled the top ranks with minor exceptions. The position of the military reflected the constitutional situation at the time, which still left the defense of Jamaica to the former imperial power. However, the interpretation of the law and especially the legal use of force within Jamaica was more controlled by expatriates than might have been expected considering the constitutional developments. This reflects in part a preoccupation of the established economic and social elites with the problems of order as self-government increased and complete independence came nearer. They considered the black lower classes increasingly to be a threat to order as the British withdrew and the Jamaican government, with more limited resources for controlling civil disorder and with fewer commitments to the old established elites, took over. With independence, a new commanding officer, born in the Bahamas, but identified as a "local," was appointed to the new Jamaican Regiment.

Almost a third of the Jamaican economic elites (including commercial, agricultural, and other) were foreign-born. This seems relatively high, but may have been accounted for in part by a colonial attitude toward commerce. For example, Broom says:

It is ironic that British colonialism, which historically has been so heavily influenced by commercial interests, should have implanted a disdain of commerce among many colonial peoples. This may be in part because a colonial may seek recognition in two places, in the colony and in the metropolitan "home." The dual striving is apparently achieved without conflict of ends most readily in the public service and, of course, some immediate status is acquired by the very identification with official functions.[13]

However, it may be less ironic than Broom thinks. Like so many things in Jamaica that were identified as being colonially induced backwardness and debilities, "a disdain of commerce" may have been less a result of colonialism per se than a British trait, a transplanted English tradition. As David Granick has recently pointed out, businessmen in England, in contrast to those in other European countries and the United States, are regarded more or less as second-string civil servants.[14] Also, the nature of enterprise in Jamaica, the problems of capital formation and investment, and the scope of economic development, contributed to maintaining, in some instances increasing, expatriates among the economic elites.

Education and health are two important areas in which expansion was necessary to bring about change in Jamaica as directed by the emergent national elites; thus an increasing need for skills in these areas developed since 1944. It is not surprising, then, to find that Jamaicans constituted only about three-fourths of the educational and medical elites. For example, the founding of the University College of the West Indies (now University of the West Indies) in Jamaica in 1948 and the development of the medical school and a university hospital have contributed to the number of (non–West Indian) expatriates among these elites. At the rate Jamaicans and other West Indians were receiving advanced education, however, the relative number of expatriates will probably be reduced within a decade even though educational and health facilities will continue to expand.[15]

The rank order of the governmental elites with respect to Jamaican birth, as shown in Table 6, is the same as shown earlier for the top governmental elites in 1954. And in each case the percentage for 1958 is even larger than that for 1954. This may show a continuation of the trend for the reduction of foreign-born persons among these groups, but the categories for 1958, as earlier stated, are defined somewhat differently than in 1954. It is interesting to note, however, that the elected political leaders in 1958 were about as likely to be Jamaican-born, with 98 per cent so classified, as was the general population of Jamaica.

METROPOLITAN RESIDENCE.—The percentages of different types of elites residing in the metropolitan Kingston–St. Andrew area serve to illustrate the concentration of elite functions in Jamaica's major city. About half or more of the different types of elites, with the exception of the elected political leaders, lived in the metropolitan area. These percentages range from 47 per cent for appointees to 87 per cent for civil servants, and compare with about 24 per cent of the general population of Jamaica who live in the Kingston–St. Andrew metropolitan area as of 1960. Only the elected political leaders, with 23 per cent residing in the urban area, approximated the distribution of the general population. Mayors and chairmen of the parish councils, of course, were located in the areas in which they held office. Also, members of the House of Representatives (MHR's) had to stand for election in the constituencies into which Jamaica was divided geographically, and their official residences were generally retained in them.[16] The House met in Kingston, however, and the MHR's spent a considerable amount of their time in the city. A few MHR's listed two addresses in *Who's Who,* one in the parish in which their constituency was located and one in the Kingston–St. Andrew metropolitan area.

OCCUPATIONAL RATING AND MOBILITY.—The occupational ratings of the different types of elites are shown in Table 6. The rating scale used is the same as that used earlier (see Appendix I). The largest percentages who had the highest occupational ratings were appointees, judges, and barristers and solicitors. Each of these groups had 100 per cent of their members in the highest occupational rank. Next were elected political leaders (94 per cent), religious leaders (94 per cent), and medical elites (93 per cent). Seventy-three per cent of the economic elites were in the highest occupational rank, followed by the social welfare elites with 57 per cent. Then came the civil servants with 45 per cent. Finally, the educational leaders had the fewest in the highest occupational rank, with only 29 per cent so classified. Of course, this is largely by definition.

With respect to upward mobility, the most mobile group were the elected political leaders, 83 per cent of whom were upwardly mobile. They were closely followed, however, by the civil servants, 79 per cent of whom were upwardly mobile. Thus, although over half of the civil servants were not of the highest occupational rank, they were a group with one of the highest rates of upward occupational mobility. Appointees were the least likely of any elite group to be upwardly mobile, with only 31 per cent so classified. This lends support to the discussion of the findings reported earlier for the 1954 top governmental elites, and shows further that elected political office and the civil service comprised routes of access to the achievement of higher socioeconomic positions for Jamaicans of relatively humble socioeconomic origins, while the *ex officio* and nominated positions tended to go increasingly, *up until 1958,* to the already entrenched higher socioeconomic classes.

With the exception of the appointees and medical elites, each of the other types of elites had over 50 per cent of their number who were upwardly mobile. This shows little about new channels of upward mobility for Jamaicans in the case of religious leaders, since so few religious leaders were Jamaican-born, but it does show that the upper classes, although greatly overrepresented, did not have a monopoly over the high positions in the economy, education, the judiciary, law, and social welfare.

SEX.—With the exception of two types of elite groups, 87 to 100 per cent of each type of elite was composed of men (see Table 6). The dominance of men over the important roles in public affairs and business is so well known as to require little further comment here.[17] The two exceptions are educational leaders, 66 per cent of whom were men, and social welfare elites, 43 per cent of whom were men.

AGE.—Supporting the conclusions for the 1954 elites given earlier, the appointees were older on the average than either the elected political leaders or the civil servants. Also, they were older than any other elite group, their median age being 61. The youngest groups were the civil servants, medical elites, and barristers and solicitors, who had median ages of 46. The other groups were as follows: educational leaders, 48; economic elites, 49; elected political leaders, religious leaders, and social welfare elites, 50; and judges, 53.

RELIGION.—In 1960, 19.8 per cent of the general population of Jamaica were Anglicans, yet among the different types of elites, the percentages of Anglicans were generally much larger (see Table 6). Seventy-three per cent of the appointees were Anglican, another reflection of the high social status and the centrality to the "established interests" in Jamaica of this type of elite at this time. Civil servants were 58 per cent Anglican; judges and barristers and solicitors, 57; educational leaders, 55; medical elites, 53; economic elites, 47; and elected political leaders, 38. Closer to the general population were social welfare elites, of whom 29 per cent were Anglican, and religious leaders themselves, of whom 25 per cent were Anglican.

Roman Catholics were a larger proportion (28 per cent) of the religious leaders than they were of any other elite group. According to the proportion of Catholics, the elites ranked as follows: economic elites (20 per cent), medical elites (18 per cent), judges (14 per cent), barristers and solicitors (13 per cent), elected political leaders and civil servants (9 per cent each), appointed officials (8 per cent), educational leaders (3 per cent), and social welfare elites (none). With the exception of educational and social welfare elites all of the elites contained a larger proportion of Catholics than would have been expected by chance alone since only 7.2 per cent of the general population of Jamaica was Catholic.[18] One reason for this was that the Catholic Church offered secondary school educational opportunities that were a route to the attainment of elite positions for some persons.

Jews, who were only about 0.04 per cent of the general population, were most overrepresented among the economic elites, of whom they constituted 8 per cent. They were also overrepresented among barristers and solicitors and religious leaders themselves (3 per cent). Although they constituted only 2 per cent of the medical elites and 1 per cent of the civil servants, the Jews were somewhat overrepresented among these groups as well.[19]

Educational leaders had the largest percentage, 7, of Atheists, Agnostics, and Independents, followed by elected political leaders with 4 per cent, medical elites and barristers and solicitors with 3 per cent each, civil servants with 2 per cent, and appointees, religious leaders, judges, and social welfare elites with none. However, Atheists, Agnostics, and Independents were underrepresented among all types of elites, since they constituted 11.4 per cent of the general population.

Additionally, there were some types of religions professed by members of the general population of Jamaica which were not present among the elites shown in Table 6 to any extent, if at all. Some of these were Hindu, Moravian, Pocomania, and the Ras Tafari Brethren.

EDUCATION.—As can be seen from Table 6, by 1958 the elected political leaders were still less educated than the appointees and the civil servants, but they were more educated than they had been in 1954. Educational comparisons between 1958 and 1954 can lead to a reliable conclusion since the 1958 group, being more inclusive of the lower rungs of the various hierarchies in the cases of elected political leaders and civil servants, should show a lesser educated group than the 1954 group unless there had been some real changes toward higher education. Also, the civil servants appeared to be better educated in 1958 than they were in 1954, and in 1958 they were more likely to have attended a university than were the appointees.

Ranked with respect to their percentages who had some university or more (from high to low), the different types of elites were: medical elites, religious leaders, judges, educational leaders, social welfare elites, civil servants, barristers and solicitors, appointees, elected political leaders, and economic elites. The elected political leaders, however, were the least educated group when the entire educational distribution is considered, having 27 per cent who had no more than an elementary education. Thus, the politicians were most like the general Jamaican public in this regard.

Table 6 also shows where elites received their university training. The dependence of Jamaica for higher education on external areas is clearly seen in the very small percentages—if not zeros—of persons who had received university training in Jamaica. Of course, the University College of the West Indies had just begun ten years before, so its effects in providing trained elites had not yet really begun to be felt. Britain dominates as the place where Jamaican elites received their higher educations. Three-fourths or more of the barristers and solicitors, appointees, judges, and social welfare elites went to universities in the United Kingdom. Of those who attended a university, however, 40 per cent of the elected political leaders did so in the United States; and 53 per cent of the economic elites, 31 per cent of the medical elites, and 23 per cent of the civil servants did so in Canada and the United States combined. With the predominance of imported English laws in Jamaica, barristers, solicitors, and judges will probably continue to be educated in Britain for some time, but for the other types of elites it is safe to predict a considerable decrease in the proportions attending universities in Britain. Not only the University of the West Indies, but also American universities will make inroads. In the case of UWI, the reasons are obvious; and in the case of American universities, they are closer, the education they offer is increasingly recognized as being more practical and useful given the needs of a developing nation, and an increase in educational grants from sources in the United States seems likely now that Jamaica is independent.

One of the more interesting and important developments in future years will be the impact of the University of the West Indies. Aside from the obvious academic implications such as the advantages of having classroom examples and illustrations selected for a West Indian student body with greater emphasis on West Indian events and conditions by West Indian instructors, there may be other consequences. What will be the effects of UWI in instilling general attitudes toward government and the political system, toward Jamaica, Trinidad, and other new nations in Africa and elsewhere, toward the global situation, toward civil, political, economic, social, and cultural equality, and so forth? The intellectual climate of Jamaica—and the West Indies generally—may change as more and more of the future elites are trained at UWI and as Jamaican and other West Indian intellectuals become a larger, more cohesive, more self-conscious, and less European-oriented group.[20]

It is difficult to overemphasize the importance of the growth of a West Indianizing West Indian university. In addition to the detailed knowledge that it can impart, it can contribute importantly to the resolution of certain ambivalences and dilemmas that have been characteristic of many Jamaican and other West Indian intellectuals. For example, among UWI students there was considerable effort, deliberate and self-conscious and often quite sophisticated, to achieve intellectual freedom. This appeared more difficult to obtain than political independence, however. Despite the emergence of Jamaican and West Indian cultural forms and unities, the West Indies represented a particular cultural hybrid that developed under the cultural hegemony of England. ENGLAND—THE GREAT POWER —stood over intellectual life like a spectre. As Scott Greer has said, Jamaica on the threshold of independence was ". . . not only itself, it was a shadow of England, but not England, the Empire, but not the Empire—high noon,

Victorian time." [21] When searching for their own identity, West Indian intellectuals often appeared to be a mixed bag of contradictions, all neatly internalized to maximize agonizing self-recriminations. Alternately, they denounced England, defended England, and pounced on each other with accusations of having a "colonial mentality." They wrote poems, stories, and plays celebrating Jamaica's awkening and nationhood, but at the same time gave voice to words that were reminiscent of England's modern "angry young men" and that were more appropriate to the sorrows of a declining nation with a golden past than to the joys of a former colony presumedly facing a new and better future. Some seemed to be finding intellectual freedom, but some still turned to England, denying part of themselves and aspiring to be a shadowy substance of what they never could have been, never can be, and few Englishmen are anymore. The University of the West Indies can help create new alternatives, not simply Jamaican (or West Indian), but models that are modern, cosmopolitan, and pan-humanitarian.

Elites and Influence, 1958

OBJECTIVE INDICATORS OF SCOPE OF INFLUENCE.—Table 7 shows the different types of Jamaican elites according to certain amounts of influence in addition to that which derived directly from their major elite positions. Two objective indicators of the scope of influence were used. The first was the percentage who occupied elite positions in three or more different institutional sectors simultaneously, the interpretation of which was discussed earlier. According to this indicator, the different types of elites rank as follows with respect to the scope of their total influence from highest to lowest: appointees, elected political leaders, barristers and solicitors, economic elites, medical elites, educational leaders, civil servants, and finally religious leaders, judges, and social welfare elites, which were tied for last place.

Note that the rank order of the three types of governmental leaders was the same as that given for 1954, the appointees with the most and the civil servants with the least scope of influence. In addition to the appointees and elected political leaders, only the barristers and solicitors and the economic elites had more than one-fifth of their numbers with wide influence according to this indicator.

The second objective indicator is membership and office-holding in formal associations (excluding business concerns and government and including mostly voluntary associations ranging from social and recrea-

TABLE 7. Percentage of Jamaican Leaders Having Certain Amounts of Influence by the Type of Elite Position, 1958

				Type of elite position						
Objective indicators of scope of influence	Elected political leaders (N=52) *	Ap-pointees (N=34)	Civil servants (N=185)	Economic elites (N=269)	Religious leaders (N=33)	Educational leaders (N=35)	Judges (N=9)	Medical elites (N=71)	Barristers and solicitors (N=36)	Social welfare elites (N=7)
% with three or more elite positions	37	56	1	22	0	3	0	10	25	0
Average % based on formal association indicators that are given below	51	73	31	35	33	42	19	26	41	48
% with at least one membership in formal associations	87	94	69	71	61	77	56	65	81	100
% who hold at least one office	46	71	19	20	24	40	0	10	22	29
% with membership in six or more formal associations	19	53	6	13	15	9	0	3	19	14

* The approximate number of cases on which the percentages are based is given in parentheses.

tional clubs to professional organizations).[22] The three indicators used (membership in at least one association, holding at least one office in an association, and membership in six or more associations) were averaged in order to construct an index of participation in the organizational membership structure. Such an index shows the relative access to organizational networks of influence and communication, and is taken as a further indication of the scope of a leader's influence.

From most to least influence, as measured by participation in the organizational membership structure, were the following types of elites: appointees, elected political leaders, social welfare elites, educational leaders, barristers and solicitors, economic elites, religious leaders, civil servants, medical elites, and judges. The rank order was fairly similar to that given for simultaneous occupancy of three or more different elite positions with appointees heading the list, followed by elected political leaders. Civil servants ranked considerably below the politicians, thus the governmental elites retained their relative rankings as shown earlier. Social welfare elites and educational leaders, however, ranked much higher by the formal association indicator than they did by the indicator of simultaneous occupancy of elite positions in different institutional structures.

During the period of tutelary democracy, the nominations to appointive office in part showed an accommodation of the new representative government to the economic and social elites of Jamaica by giving them a voice in government which most of them could not have obtained by running for elective office. Also, a position in the top circles of influence in Jamaica, while not a precondition to appointment, was certainly a consideration of importance in the selection of appointees. Judging from the appointments to the Legislative Council made in 1958, however, political considerations and racial characteristics of members were also taken into account. Three such appointments included a top reputational influential (see below) from the economic-commercial sector who was ethnically identified as a Syrian, a second-echelon reputational influential from the economic-commercial sector who was ethnically identified as being light to medium brown, and a retired educator and civil servant who was not among the reputational influentials at all (although he occupied several elite positions simultaneously and belonged to several formal associations) and who was ethnically identified as dark brown or black. Appointments made since 1958 showed the increasing importance of political considerations in appointed positions.

It was reported earlier that the elected political leaders had their power increasingly confined to the governmental structure from 1939 to 1954, yet in 1958 they still ranked higher by two objective measures of scope of influence than any other type of elite except for appointees. By then, the participation of the elected political leaders in the organizational membership structure and to some extent their interlocking occupancy of elite positions in different institutional structures had increased and was more the result of their governmental position than a cause of it—to the extent to which these can be untwined in this context. That is, the elected political elites were in part being coöpted by the preëxisting and established social and economic elites. This should not be overemphasized in that it has been a two-way flow of communication and influence—the old established elites recognizing the new power of the elected political leaders by including them in some of their associations, both formal and informal, and being subsequently affected by their membership. In turn, the elected political leaders have become somewhat circumscribed in new and unanticipated ways by their new associations. For example, a few social and recreational clubs had a near monopoly on the validation of certain kinds of prestige. Accommodating to the shifts in political power, they included a few elected political leaders who would not have been acceptable before their rise to political power. This accommodation constituted a change in the system of social stratification by altering the criteria of differential evaluation—by reducing the relative importance of family background and other ascriptive variables while increasing the relative importance of achieved characteristics. Also, some control over the new additions to the power elite—the politicians—may be exerted in return for this conferral of prestige. The elected political leaders were far from fully coöpted, but there was some indication that some of them to a certain degree had been. Coöptation of the new political leaders contributed to social stability in that it reduced cleavages and antagonisms, while promoting coöperation, between different types of elites. But it produced potential instability to the extent to which it left inarticulate or unattended the discontents of the lower classes.

INSTITUTIONAL SECTORS AND REPUTATIONAL INFLUENCE.—In the late spring and summer of 1958, the basic sample of 803 Jamaican elites were sent mail questionnaiers, as described in Appendix II. One of the questions asked was as follows:

Considering all aspects of Jamaican life, who would you say are the most influential *individuals* on the entire island? That is, who are the people who can really get things done and who are really most important in influencing major economic and political decisions which affect all of Jamaica? In each case, does the person usually stay behind the scenes or is he in the forefront of affairs? (PLEASE LIST 10 INDIVIDUALS IN ORDER OF THEIR IMPORTANCE) [23]

A hundred and twenty-five persons were nominated as being among the top ten influentials of Jamaica by the 208 respondents who answered this question. Forty-one of them, however, were nominated by only one respondent each and twelve of them were nominated by only two respondents each. These were discarded from the analysis and the remainder of seventy-two—persons nominated by three or more respondents—are shown in Table 8 according to various social characteristics.[24]

From Table 8, note that the two most highly ranked reputational leaders were elected politicians. Their high rankings in reputational influence are themselves significant indicators of the transfer of power and the shift in influence toward greater representation and participation of the mass of Jamaicans. For example, the first person is Norman W. Manley, then Chief Minister of Jamaica and Minister of Development, founder and president of the People's National Party, and founder of Jamaica Welfare, Ltd. The second person is Sir William Alexander Bustamante, then Leader of the Opposition, former Chief Minister of Jamaica, founder and president of the Bustamante Industrial Trade Union, and founder and leader of the Jamaica Labour Party. These men were the two great Jamaican leaders, as pointed out in Chapter I, who emerged from the riots, strikes, and disturbances of 1937 and 1938 and who became spokesmen of the people. More than any other Jamaican leaders they were associated with these significant events, and their efforts for twenty-five years identified them with the trends toward the economic betterment of the general population, civil and political equality (including self-government), and equal access to facilities, services, and social institutions. The rankings of Manley and Bustamante can be compared to that of the last British Governor of Jamaica, Sir Kenneth Blackburne, who was tied for nineteenth place in reputational influence. Considering how much the Governor's formal powers had been reduced by 1958, one may wonder that Sir Kenneth was ranked as highly as he was. However, compared to the paramount importance of the powers of the Governor before 1944 under the crown colony form of government, his ranking in reputational influence in 1958 must be considered relatively low. Since 1958, the formal powers of the Governor have continued to dwindle, and so has his reputational influence.

Because of the predominance of political and economic elites among the seventy-two top reputational leaders, a somewhat different classification of institutional sectors was used than was used earlier. The leaders of the then-majority political party (PNP) were differentiated from the leaders of the then-minority party (JLP), and economic elites in agriculture were separated from economic elites in other spheres (mostly in commerce). Also, members of the Legislative Council and other nominated persons were classified according to their major activity, and a few other changes were made for convenience.

According to the *percentage of top reputational leaders* contained within them, the sectors ranked as follows: (1) economic—commerce, 30.4 per cent; (2) majority party, 18.1 per cent; (3) economic—agriculture, 15.3 per cent; (4) minority party, 9.8 per cent; (5.5) civil service (including the Governor) and religion, 5.6 per cent each; (7) professions, 4.2 per cent; (9) mass media, education, and social welfare, 2.8 per cent each; and (11.5) labor and arts, 1.3 per cent each.

An even better indicator of the relative reputational influence of each sector may be the percentage of total nominations contained within the sectors. Thus, a sector that had fewer persons who were frequently nominated might rank above a sector that had more persons who were infrequently nominated. Such does occur with respect to the relative ranking of majority political party leaders and the economic-commercial elites, as can be seen by the following ranking based upon the *percentage of nominations* contained in each sector: (1) majority party, 29.5 per cent; (2) economic—commerce, 27.7 per cent; (3) economic—agriculture, 15.8 per cent; (4) minority party, 12.3 per cent; (5) religion, 4.1 per cent; (6) civil service, 3.6 per cent; (7) education, 1.8 per cent; (8) mass media, 1.6 per cent; (9) professions, 1.4 per cent; (10) labor, 1.3 per cent; (11) social welfare, 0.5 per cent; and (12) arts, 0.4 per cent.

Clearly, the most influential sectors by this measure were the four political and economic groups. Combined, they accounted for 73.6 per cent of the 72 reputational leaders and 85.3 per cent of the total nominations. The reader should be reminded again that the low ranking of labor should not be interpreted as indicating little influence for this sector. Rather, labor was represented by the political parties. As indicated, the leader of the JLP was also president of one trade union, and a son of the then-Chief Minister was first vice-president of another, the National Workers Union.

The importance of the political and economic sectors was not entirely due to the use of the terms "economic and political" in the question that was used to elicit the identities of influentials. Key informants agreed that these sectors were the most important ones that affected *all* of Jamaican life, and the study done in 1961–1962 by Charles C. Moskos, Jr., showed the same four sectors to be most important compared to other sectors, according to his respondents, even though "political and economic" were not specified in the question used by him to locate reputational leaders.[25]

In 1958, the economic elites in agriculture were not "playing politics" nearly as much as the economic elites in commerce, an exception being in the rather narrow case of negotiations between management and labor

TABLE 8. *Selected Characteristics for Each Reputational Leader Who Was Nominated for Inclusion among the Ten Most Influential Persons in Jamaica, 1958*

No. of times nominated (out of a total of 208)	Rank order	Institutional sector of major elite position	No. of elite positions	No. of memberships in formal associations	Percentage of nominations reputed to work behind the scenes
194	1	Majority party *	2	5	2
150	2	Minority party	3	6	2
132	3	Economic—commerce †	7	8	42
122	4	Majority party	2	9	19
117	5	Economic—agriculture †	3	8	29
107	6	Majority party	1	0	1
73	7	Economic—commerce (federal Senator)	7	11	42
59	8	Economic—agriculture †	4	7	18
57	9	Majority party	1	1	4
48	10	Economic—agriculture	7	0	64
45	11	Economic—commerce	7	5	91
41	12	Religion †	2	0	48
31	13.5	Economic—commerce	7	0	77
31	13.5	Economic—commerce †	7	6	36
30	16	Economic—commerce	7	5	85
30	16	Economic—commerce	2	8	89
30	16	Economic—commerce	5	3	86
28	18	Education †	2	2	57
26	19.5	Minority party	2	1	5
26	19.5	H.E., The Governor	1	12	58
25	21.5	Economic—agriculture	3	10	57
25	21.5	Mass media	1	2	48
24	23	Labor	1	6	13
21	24	Economic—commerce †	6	10	53
20	25	Religion	1	2	75
19	26.5	Professions †	2	12	67
19	26.5	Civil service	2	0	88
18	28	Majority party	2	7	27
17	29	Economic—commerce	7	8	93
16	30	Civil service	1	2	100
12	31.5	Minority party (federal elected pol. leader)	3	2	27

No. of times nominated (out of a total of 208)	Rank order	Institutional sector of major elite position	No. of elite positions	No. of memberships in formal associations	Percentage of nominations reputed to work behind the scenes
12	31.5	Minority party	2	6	8
11	34	Economic—commerce (Privy Council)	7	2	100
11	34	Economic—agriculture (Custos)	4	3	73
11	34	Majority party	1	7	10
10	36.5	Economic—agriculture	5	2	100
10	36.5	Minority party	3	3	38
8	38	Arts	1	1	100
7	42	Economic—commerce	7	8	100
7	42	Economic—commerce	4	9	83
7	42	Minority party (party officer)	2	0	33
7	42	Economic—commerce	2	8	43
7	42	Majority party	2	1	0
7	42	Religion	1	1	83
7	42	**Religion**	1	2	86
6	48.5	Economic—commerce	2	7	100
6	48.5	Social welfare †	1	1	67
6	48.5	Economic—commerce	7	10	75
6	48.5	Minority party (party officer)	1	6	17
6	48.5	Economic—commerce †	2	8	75
6	48.5	Economic—agriculture	2	6	60
5	53	Civil service	2	1	80
5	53	Mass media	2	5	0
5	53	Education	1	6	100
4	56.5	Majority party (party officer)	2	3	100
4	56.5	Majority party (party officer)	1	3	100
4	56.5	Social welfare †	1	7	25
4	56.5	Majority party (mayor)	‡	‡	67
3	65.5	Majority party (party officer)	2	1	100
3	65.5	Economic—agriculture	3	1	67
3	65.5	Economic—agriculture	3	10	33

TABLE 8. *Selected Characteristics for Each Reputational Leader Who Was Nominated for Inclusion among the Ten Most Influential Persons in Jamaica, 1958 (continued)*

No. of times nominated (out of a total of 208)	Rank order	Institutional sector of major elite position	No. of elite positions	No. of memberships in formal associations	Percentage of nominations reputed to work behind the scenes
3	65.5	Majority party (party officer)	1	1	100
3	65.5	Professions †	2	9	50
3	65.5	Economic—commerce	7	5	100
3	65.5	Economic—agriculture	7	9	50
3	65.5	Professions †	2	12	50
3	65.5	Majority party	1	1	0
3	65.5	Economic—agriculture	3	7	33
3	65.5	Economic—commerce	7	5	100
3	65.5	Economic—commerce	6	3	100
3	65.5	Economic—commerce †	7	7	100
3	65.5	Economic—commerce †	7	3	33

* All persons who are shown to be part of the majority or minority parties are members of the House of Representatives except where otherwise indicated.

† These persons were also members of the Legislative Council.

‡ This person was not listed in *Who's Who,* 1957, owing to an oversight in the preparation, thus these data are unknown.

in sugar where the implications of the PNP–NWU and JLP–BITU alignments did not go unnoticed. Sugar was the dominant industry in agriculture, and its importance to the economy was so well recognized that both political parties saw to it that the sugar industry survived. At the same time, although the economic-agricultural elites were powerful, they were confronted with a heavily unionized labor force and their influence could be counterbalanced by trade union activity. Also, the agricultural sector was already being squeezed by wage increases. On the other hand, the mercantile class had considerably more freedom within which to exercise influence. The labor force in the commercial sector was less organized than in the agricultural sector and the imposition of controls on the commercial elites had to be carried out more by the use of governmental authority than by labor-management negotiations. Also, the expansion of commercial and industrial activities, the angling for markets, and the importance of governmental policies for stimulating economic development spurred the commercial elites' interest in politics and government. In this situation, it is understandable that the economic-commercial elites were very active behind the scenes trying to influence policies to conform to their views— sometimes to serve a narrow sectional interest and sometimes for the public good.

The economic-commercial elites shown in Table 8 were most influential according to the average number of elite positions that they simultaneously occupied ($\overline{X} = 5.8$) and they were higher than any sector except for the professions in average number of formal association memberships ($\overline{X} = 6.3$). The economic elites discussed earlier in connection with Table 4 did not show up as being so influential because they included quite a number of relatively small and middle-sized operators and because the appointees among them were given a separate category. The reputational economic-commercial elites as shown in Table 8, however, contain only the largest operators, and as noted they were very high on each of the three indicators of influence employed. Also, the then-chairman of the Board of Directors of The Gleaner Company, which owns the only two daily newspapers in Jamaica, was an economic-commercial elite, as was every other member of the Board. Finally, of the seventeen appointees shown in Table 8, eight were economic-commercial elites.

These economic elites generally preferred the JLP to the PNP. It is true that each of the major political parties drew heavily on laboring-class and small-independent-farmer support with an edge perhaps to the PNP among the former and an edge to the JLP among the latter. Also, each party had some support from among the members of every social class, notably so with respect to a few well-known top economic elites, but differentially so with respect to the overall proportion of support received from the different social classes. The PNP had more support among middle-class intellectuals and professionals than the JLP. For example, the 1958 mail questionnaire survey showed much more support for the PNP than for the JLP among lawyers, civil servants, educational leaders, social welfare elites, doctors, and religious leaders. However, among the economic elites (including both small and large operators) the PNP received little support. Only 21 per cent of the economic-commercial elites and 7 per cent of the economic-agricultural elites preferred the PNP compared to 48 and 50 per cent respectively of the same groups who preferred the JLP.

Finally, note from Table 8 that the economic-commercial elites were generally reputed to work more behind the scenes than in the forefront of affairs, the average of such designations being 77.4 per cent. Civil servants, religious leaders, and educational leaders shown in Table 8 were also much more likely to work behind the scenes than in the forefront of affairs. Of the remaining large sectors, economic-agricultural elites were about as likely to work in the forefront of affairs as behind the scenes, and of course, elected political leaders worked almost entirely in the forefront of affairs, although many of the party officers of the PNP were "back-room boys" who worked mostly behind the scenes.

Elites and Ethnicity

Historically, ethnic differences were of considerable importance in differentiating Jamaican society into segments of persons having differential rights and duties. Color, of course, differentiated slaves from free persons at one period, and nationality background and religion were important differentiating factors also. Ascription on the basis of ethnicity had been reduced by 1958 as had ascription on the basis of other criteria, but ethnicity had not yet become completely irrelevant to the distribution of elite functions in Jamaica.

Table 9 contains distributions of the members of the House of Representatives and the Legislative Council by color for 1951 and 1958. For both years the members of the House were much less likely to be white or light than were the members of the Legislative Council. Conversely, they were much more likely to be dark brown or black. As Broom points out in his discussion of the 1951 data, the House of Representatives ". . . is more representative of the color characteristics of Jamaica than is any other high-status group. Even so, the darker elements are under-represented, if one's sole criterion is proportionality." [26] This was still true in 1958.

For the House of Representatives in 1951 the color of four members was unknown, so the differences between 1951 and 1958 cannot be accepted without caution. It appears from Table 9, however, that the relative number of black MHR's increased while the relative number of dark brown MHR's decreased. But for both times the percentage of dark brown and black persons combined was about the same, about 50 per cent. Also, the percentage of white, light, olive, and light brown MHR's combined stayed about the same.

There was a decrease in the percentage of white and light persons in the Legislative Council from 1951 to 1958, from 86 to 47 per cent. The largest increase was in the percentage of olive and light brown persons, from 7 to 29 per cent; but there were also increases in the percentage of dark brown persons, from 7 to 18, and an increase in the percentage who were black, from 0 to 6 per cent. In the sense of proportionality, the Legislative Council members were somewhat more representative of the general population of Jamaica in 1958 with respect to color than they were in 1951, but they were still grossly dissimilar—and much more dissimilar to the general population than were the members of the House. As indicated earlier, however, trends detected in such appointments probably will make the members of the Legislative Council (at independence the Senate) still more similar in color and other social characteristics to the members of the House.

TABLE 9. *Percentage of Members of the House of Representatives and the Legislative Council According to Color, 1951 and 1958*

Color	House of Representatives		Legislative Council	
	1951 (Per cent)	1958 (Per cent)	1951 (Per cent)	1958 (Per cent)
White and light	11	9	86	47
Olive and light brown	36	41	7	29
Dark brown	42	28	7	18
Black	11	22	0	6
Total	100	100	100	100
Number of cases	(28)	(32)	(15)	(17)

Source: 1951 data adapted from Leonard Broom, "The Social Differentiation of Jamaica," *American Sociological Review,* 19 (April, 1954), p. 125. Unfortunately, Broom has data for only 28 of the 32 members of the House in 1951, thus the percentage distribution is approximate and has been computed here under the assumption that the "unknowns" were distributed with respect to color just as the "knowns." All members of the Legislative Council are classified.

1958 data from personal observation or from informants or both. All members of both the House and the Legislative Council are classified.

The numerical distribution of the top reputational leaders by sector and color is given in Table 10. No Chinese were among the reputed influentials despite the fact that they were differentiated in the larger society. Also, none of Jamaica's East Indians were nominated. For all seventy-two influentials the percentage distribution by color was as follows: 11 per cent white (foreign-born), 40 per cent Jamaican white and practically white, 28 per cent light and medium brown, and 21 per cent dark brown and black. Thus, the observation must be made again that the dark brown and black segments were underrepresented.

Color distributions by sector were quite dissimilar. For example, comparing the four most influential groups, one can see that the political elites of both parties were most similar to the general population with respect to color. None of them were foreign-born whites, only four were Jamaican whites or near-whites, eight were light or medium brown, and eight were dark brown or black. Thus, the constitutional changes increasing the number of elected offices, enhancing the power of the elected positions, and permitting the introduction of mass political parties, also meant a shift in power to the colored and black segments of the population.

The economic elites were quite different. Although three economic-agricultural elites were dark brown or black, seven of the others were Jamaican whites or near-whites and one was foreign-born white. The economic-commercial leaders were even more unlike the general Jamaican population than the economic-agricultural elites. None of them was dark brown or black, only four were light or medium brown, fourteen were Jamaican whites or near-whites, and four were foreign-born whites. Thus economic power largely remained directly in the hands of whites or near-whites, although it was limited, as discussed earlier, by the power of trade unions, political parties, and government—and such power was for the most part directly in the hands of brown or black leaders.

TABLE 10. *The Number of Top 72 Reputational Leaders by Sector and Color*

	Color				
Sector	White * (foreign-born)	Jamaican white & practically white	Light & medium brown	Dark brown & black	Total
Majority political party ...	0	2	6	5	13
Economic—commerce	4	14	4	0	22
Economic—agriculture ...	1	7	0	3	11
Minority political party ...	0	2	2	3	7
Religion	1	0	1	2	4
Civil service	2	0	1	1	4
Education	0	0	2	0	2
Mass media	0	0	1	1	2
Professions	0	2	1	0	3
Labor	0	0	1	0	1
Social welfare	0	1	1	0	2
Arts	0	1	0	0	1
Total	8	29	20	15	72

* Excludes a few foreign-born whites and near-whites who are known to have Jamaican parentage. Such persons are included with the Jamaican white and practically white.

Additionally, the economic-commercial influentials were ethnically differentiated from the other types of influentials further in that two of them were Syrian, eight were Jews, and three had Jewish backgrounds. (These persons are classified as Jamaican whites or near-whites in Table 10.) Unlike the Chinese, who were also overrepresented in commercial activity (but more concentrated in retail trade), the Syrians and Jews tended not to be ethnically exclusive in their associations, they performed many elite functions, and they were not isolated from the blacks, colored, and the other ethnics of similar social-class levels. Their rise to economic prominence was itself a measure of increasing internal inclusiveness in that the Jews had been legally discriminated against in the past.

As Broom points out:

Like the Chinese, the Syrians are concentrated in commercial activity. Unlike the Chinese, at the turn of the century they entered into competition with the relatively well established dry goods and wholesale firms run by creole whites and colored. In large part through the skill of a single family, the Syrians have become a major economic force, tightly integrated and with close ties to the Syrian community in North America and throughout the Caribbean. . . .

The Jews of Jamaica . . . have never exceeded a few hundreds. They were originally of Spanish and Portuguese origin and were important in the entrepot trade with the Spanish Caribbean. Along with the Scots, they dealt in plantation stores, a large scale business in which sales were made in bulk. In the 17th and early 18th centuries Jews suffered from discriminatory taxation and civil disabilities. The special taxes were rescinded first, and then, early in the 19th century they were relieved of the remaining impediments. As the colored population became urbanized and achieved some vertical mobility, intermarriage and concubinage with Jews as well as with other whites took place. . . . The group is the most fully integrated of all the ethnic minorities into Jamaican society. Like the colored, many of their number perform elite functions.[27]

Two of the persons classified in Table 10 as civil servants were foreign-born whites. One was the Governor and one was a special United Nations economic and social adviser to the Chief Minister. The latter person has since left the island, and soon after independence a new Governor-General was appointed who was a dark-skinned Jamaican.

Thus, recent political developments, economic transformations, and social changes altered the Jamaican leadership structure, and a new elite emerged. The social characteristics and social differentiation of Jamaican leaders and some of the ways they changed were described in this chapter. Such a description tells us in considerable detail about some of the structural effects of the political transformation of Jamaica from colony to nation. In order to obtain a more complete picture of the overall consequences of the emergence of the new Jamaican elite, however, the important ideas held by them must be described and analyzed. The ideologies of Jamaican leaders, their beliefs and attitudes on some of the important decisions facing Jamaica, are examined in detail in the remaining chapters.

Chapter IV

What Kind of
Social Structure Should
Jamaica Have?

UNDER THE CROWN COLONY form of government decisions that affected the development of Jamaican society were ultimately made in the United Kingdom, not in Jamaica. As has been pointed out, the elected representatives to the Executive Council from 1884 to 1944 were relatively powerless and they were generally an irresponsible, querulous, and negative opposition with little opportunity to experience the maturing effect of accountability for the formulation and implementation of policy.

The transition to independence from 1944 to 1962 resulted, however, in the rise of a new national elite into whose hands were placed both legitimate power and responsibility. Conscious direction of the polity, economy, and society became the preoccupation of the new indigenous elite. What should be done? How should it be done? What should Jamaica's national goals be? How can they be best achieved? Actions were taken and policies were formulated by the new national elites in the process of acquiring sovereignty which decisively affected the course of developments of the new national society. We have called these actions and policies the "big decisions of nationhood," although neither the alternative choices regarding a particular policy area nor the total configuration of "big decisions" should be regarded as peculiar to the new nations.[1] In fact, similar processes are constantly going on in the older nations, which are themselves reformulating goals and devising different and more effective means of achieving them; for the older nations too are in a state of flux, of development, of constant change from past to future. Nonetheless, the transfer of power from a colonial to an indigenous regime forcefully raises a large number of societal policies that become highly problematic, subject to change, and, most of all, potentially amenable to manipulation in accordance with the collective will of the citizens and the leaders of the new nations.

One of the critical big decisions of nationhood is, "What kind of social structure should the new nation have?" We cannot, of course, expect a nation to alter its social structure overnight in accordance with its ideals concerning the "good society." The social structure that a society has at any given time sets certain limits on the tempo and direction of possible change. Yet in developing societies, such as Jamaica, where professed change-leaders came into power, rapid and *planned* change was not only possible, but actually occurred. For example, social change in Jamaica during the last decade was little short of phenomenal and again and again the limitations on change imposed by existing social institutions were transcended. If this rapid change continues during the next decade, a social structure will emerge in Jamaica that will conform more closely to the kind of social structure Jamaicans, and especially Jamaican leaders, think that Jamaica ought to have, rather than to the kind of social structure that Jamaica now has. That is, ideologies regarding the ideal Jamaican society will result in actions and policies that will further mold and transform actual Jamaican society toward the ideal. I am assuming that catastrophes in excess of temporary setbacks do not occur, that our knowledge of social forces, causes and effects, continues to increase, and that the leaders take the actions necessary to bring about the desired change.

Jamaican social structure being what it was as Jamaica approached independence, the most important aspect to the question, "What kind of social structure should Jamaica have?" was contained in the question, "How soon and to what degree should the lower socio-economic-racial groups in Jamaica be included in the larger society on the basis of more equality than before?" Thus, in this chapter we return to the question of the trend toward equality, but now we are interested not in its past but in its probable future. In the face of renewed lower-class demands for equality, the future extension of equality in Jamaica depended a great deal on the attitudes toward equality held by the Jamaican elites. If the elites generally favored the further extension of equality, if they believed that the structures that gave rise to and maintained the existing inequalities were no longer legitimate when viewed from the perspective of the ideology and morality of equality, then structural changes could result extending equality still further without violence and other debilitating disruptive effects. That is, if elites accept the doctrine of equality and if they are courageous enough to act on it, then the trend toward equality may continue while social integration is increased. However, if the new Jamaican leaders should feel that the current inequalities are right and fair and that the trend toward equality has already gone far enough, if they should believe current inequalities ought to remain, then the trend toward equality may not continue at all or it may continue only at the expense of social integration and with violence and the use of force.

An Index of Equalitarianism

Attitudes toward equality among Jamaican leaders were measured by an Index of Equalitarianism that was adapted from the work of Seeman and his associates.[2] The original instrument was used in connection with a study of leadership in the United States and was constructed to measure attitudes toward prestige differences in occupations, racial discrimination, social and economic barriers, and the like. Its application to Jamaica appears particularly apt and valid. In the first place, it was designed from a consideration of the value premise of equality in American culture—a value premise generally shared by Jamaica and all Western civilization. Although the United States is a relatively rich country and Jamaica relatively poor, there are large-scale inequalities in the United States, as in Jamaica, and Seeman explicitly had such inequalities in mind when he constructed his attitude scale. That is, he was mindful both of the spread of the idea of equality and the realities of social stratification.

In the second place, the seven questions included in the final index here, as shown in Table 11, do not contain questions about civil and political rights but concentrate on questions about economic and social rights. The struggle over the *legitimacy* of civil and political equality was pretty much over in Jamaica, athough the continuation of civil liberties and political democracy in independent Jamaica, as will be discussed in the following chapter, may be problematic. Nonetheless, the battle lines in the last few years, and in the immediate future, were drawn, and will increasingly be drawn, with respect to the extension of social and especially economic equality. Thus, the Index of Equalitarianism used in this study measured attitudes relevant to the conflict between different segments of the population over the distribution of social and economic goods, services, and opportunities.

In the third place, from informants and informal interviews with leaders at various times from 1956 to 1962, I am satisfied that the Index, as used in Jamaica, is valid; that is, it did a pretty good job of measuring what it

TABLE 11. *Percentage Distribution of Responses for the Items Comprising the Index of Equalitarianism for Jamaican Leaders and UCLA Students*

1. The incomes of most people are a fair measure of their contributions to human welfare.

		Jamaican leaders	UCLA students
5 Strongly disagree	(Equalitarian) *	62	67
4 Somewhat disagree		20	24
3 Undecided		8	7
2 Somewhat agree	(Nonequalitarian)	7	1
1 Strongly agree		3	1
Total		100	100
Number of cases		(229)	(91)
No answer		(9)	(0)

2. Social clubs which restrict membership on a racial basis ought to be considered as being against Jamaican (American) principles.

		Jamaican leaders	UCLA students
1 Strongly agree	(Equalitarian)	80	41
2 Somewhat agree		6	11
3 Undecided	(Nonequalitarian)	2	10
4 Somewhat disagree		3	15
5 Strongly disagree		9	23
Total		100	100
Number of cases		(233)	(91)
No answer		(5)	(0)

3. We should not be too concerned if there are many people in low positions in Jamaica (our society) since most of them do not want the responsibility of higher positions.

		Jamaican leaders	UCLA students
5 Strongly disagree	(Equalitarian)	45	37
4 Somewhat disagree		24	34
3 Undecided		4	11
2 Somewhat agree	(Nonequalitarian)	15	12
1 Strongly agree		12	6
Total		100	100
Number of cases		(227)	(91)
No answer		(11)	(0)

4. Differences in prestige among the various occupations in Jamaica (America) should be reduced.

		Jamaican leaders	UCLA students
1 Strongly agree	(Equalitarian)	39	4
2 Somewhat agree		24	18
3 Undecided		13	13
4 Somewhat disagree	(Nonequalitarian)	10	30
5 Strongly disagree		14	35
Total		100	100
Number of cases		(230)	(91)
No answer		(8)	(0)

5. Differences in rank among people are acceptable since they are chiefly the result of the way individuals have made use of the opportunity open to them.

		Jamaican leaders	UCLA students
5 Strongly disagree	(Equalitarian)	10	14
4 Somewhat disagree		11	29
3 Undecided		4	9
2 Somewhat agree		30	34
1 Strongly agree	(Nonequalitarian)	45	14
Total		100	100
Number of cases		(228)	(91)
No answer		(10)	(0)

6. People of about the same social or economic position ought to pretty much mingle with their own kind.

		Jamaican leaders	UCLA students
5 Strongly disagree	(Equalitarian)	33	21
4 Somewhat disagree		17	20
3 Undecided		8	14
2 Somewhat agree	(Nonequalitarian)	21	29
1 Strongly agree		21	16
Total		100	100
Number of cases		(225)	(90)
No answer		(13)	(1)

TABLE 11. *Percentage Distribution of Responses for the Items Comprising the Index of Equalitarianism for Jamaican Leaders and UCLA Students (continued)*

7. High social or economic position in Jamaica (America) is a pretty good sign of an individual's superior ability or efforts.

		Jamaican leaders	UCLA students
5 Strongly disagree	(Equalitarian)	35	30
4 Somewhat disagree		21	29
3 Undecided	(Nonequalitarian)	6	5
2 Somewhat agree		18	26
1 Strongly agree		20	10
Total		100	100
Number of cases		(231)	(91)
No answer		(7)	(0)

* The responses are labeled in parentheses according to the meaning attached to them with respect to equalitarianism.

was supposed to measure. One or two cases where its validity may be in doubt with respect to certain subgroups are pointed out below, but these do not seriously affect the findings.

Seeman named his index the *status-attitude scale,* but I prefer to call it an *index of equalitarianism* after the meaning Seeman attaches to the responses of persons who score low in status-attitude. These people he calls "equalitarians" and I have simply reversed his scoring to obtain an Index of Equalitarianism. Thus, at one end of the continuum a respondent thinks that economic and social equalities are acceptable, right, fair, moral, in accordance with national principles, and so on. At the opposite end of the continuum are the antiequalitarian respondents who indicate that social and economic equalities are wrong, unfair, pernicious, contrary to national principles, and so on.

The data on Jamaican leaders are from the 1958 questionnaire survey, which is discussed in Appendix II. Also another set of data is discussed briefly and compared at one point with the data for Jamaican leaders. These were collected by James A. Mau among a group of students at the University of California, Los Angeles, in 1959.[3] Mau selected a fairly representative cross-section by using students in a lower division course in

the history and appreciation of music which satisfies a liberal arts requirement for all majors in the university.

In accordance with conventional procedures designed to test the adequacy
of indexes of this sort, the nine items selected to compose the Index of
Equalitarianisms from the eighteen that Seeman used in his study, were
subjected to the Cornell scaling technique.[4] During the scaling of the responses of Jamaican leaders, two of the items were dropped because they
failed to scale. These are:

Differences in rank within an organization should be kept clearly before the
members to increase their incentive to do good work and rise within the organization.

It is unwise to try to run a business on a completely democratic basis where
all members have an equal voice in the making of decisions.

Each of these rejected items refers to attitudes toward equality within
an organization rather than to attitudes toward equality in the society at
large. The seven items remaining after the final trial all refer to attitudes
toward economic or social equality (or inequality as the case may be)
within the whole society.

Table 12 summarizes the final results of the application of scale analysis
to the Index of Equalitarianism for Jamaican leaders. The coefficient of
reproducibility is .86, which is not sufficiently high to meet the criterion
of .90 established by Guttman; however, this coefficient shows improvement over the minimum marginal reproducibility of .67.[5] And the range of
marginal percentages is not extreme enough to produce a spurious level of
reproducibility, but is sufficiently nonuniform to result in an adequate range
of scores.

Inspection of the scalogram reveals that the Index of Equalitarianism
contains thirty-five nonrandom errors, which occur in six segments. In
addition, three out of fourteen response categories contain more error than
nonerror.

Thus, one cannot conclude that unidimensionality has been definitely
established for the universe of content defined as "equalitarian attitudes,"
because the response error cannot be considered completely random. Yet
the response pattern does approximate the parallelogram as described
by Guttman, and the coefficient of reproducibility is considerably higher
than the coefficient of minimum marginal reproducibility. The scale types
based on the combination of response categories as dichotomized in Table
12 have been used to comprise the Index of Equalitarianism in the analysis
to follow.

TABLE 12. *Scale Criteria Related to the Index of Equalitarianism for Jamaican Leaders*

Scale criteria	Jamaican leaders (N = 211)
1. Coefficient of reproducibility	.86
2. Range of marginal frequencies	The extreme modal categories contain 65 and 82 per cent of the responses. Four of the response categories have marginals falling between 45 and 55 per cent. The spread is sufficient to provide a range of scores.
3. Minimum marginal reproducibility	.67
4. Number of items and response categories ...	Seven dichotomous items.
5. Pattern of error	Thirty-five of 206 errors are nonrandom. These occur in six segments.
6. Error-to-nonerror ratio: Ratio for all items	Three out of 14 answer categories have more error than nonerror.

Item by item	Response category *	Error	Nonerror
1	4–5	0	173
	1–3	33	5
2	1	0	170
	2–5	25	16
3	3–5	2	147
	1–2	34	28
4	1–2	4	134
	3–5	21	52
5	2–5	11	104
	1	11	85
6	4–5	32	70
	1–3	4	105
7	5	29	46
	1–4	0	136

Source: This table is from James A. Mau, Richard J. Hill and Wendell Bell, "Scale Analyses of Status Perception and Status Attitude in Jamaica and the United States," *Pacific Sociological Review*, 4 (Spring, 1961), p. 40.

* The response categories are here dichotomized according to the results of the scaling procedures. The numbers refer to the response categories given in Table 11.

Overall Level of Equalitarianism

Table 13 shows the distribution of scale types according to the final scaling trial for the entire sample of Jamaican leaders. Note that the distribution tends toward skewness with the larger number of cases falling near the proequalitarian end of the scale. The median falls within scale type six. This is relatively high with respect to favorable attitudes toward economic and social equality. For example, a respondent must have given an equalitarian response to five of the seven items in order to fall in scale type six. *Thus, although there were Jamaican leaders in each of the scale types, more of them were proequalitarians than antiequalitarians based upon their absolute distribution among the scale types.*[6]

TABLE 13. *Percentage Distribution of Scale Types on the Index of Equalitarianism for Jamaican Leaders*

Scale type	Per cent	Number of cases
8 (Pro-equalitarianism)	20.17	(48)
7	12.61	(30)
6	19.75	(47)
5	17.65	(42)
4	12.18	(29)
3	7.14	(17)
2	5.04	(12)
1 (Anti-equalitarianism)	2.52	(6)
No answer	2.94	(7)
Totals	100.00	(238)
As dichotomized:		
6–8		
(Equalitarians)	54.11	(125)
1–5		
(Nonequalitarians)	45.89	(106)
Totals	100.00	(231)

The overall level of equalitarianism among the Jamaican leaders can be assessed further by returning to Table 11. Here the percentage distribution of responses of Jamaican leaders for each of the seven items that compose the Index of Equalitarianism can be compared one by one with similar responses from students at the University of California, Los Angeles. Although the comparison was made in an attempt to get some idea of how the Jamaican leaders compared to Americans with respect to attitudes toward equality, it is quite clear that the samples were far from comparable. Considering the factors of age and education, I would guess that the UCLA students were generally more equalitarian than their parents. How they compared to American leaders generally is difficult to say, although the expatriate Americans living in Jamaica who were included in the questionnaire survey were more equalitarian than the UCLA students and they were more equalitarian than the average for Jamaican-born leaders also (see Table 14).

Jamaican leaders and UCLA students were markedly different on three of the seven items, slightly different on three others, and about the same on one with respect to their equalitarian responses. Of the three large differences, two show the Jamaican leaders to have been more equalitarian than the UCLA students. These items are:

2. Social clubs which restrict membership on a racial basis ought to be considered as being against Jamaican (American) principles.
   80 per cent of Jamaican leaders and
   41 per cent of UCLA students "strongly agree."

4. Differences in prestige among the various occupations in Jamaica (America) should be reduced.
   63 per cent of Jamaican leaders and
   22 per cent of UCLA students "strongly or somewhat agree."

One of the large differences between Jamaican leaders and UCLA students, however, shows that the American students gave more equalitarian responses (86 per cent) than the Jamaican leaders (55 per cent). This difference occurs on the following item.

5. Differences in rank among people are acceptable since they are chiefly the result of the way individuals have made use of the opportunity open to them.

On the three items showing small differences between leaders and students, the former were more equalitarian than the latter only on one.

A close inspection of Table 11 reveals that Jamaican leaders were more opposed to economic and social inequalities than were the American students (compare responses to questions 2, 4, and 6). There was, in addition, a tendency for the American students to be less willing to go along with the usual rationalizations for the existence of such inequalities (compare responses to questions 1, 3, and 5). This may be an important clue to the attitudes of the Jamaican leaders. While they appeared definitely more in opposition to economic and social inequalities than American students, they were at the same time somewhat more susceptible to the usual explanations for the existence of such inequalities which put the onus, not upon society, but upon the individuals involved.[7]

One final word is necessary regarding the overall level of equalitarianism. Some of my informants and others told me that they thought that my data generally overestimated equalitarian attitudes among Jamaican leaders. They felt that, as an American, I may have received more equalitarian responses than I rightly should have since Jamaicans looked upon American ideology as including the ideas of economic and social equality. Thus, according to this view, some of my respondents might have altered their real attitudes in deference to what they thought the researcher would think were the "right answers." I doubt very much if this significantly affected these findings. Included in the questionnaire were two questions asking the respondents to evaluate the United States comparatively with the Soviet Union. In the first place, from the severe knocks that the United States received from the respondents in answer to these questions I see no evidence to support the contention that the respondents were falsifying their attitudes out of any concern for my sensibilities; and in the second place, it is clear from these same responses that many of the respondents were concerned with "witch-hunting," racial discrimination, and other violations of civil, political, economic, or social rights in the United States, which places in doubt the assumption that Jamaican leaders viewed America without reservations in this regard.[8]

Other informants told me that they thought the equalitarianism of Jamaican elites had been underestimated by my data. They argued that the American tourists who come to Jamaica—especially to the North Coast—and the American businessmen who come as possible investors do not generally give the impression that they are equalitarians or that they wish Jamaicans were equalitarians. In fact, American businessmen, so I am told, would not invest their money in Jamaica if they thought that Jamaican leaders were strongly in favor of economic and social equality. They would think that this was socialistic and would fear confiscation of their investments. Thus, according to this view, Jamaican leaders would not want me to document their favorable attitudes toward (especially) economic equality and they may have falsified their attitudes by making them appear less equalitarian than they really were. Again, by looking at other responses of the Jamaican elites, I doubt very much that attitudes were significantly altered in this way. The one exception, perhaps, may be in the case of the elected political leaders and higher civil servants, who were more sensitive to this problem than any other type of elite.

A few other informants told me that they thought my data were pretty good estimates of the level of equalitarian attitudes among Jamaican leaders. Considering all my sources of information, I think that this is true. One exception is the possible underestimation of equalitarianism among politicians and civil servants, mentioned above, and another is that the correlation between equalitarianism and education, to be discussed below, combined with the fact that there was a response bias favoring the more educated persons, results in a slightly inflated estimate of overall equalitarianism.

Elite Differentiation and Equalitarianism

In general, the Jamaican elites were fairly favorably disposed toward economic and social equality, both when their absolute scores were considered and when they were compared with a sample of American students. This suggests a relatively favorable climate of elite opinion for the further extension of equality in Jamaica. Much depends, however, upon the characteristics of those elites who hold the most favorable attitudes toward equality when compared with those who hold the least favorable attitudes. Obviously, some elites are more strategically placed than others to articulate and aggregate economic and social interests, and some are more strategically placed to make and execute policies designed to bring about economic and social change. Also, the locus of structural support for, or opposition to, the spread of economic and social equality is of theoretical interest.

Table 14 shows the percentage of Jamaican leaders who were equalitarians by selected social characteristics. Starting with the first characteristic given, one can see that equalitarianism decreases with age. Young elites were more likely to have equalitarian attitudes than the oldest group of elites, with the middle-aged group falling in between. Perhaps, this merely reflects the increasing "conservatism" that develops with increasing age, or perhaps new and more liberal generations are being added to the age distribution at the bottom, each generation retaining certain characteristic habits of belief and attitude throughout its life. In any event, this correlation between age and equalitarianism may augur well for the continued spread of equality. There were already indications that Jamaica was moving into a period in which power was passing into the hands of a younger generation. This was clearly the case among political leaders. Most of the old crowd who dominated the leadership structure of the major parties, in part owing to their participation in the significant events of 1938, could not hold on much longer. Thus, younger leaders were getting more and more of a chance to put their ideas for extending economic and social equality into action. It should be pointed out, however, that some of the younger elites who most favor economic and social equality were among the persons who may be less committed to political democracy, to equalities of civil and political rights, at least to the extent to which they perceived these things as hindering large-scale efforts for economic betterment.

TABLE 14. *Percentage of Jamaican Leaders Who Are Equalitarians by Selected Social Characteristics*

Selected social characteristics	Per cent who are equalitarians	Number of cases on which the per cent is based
Age:		
55 and over	46	(67)
40–54	54	(114)
25–39	64	(50)
Sex:		
Men	52	(213)
Women	78	(18)
Occupational rating:		
1 (highest)	58	(133)
2	49	(82)
3 and 4 (lowest)	50	(16)
Education:		
Graduate school	69	(49)
Completed college	65	(43)
Some college	49	(35)
Secondary or training school	47	(87)
Elementary only	29	(17)
Annual income:		
£2,000 and more	49	(98)
£1,999 and less	58	(114)
R's perception of his financial mobility:		
R. better off than father	54	(167)
R. same as father	52	(33)
R. worse off than father	60	(25)
Religious preference:		
None	40	(10)
Catholic	36	(25)
Jewish	42	(12)
Protestant	59	(176)

TABLE 14. *Percentage of Jamaican Leaders Who Are Equalitarians by Selected Social Characteristics* (*continued*)

Selected social characteristics	Per cent who are equalitarians	Number of cases on which the per cent is based
Political party preference:		
None	53	(64)
People's National Party	59	(100)
Jamaica Labour Party	44	(63)
Country of birth:		
Jamaica	53	(167)
British Caribbean other than Jamaica	36	(11)
Other Caribbean	50	(4)
British Isles	59	(29)
Canada and the U.S.	77	(13)
Other (including Middle East, Far East, USSR)	57	(7)
Number of foreign countries lived in for at least one year (Jamaican-born only):		
2 or more	52	(48)
1	61	(49)
None	46	(69)

Seventy-eight per cent of the women were equalitarians compared to 52 per cent of the men. These women, of course, were persons who were elites in their own right and not persons who were merely wives of elites. This finding may or may not have implications for the trend toward equality. The correlation may be spurious since women are overrepresented in those elite positions whose occupants are most likely to be equalitarians (see Table 15). It may not be entirely spurious; the number of cases is too small to tell for sure. If the correlation is not spurious, then more favorable attitudes toward economic and social equality may be introduced into the elite structure as more women become elites in their own right. (I am assuming that Jamaica will reflect what seems to be a world trend toward the increasing participation of women in all aspects of political, economic, and social life, including membership in leadership groups.) [9]

The differences in equalitarian attitudes by occupational rating, annual income, and the respondents' perceptions of their financial mobility were each relatively small. Such small differences may be due in part to the relative lack of variations in the socioeconomic level of the respondents (for example occupational ratings 5, 6, and 7 are not represented), the respondents being elites by selection. Nowak found attitudes toward equal-ity to be related to self-interest in a study of Warsaw students.[10] Although this phenomenon did not appear strikingly evident when one considers occupational rating, income, and perceptions of financial mobility, it did seem to enter in when type of elite position is considered. This is discussed below.

Differences by educational level were quite marked. Sixty-nine per cent of the highest educational group, persons who had attended postgraduate school, had equalitarian attitudes, compared to only 29 per cent of the persons who had only an elementary school education, the persons with the least education. The intermediate educational levels had correspond-ingly intermediate positions with respect to attitudes toward economic and social equality. It seems reasonable to assume that Jamaican elites will be increasingly better educated in the future, thus this finding suggests a favor-able prognosis for the trend toward equality. Also, an increase in educa-tional levels can be expected in Jamaica as a whole; thus, if the correla-tion between education and equalitarian attitudes exists in the general population as it did among the leaders, then we can expect increases in equalitarian attitudes throughout the society. Education is clearly an im-portant factor in the trend toward equality. It is itself a measure of equality, it is highly correlated with attitudes toward equality, it is subject to manip-ulation in a way many other variables are not, and most important, it seems to be a part of a circular causal process: rising education levels result in more favorable attitudes toward equality, and more favorable attitudes toward equality can result in further extensions of equality including addi-tional increases in educational levels, and so on around. This is underlined by the fact that educational leaders have the most favorable attitudes to-ward equality of all types of elites (see Table 15).[11]

The Protestants were more equalitarian than any of the other religious groups as shown in Table 14. The Jews, Catholics, Agnostics, Atheists, and Independents were all less equalitarian than were Protestants. This finding may be surprising if one considers Calvinistic doctrines underlying the Protestant Ethic as specified by Max Weber. One might rather have expected the Protestants to be least equalitarian in their belief that material success and its symbols were the signs of good works and the indications of heavenly destiny and that the lack of same were indications of sloth and sin. Thus, justifications of inequalities are ready and applicable in Protestantism. Frankly, the implications of this finding for future develop-ments toward more equality seem unclear.

Elites who preferred the People's National Party (PNP) were most likely to have equalitarian attitudes while those who preferred the Jamaica

Labour Party (JLP) were least likely to be equalitarians. Persons with no political party preference were in between. The JLP won the April, 1962, general elections and formed the government that led Jamaica into her first years of independence. From these attitudinal data alone one must conclude that the trend toward economic and social equality might have been advanced faster had the PNP won a majority in the last elections. The fact that PNP supporters were most likely to be equalitarians combined with the fact that the transition to political independence dramatized the past trend toward equality and affirmed the desire for more equality as a national goal might have resulted in a spurt of accelerated changes toward increasing equality.

This judgement, however, is in part mitigated by other considerations. It is true that there were more powerful conservative economic influences behind the JLP than behind the PNP—and these may reassert themselves now; *but* (1) the platforms of the two parties were not significantly different with respect to their espousal of equality, (2) there was a new emergent group among the JLP politicians which was particularly dedicated to the further extension of economic and social equality, (3) some equalitarians may have switched their support from the PNP to the JLP since 1958 because of the PNP's failure to improve economic and social conditions more, and (4) the new JLP government was free from some of the debilitating entanglements in which the PNP had become involved after seven years of rule and which resulted in the "watering down" of many PNP policies, perhaps conceived in dimming memories of socialistic theories but issued forth, unrecognizable, in fear of alienating the articulate and economically established members of the society, and in fear of alienating potential foreign investors.[12] Also, the spur of independence remained regardless of the party in power.

Equalitarian attitudes by country of birth are also given in Table 14. Most of the leaders in Jamaica were Jamaican-born persons, but some were not. Persons born in the United Kingdom, elsewhere in the Caribbean, in Canada and the United States, and a few other places were among the elites of Jamaica. In my studies, I counted them all as "Jamaican leaders" since they were persons playing elite roles with *direct relevance* to Jamaican social structure. Also, expatriates in some roles increased with economic advancement even though the civil service and political system were "Jamaicanized" as a result of deliberate policy.

Elites born in Canada and the United States had the most favorable attitudes toward equality and those born in the British Caribbean other than Jamaica had the least, with other groups, including Jamaican-born elites, having an intermediate position. Future developments may bring still more Americans and Canadians to Jamaica, at least changes from 1956 to 1962 suggest that this may be so. If so, then additional supports for a favorable attitude toward economic and social equality may be introduced into the elite structure of Jamaica, even though some of the expatriates may have little impact on the local situation.

Another consideration is the fact that the official positions of the representatives of the United States Government in Jamaica reflected at independence the Alliance for Progress of the United States administration. Among the avowed purposes of the Alliance for Progress is the promotion of economic and social development of the less privileged classes throughout Latin America and the Caribbean. Also, although there are poorer countries than Jamaica in Latin America and the Caribbean, there are few others in which political, economic, and social conditions are more favorable to the successful achievement of the goals of the Alliance for Progress. Therefore, the efforts of an independent Jamaica to achieve economic and social development may be reinforced by additional American assistance.

Although migration to England was reduced for members of the Jamaican lower classes, Jamaican elites probably will continue at an increasing rate to travel and live for periods of time in other countries. The flow to foreign countries of students, persons on study leaves, those giving or receiving technical advice or assistance, and others will undoubtedly increase in future years. This may result in an increase in equalitarian attitudes in Jamaica. Consulting Table 14, one can see that living in a foreign country (for Jamaican-born persons only) for at least a year resulted in more equalitarian attitudes than not doing so, although the maximum advantage seems to be attained at the point of living in one country for at least a year rather than two or more countries for at least a year each.

The importance of education in contributing toward the trend toward equality has already been discussed. Bendix points out that compulsory education is perhaps the earliest example of prescribed minimum levels of living which are enforced by the powers of the state and suggests that equal access to educational facilities is an act of liberation that may be a precondition to the effective enjoyment of all other rights under the law.[13] In Jamaica, effective compulsory education for all awaited the creation of more school places, but it was a stated goal and during recent years many steps toward its achievement were made. In addition, governmental actions were taken to increase equality of access to educational institutions.[14] So it is not surprising to see, Table 15, that educational leaders, persons who occupy the line and command posts of the educational institutions, were more equalitarian than any other type of elite, with 93 per cent of them being favorable to the ideas of economic and social equality. The function of the role they are formally required to play was perfectly consistent with their own personal attitudes. And this fact should increase their effectiveness as agents of the trend toward equality.

TABLE 15. *Percentage of Jamaican Leaders Who Are Equalitarians by Type of Elite Position*

Type of elite position	Per cent who are equalitarians	Number of cases on which the per cent is based
Educational leaders	93	(14)
Religious elites	80	(10)
Social welfare elites	75	(4)
Medical elites	74	(23)
Legal elites	55	(11)
Appointed officials	54	(13)
Economic elites, agricultural	50	(12)
Elected political leaders	47	(19)
Civil servants	46	(67)
Economic elites, commercial	41	(56)

Religious leaders also were likely to be equalitarians, 80 per cent of them being so classified in Table 15. They, like the educational leaders, were consistent with their professional roles in this regard. Of course, the church has not consistently been a force for liberty and freedom. The churches in Jamaica, however, have been agencies through which education was spread and social welfare was dispensed. The religious missionaries at several times in Jamaican history were important influences for the spread of equality. We are prone to forget that the dignity of man and the equality of all men in some respects are important parts of Christian ethics, and that such ethics in turn are part of the value premises of Western civilization.

Social welfare elites were, like the educational leaders, part of secular organizations for the most part rather than sacred organizations like the religious leaders. But like both educational and religious leaders, social welfare elites had as part of their job specifically to aid in the spread of equality, and three out of four of them were equalitarians.

Medical elites (mostly doctors) were also generally favorable toward economic and social equality, but other types of elites were considerably less favorable. Legal elites (mostly barristers and solicitors) came next with 55 per cent categorized as equalitarians. About the same percentage,

54, of the appointed officials (mostly members of the Legislative Council) and 50 per cent of the economic elites in agriculture (planters, agents, managerial, or other top personnel) were equalitarians.

For a country in which governmental policies were increasingly directed toward change, toward economic and social development, and toward increasing civil and political equality, it seems surprising that elected political leaders and higher civil servants were not more equalitarian than they are shown to be in Table 15. Even though these responses may somewhat underestimate the actual equalitarian attitudes of these elites (see above), they were far less equalitarian than one might expect change-leaders in a new and modernizing nation to be. These elites held legitimate change most directly in their hands, yet they were not overwhelmingly and strongly favorable to economic and social equality.

The least equalitarian of all the elite groups were the economic elites other than those in agriculture. Most of these elites were in commercial activities. Only 41 per cent of them were equalitarians. The principle of perceived self-interest, as enunciated in Nowak's study of Warsaw students cited above, may explain this. Many commercial economic elites thought— probably erroneously in the long run if the truth were known—that they had most to lose by the spread of economic and social equality.

Commercial economic elites did not generally agree with the economist, Gunnar Myrdal, but if they did they might become considerably more favorable to the spread of economic equality. He says,

> If we seek to learn from what has actually happened in the richer countries which during the last half-century have proceeded far in the direction of greater equality of opportunities we reach . . . a dynamic theory: that the realisation of more equal opportunities has been needed to spur and sustain economic progress as well as to make good the assumptions of social democracy. A corollary to this is the important fact that in a progressive society—characterised by both redistributional reforms and economic growth as the two types of social change mutually support each other by circular causation—*the improvement of the lot of the poor can often be won without substantial sacrifices from those who are better off and is sometimes not only compatible with, but a condition for, the attainment of higher levels in all income brackets, including the higher ones.*[15]

Conclusion

In this chapter, I have described and analyzed attitudes of Jamaican leaders toward economic and social equality. Just as in the past, such attitudes will shape the emergent Jamaican social structure. Thus, the distribution of attitudes of modern-day Jamaican elites is an important indicator of the chances for future structural changes that will continue the trend toward equality, and the manner—planned change or revolution or static oligarchy—of their accomplishment or retardation.

The probability of any single event occurring in a particular way is either zero or one—the frequency definition of probability requires a class of events for its proper application. Thus, the chances of Jamaica pursuing a course of rapid, peaceable change toward increasing minimums of economic and social rights for all Jamaicans in the coming decades might be as high as ninety-nine to one, but that one in a hundred chance may be the one that in fact occurs. Thus, prediction of a given case is risky.

The data presented here, however, suggest that a generally favorable climate of elite opinion for the further extension of economic and social equality existed. The overall level of equalitarianism among the leaders as a whole appeared to be relatively high, and variations by subgroups generally support the contention that equalitarianism among the elites may be expected to increase in future years. Furthermore, the Jamaican representative to the United Nations in one of his first official acts proposed, in accordance with the equalitarian image of the future, an International Human Rights Year. Yet the attitudes of elected political leaders and higher civil servants, who are directly involved in planning change through governmental actions, were not overwhelmingly in favor of economic and social equality.

The questionnaire data reveal patterns of differential distributions of equalitarian attitudes within the Jamaican leadership group. Equalitarians among the elites were more likely to be young than old, women than men, highly educated than poorly educated, and Protestants rather than persons who have other religious preferences. Also, they were more likely to be supporters of the PNP than to be persons having other political preferences; they tended to be expatriates from Canada and the United States, and they were underrepresented among Jamaican-born persons who never lived abroad for as long as a year. Additionally, equalitarians were most likely to be educational, religious, social welfare, and medical elites, and least likely to be commercial economic elites, higher civil servants, or elected political leaders.

Finally, the data presented here from the questionnaire survey are attitudinal. They are not based upon observations of elites' day-to-day behaviors with respect to economic and social equality or inequality. Thus, the usual caution regarding the tenuousness of the link between an attitudinal measurement obtained in one situation and behavior in other situations must be made. But we must not forget that ideas about equality are ideas for which men have fought and died.

Chapter V

Should Jamaica Have a
Democratic Political System? [1]

FOR THE MOST PART, the new nations since World War II emerged from the political domination of the Western democracies, and it was no accident that the ideologies that were invoked to justify claims for political *independence* were heavily larded with the rhetoric of the theory of political *democracy*. Thus, in a sense the colonial powers were hoisted with their own petards, having had their own professed beliefs concerning public liberties and parliamentary government turned against them by the emerging nations during the struggle for "freedom," that is, the struggle for political independence. In crude terms, the demand for government of the people, by the people, and for the people was in the older nations an imperative for the end of political domination of some social classes by others within a given nation, but within the context of the former colonial areas it shifted in emphasis and connotation and became a demand for the end of the political domination of the people of one nationality, even though nascent, by the people of another nationality. It was not inevitable that the empires would crumble and that new nations would emerge, but to have prevented it would have required such a profound change in the fundamental beliefs and values of the Western democracies themselves that these societies would have been thoroughly shaken.[2]

To the dismay of many persons in the Western democracies it has become increasingly clear that the apparently heartfelt appeals to democracy that were made to justify the demands for independence have done little, ironically, to insure the establishment and continuation of democratic political systems in the new nations once independence was achieved. For example, leaders of the emergent nations toured England, the United States, and other countries, and with apparent sincerity they dramatized their political oppressions and called for "one man, one vote," for democracy, *for independence,* only to return in some cases to their newly created countries and the businesslike and not infrequently ruthless elimination of political opposition in the name of everything from national consolidation to economic advancement and from social reform to even "democracy" itself. To say that the future of democracy in the new states is uncertain is an understatement. More correctly, one-party "democracies," semimodern dictatorships, reversions to near-feudal systems, fragmented and quarreling regional aristocracies, and other variations of undemocratic political systems with or without some of the superficial trappings of democracy have formed within some, if not most, of the new nations.

Thus, another of the big decisions of nationhood is, "What form of government should the new nation have?" And for the new nations since World War II, the most significant aspect of this decision was whether or not to have a democratic political system modeled after those of the Western democratic countries. The new national elites, of course, often had little freedom of choice in reaching a decision about the form of their own governments until after independence was actually achieved, since the colonial powers imposed a particular form of government on them. In Jamaica, for example, the period from 1944 to 1962 was a time of tutelary democracy during which the British established a parliamentary system like their own. If the emergent elites had rejectetd it, Jamaica might not be independent today. For instance, British Guiana suffered a constitutional setback and its independence was delayed in part because it appeared that the control of government was in the hands of a section of the new national elite which found Western democratic forms uncongenial.

The purpose of this chapter is to discuss the chances for the continuation of a democratic political system in Jamaica. As independence approached, did the Jamaican elites believe in democracy? Would they try to make it work? Or did they believe that it would never work in Jamaica? There are other aspects to the problem of democracy than the one selected for examination, of course, but I believe it to be a crucial one. It is the *attitudes toward the electorate held by elite groups.* Such attitudes bear on problems of democracy in that they reveal the extent of basic commitments and underlying sentiments toward some of the institutions and rules that sustain and give form to democratic procedures—the political campaign and election. If the elites in Jamaica believe basically that the electorate acting collectively are fools to be tricked, herded, or grossly manipulated, if they are contemptuous and disrespectful of the voters, if they think the voters are incompetent, if, in other words, they are generally *cynical* about one of the fundamental elements of political democracy, then the foundations on which a democracy can be erected may be shaky indeed.

An Index of Political Cynicism

Table 16 contains the four items which were used to measure political cynicism among Jamaican leaders. They each describe two alternative forms of campaign strategies, one that involves a contempt for the voter and which Charles R. Nixon and Dwaine Marvick refer to as a cynical or manipulative response, and another that involves considerably more respect for voters' powers of judgment and competence and that is designated the idealistic response. The cynical alternative is subversive of democratic procedures in that it reveals a lack of respect for one of the major pillars of democracy—the institutions and rules that define the selection of political leaders. Additionally, the normative standard of the democratic process demands that campaign appeals and charges should be disciplined and regulated fundamentally out of deference to the wisdom of the people acting collectively as an electorate.[3]

In addition to the data from the 1958 questionnaire survey of Jamaican leaders, another set of data is discussed briefly and compared at one point with those for Jamaican leaders. These data were collected by Nixon and Marvick among active campaign workers in the Los Angeles area during the American political campaign that culminated in November, 1956.[4] No claim is made for the representativeness of these data nor for their comparability to the data for Jamaican leaders, but they are worth reporting to give some perspective to the responses of the Jamaican leaders with respect to their overall level of political cynicism.

Each Jamaican leader in the sample was asked to rate the cynical alternative campaign strategy as being "good, fair, or poor strategy, thinking specifically of Jamaican voters." In order to establish firmly the political context of Jamaica rather than some democracy in theory or in reality under different conditions than those in Jamaica as the frame of reference of the respondent, "thinking of Jamaican voters" was repeated in each item. The responses of the Jamaican leaders are given in Table 16, and they can be compared with the responses of the American campaign workers. On each of the items, the Jamaicans were more likely than the Americans to think that the cynical alternative was good strategy, the average difference for the four items being 20 per cent. Although it requires herculean assumptions to infer much from this comparison, the difference is what one would expect considering that social and cultural differences between elites and nonelites were greater in Jamaica than in the United States. The American campaign workers, however, were self-selected and this fact may explain the differences shown in Table 16.

TABLE 16. *Beliefs of Jamaican Leaders and American Campaign Workers Concerning Political Campaign Strategies*

"In campaigning, the thing to do is to point out how different issues affect the voter's pocketbook instead of how issues affect the whole society and economy. . . ."

	Jamaican leaders	American campaign workers *
Good strategy (cynical)	71%	53%
Fair strategy	14	24
Poor strategy (idealistic)	15	23
Total	100%	100%
Number of cases	(227)	(251)

". . . the thing to do is to lash out at the opposition's record and program instead of calmly presenting your own side's records and plans. . . ."

	Jamaican leaders	American campaign workers
Good strategy (cynical)	54%	25%
Fair strategy	21	32
Poor strategy (idealistic)	25	43
Total	100%	100%
Number of cases	(226)	(253)

". . . the thing to do is to stir up strong emotions, hates and fears instead of presenting a careful discussion of complex problems facing the country. . . ."

	Jamaican leaders	American campaign workers
Good strategy (cynical)	36%	17%
Fair strategy	16	13
Poor strategy (idealistic)	48	70
Total	100%	100%
Number of cases	(225)	(253)

". . . the thing to do when the other side makes a smear attack is to level fresh charges against them instead of making a reasoned explanation of the facts. . . ."

	Jamaican leaders	American campaign workers
Good strategy (cynical)	29%	15%
Fair strategy	15	25
Poor strategy (idealistic)	56	60
Total	100%	100%
Number of cases	(228)	(252)

* Data on Americans are from Dwaine Marvick, "Active Campaign Workers: The Power Structures of Rival Parties," unpublished paper, University of California, Los Angeles.

In general, Table 16 shows that a substantial proportion of the Jamaican elites were lacking in a sense of respect for the competence of the Jamaican electorate. However, the level of political cynicism, as measured by these items, although relatively high, was not as high as it could be. Forty-eight per cent of the Jamaican leaders rejected the efficacy of stirring up strong emotions, hates, and fears, and 56 per cent of them rejected leveling fresh charges against the other side instead of making a reasoned explanation of the facts when faced with a smear attack.

The four items shown in Table 16 were combined to construct an Index of Political Cynicism. The responses to each item were simply added together for each respondent, by giving two points for a response of "good strategy," one point for "fair strategy," and zero for "poor strategy." Thus, the possible scores on the Index run from 0 to 8, with 0 representing the least cynical and 8 the most cynical response. The percentage distribution of Jamaican elites according to their scores on the Index of Political Cynicism is given in Table 17.

The Index of Political Cynicism was dichotomized as shown in the lower portion of Table 17. Arbitrarily, persons with scores of 5 or more were classified as "cynical" or "undemocratic" and those with scores of 4 or less were classified as "idealistic" or "democratic." This dichotomy is used throughout the remainder of the analysis.

In addition to the items used to measure political cynicism, there was an item in the questionnaire asking the respondents' opinions regarding the importance of factors that influence the average Jamaican voter. The responses to one of these factors, "serious consideration of the issues involved," permit a tentative evaluation of the validity of the Index of Politi-

TABLE 17. *The Distribution of Jamaican Leaders According to Their Scores on the Index of Political Cynicism* *

Index score	Per cent
8 (most cynical)	20
7	6
6	14
5	10
4	16
3	10
2	7
1	6
0 (most idealistic)	11
Total	$\overline{100}$
Number of cases	(231)
No answer	(7)
As dichotomized:	
5 to 8 (cynical)	50
0 to 4 (idealistic)	50
Total	$\overline{100}$

* The index is based on the responses given in Table 16: good strategy = 2; fair strategy = 1; and poor strategy = 0.

cal Cynicism. If the Index measured what it was intended to measure, then respondents who thought that serious consideration of the issues was very important should have been less cynical than those who thought it was not very important. That such was the case is shown by Table 18. Thirty-one per cent of those leaders who said this factor was very important were politically cynical compared to 66 per cent of those who said that it was not very important. Thus, on the basis of one external criterion, the validity of the Index can be accepted tentatively.[5]

Of course, leaders who were politically cynical claimed to be simply realistic. That is, they argued that their cynicism was merely the result of their own knowledge and experience and that their misanthropic view of the Jamaican voter was factually correct. That most of the cynics believed this seems true enough, but this seems insufficient grounds for giving up the concept of cynicism in favor of realism. First, the idealistic persons also argued that their views were based upon facts; *their* knowledge and experience led them to an opposite view of the average Jamaican voter than that held by the cynics. Thus, similar claims for realism were made alike by cynics and idealists. With a few exceptions, each seemed generally aware of the same "reality"—in the sheer perceptual sense; but each made different inferences and generalizations from it giving weight to different aspects of reality and credence to different assumptions.

Second, the question of amount of realism, objectively determined, in the cynical versus the idealistic view, although an important one, is beyond the purpose of this book. It appears to me, on the basis of very little systematic evidence, that there are data to support both views, and some that conflict with both. Whichever view is more justified in reality, negative attitudes about the electorate, which I have called political cynicism following Marvick and Nixon, remain contrary to the theory of political democracy and inimical to the operative ideals that help make democracy work in fact as well as it does. Especially in a country like Jamaica in which democracy is getting a trial, the spread of political cynicism, even though largely unrealistic, can undermine democracy; and conversely, the avoidance of political cynicism can result in the future transcendence of whatever truth there may presently be in the cynical attitude.

TABLE 18. *The Percentage of Jamaican Leaders Who Are Politically Cynical by Their Opinions Regarding How Important Serious Consideration of the Issues Is in Influencing the Average Jamaican Voter*

Serious consideration of the issues is:	*Per cent who are politically cynical*	*Number of cases on which the per cent is based*
Very important	31	(51)
Somewhat important	44	(79)
Not very important	66	(95)

Correlates of Political Cynicism

Table 19 gives the percentage of Jamaican leaders who are politically cynical by selected social characteristics. There are only slight differences by age, with the group between ages 40 and 54 being most cynical and the oldest group, age 55 and over, least cynical. Persons age 39 or less were intermediate in cynicism. Men were somewhat more likely than women to be cynical, although the small number of women in the sample reduces the confidence with which this statement can be made. Elites born in Jamaica were least cynical followed closely by Canadians and Americans. Persons born in the British Caribbean other than Jamaica and persons born in the British Isles were somewhat more cynical, but the most cynical persons were those born in the non-British Caribbean, the Far East, Middle East, and other places.

Political cynicism was related to amount of education, but not monotonically. Only 19 per cent of the elites with an elementary education were cynical, and the percentage increases with increasing levels of education up to 64 per cent for those who have completed college. Among persons who had attended postgraduate school, however, the percentage who were cynical dropped to 45.

Differences in political cynicism by annual income and occupational rating were inconsequential. Religion appeared to be somewhat related to cynicism with the Catholics being the most cynical and persons with no religious preferences, Independents, Agnostics, and Atheists, being the least cynical. Protestants were practically as cynical as the Catholics, but Jews were somewhat less cynical.

Among Jamaican-born elites, there was a slight increase in cynicism with the number of foreign countries lived in for at least one year, a measure of cosmopolitanism. Political party preference entered into amount of political cynicism in that persons with no party preference and supporters of the PNP were more likely to be politically cynical than were supporters of the JLP. The PNP was in power at the time and the JLP was out of power, but the PNP had just suffered a setback in the federal elections of 1958.

TABLE 19. *The Percentage of Jamaican Leaders Who Are Politically Cynical by Selected Social Characteristics*

Selected social characteristics	Per cent who are politically cynical	Number of cases on which the per cent is based
Age:		
55 and over	45	(69)
40–54	55	(112)
25–39	50	(50)

Selected social characteristics	Per cent who are politically cynical	Number of cases on which the per cent is based
Sex:		
Men	52	(213)
Women	39	(18)
Country of birth:		
Far East, Middle East, and other	86	(7)
Caribbean other than British Caribbean	80	(5)
British Isles	63	(27)
British Caribbean other than Jamaica	60	(10)
Canada and the United States	50	(12)
Jamaica	46	(170)
Education:		
Graduate school	45	(47)
Completed college	64	(44)
Some college	56	(34)
Secondary or training school	52	(89)
Elementary only	19	(16)
Annual income:		
£3,000 and over	48	(46)
£2,000–2,999	53	(49)
£1,999 and under	49	(114)
Occupational rating:		
1 (highest)	51	(132)
2	49	(83)
3 and 4 (lowest)	56	(16)
Religious preference:		
Catholic	56	(25)
Protestant	51	(176)
Jewish	45	(11)
None	30	(10)
Number of foreign countries lived in for at least one year (Jamaican-born only):		
2 or more	54	(41)
1	51	(47)
None	44	(71)
Political party preference:		
None	54	(63)
People's National Party	54	(100)
Jamaica Labour Party	39	(64)

Additional data are given in Table 20. Here, the percentage of Jamaican leaders who were politically cynical is given by the major type of elite position that was occupied by each elite. By far the most cynical of all the different types of elites are the legal elites, a category containing judges, barristers, and solicitors.[6] Seventy-three per cent of them were cynical. Next were the economic elites in agriculture and the higher civil servants, with 58 per cent each who were cynical. Having about 50 per cent of their number who were politically cynical, educational elites, religious elites, social welfare elites, and economic elites in commercial activities came next. Medical elites were less cynical, with 43 per cent being so classified; and finally, the least cynical of all the types of elites were the nominated officials (36 per cent) and the elected political leaders (35 per cent).

TABLE 20. *The Percentage of Jamaican Leaders Who Are Politically Cynical by Type of Elite Position*

Type of elite position	Per cent who are politically cynical	Number of cases on which the per cent is based
Legal elites	73	(11)
Economic elites (agriculture)	58	(12)
Civil servants	58	(66)
Educational elites	53	(15)
Religious elites	50	(10)
Social welfare elites	50	(4)
Economic elites (commercial and other)	49	(57)
Medical elites	43	(23)
Nominated officials	36	(11)
Elected political leaders	35	(20)

Finally, the percentage of Jamaican leaders who were politically cynical is given in Table 21 by four measures of social influence. The measures of influence used were (1) amount of political activity, (2) a respondent's self-evaluation of his influence in Jamaican affairs, (3) the total number of elite positions that a respondent simultaneously occupied, and (4) the number of books, articles, or pamphlets that the respondent had written during the last ten years. Although the differences are small, they consistently show that the less influential elites were more likely to be politically cynical than were the more influential. Each of these relationships held up, that is remained, when country of birth and educational level were controlled.

TABLE 21. *The Percentage of Jamaican Leaders Who Are Politically Cynical by Four Measures of Influence*

Measures of influence	Per cent who are politically cynical	Number of cases on which the per cent is based
Amount of political activity:		
Active	32	(34)
Inactive	54	(196)
R's self-evaluation of his own influence in Jamaican affairs:		
Much influence	48	(136)
Little influence	55	(95)
Number of elite positions simultaneously occupied by R:		
4 or more	46	(61)
3	47	(32)
2	49	(47)
1	56	(91)
Number of books, articles, or pamphlets published during last ten years:		
Many	41	(39)
Some	46	(37)
None	54	(153)

Causes of Political Cynicism

Three hypotheses, each specifying a cause of political cynicism, are suggested by these correlations and by other information. The hypotheses are interrelated, but in complex ways. Two of the causes of cynicism generally occur together and reinforce each other, but another factor that produces cynicism is operative primarily when the other factors are not. Additionally, the causes that are specified below appear to cut across most of the variables shown in Tables 19 and 20, and as a result, confound the relationships between such variables and cynicism.

Hypothesis 1: powerlessness. Feelings of powerlessness and the sense of losing relative power with respect to public affairs produce political cynicism. It is hypothesized that powerlessness, however it may develop, produces cynicism. In Jamaica it is obvious that the major social process that affected the redistribution of power, the waxing and waning of different elite groups, and feelings of gaining or losing relative power,was the transfer of political power that came with self-government. Before the beginnings of self-government in 1944, Jamaica was run by the Governor and a small handful of officials responsible to the British Colonial Office and by local economic elites both in agriculture and commerce. The Governor and his officials had formal responsibility, but they listened to the advice of the economic dominants. In general, this group was concerned that things should run smoothly, that order should be maintained, and that the interests of the *status quo* should be served but preferably not by any acts of governance that were barbaric or inhuman. This group was largely oriented to British culture, composed in part of persons whose formal positions necessitated giving highest allegiance to England not to Jamaica, and contained persons who were primarily white or nearly white. Their power was not seriously challenged by a few brown or black-skinned leaders with popular followings of various sizes.

With the coming of universal adult suffrage, however, the legality of trade unions, and the transfer of formal power from Governor and appointed officials to the Cabinet and the elected House of Representatives, this near-monopoly of power was broken. As a result of official British policy, the power of the Governor and his officials began to wane and the target of complete independence was established. Elected political leaders, trade union leaders, new *Jamaican* higher civil servants, and other emergent elites, encouraged by the new British policy, began to pull the reins of government toward development, reform, redistribution, and toward other national goals that many of the former local elites could only view with distress, if not horror. A minority of the former established elites, feeling that they had been deserted by the British government, were still not reconciled in 1958 to an independent Jamaica, to rule by the "ignorant masses" and their "agitators," and to the "ruinous" policies that were resulting. Most of the former elites, however, primarily big planters and traders, whatever private regrets and querulousness some of them still had, were reconciled to independence, that is to political democracy based upon the universal adult suffrage that independence implied. They were reconciled also to the loss of the reassuring protection of Britain against the nightmarish possibility of their becoming victims of violence at the hands of rebelling members of the black lower classes. During the transition to independence, they had worked to establish channels of communication and influence between themselves and the emergent elites and they had adopted policies primarily of accommodation, but secondarily of coöptation when it proved possible, and even, although infrequently, of assimilation. In addition, recent governmental policies generally did not deprive them of their nongovernmental sources of power, and in more than a few cases helped them to expand their economic activities or to establish new activities. Some of them even received windfall business profits as a result of the new policies.

The established elites in Jamaica with few exceptions lost relative power over public affairs with the coming of self-government. At worst, some of them no longer attempted to participate in the major affairs of the society but complained bitterly of recent political developments, heaped invectives on the heads of both the electorate and the new politicians, and in general deplored the present democratic system in Jamaica. Such persons became extremely cynical, but they no longer posed any serious threat to Jamaican democracy—although such groups appear to be important in some of the other emerging nations, for example such as the white settlers of East Africa.[7]

At best, some of the former established elites merged their efforts with those of the new elites, and although they were forced to take account of new and competing centers of power, they were playing hard, and not without some success, at the new game of popular government. Although for the most part decreasing in *relative* power or proportion of total power in relation to other groups, some of these elites—especially some economic-commercial elites—actually had more power in absolute terms than they had before.[8] Other things (that is, the other two causes of cynicism to be specified below) being equal, such elites were not politically cynical. And they represented an important group in nearly independent Jamaica.

The hypothesis under discussion is most directly tested by the data given in Table 21, which show that on each of four measures the more influential elites were less likely to be politically cynical than were the less influential elites.[9]

The hypothesis is not directly tested by the variables in Table 19 but it may help to explain the relationships between political cynicism and country of birth (because Jamaican-born elites were ascendant, Americans and Canadians had new opportunities, especially in industry and commerce, and persons born in the British Isles were in relative decline), and political party preference (because the PNP, although still in power within Jamaica, had just been rejected by the electorate in the federal elections). Also, it may help to explain some of the differences in cynicism between different types of elite groups shown in Table 20, such as the relatively low amount of cynicism among elected political leaders and nominated officials, the latter by 1958 representing official British policy regarding independence and democracy and being increasingly appointed upon the recommendation of the elected political leaders, and the relatively high amount of cynicism among the economic elites in agriculture.

Hypothesis 2: social distance. Feelings of social distance from the subordinate socio-economic-racial groups in Jamaica produce political cynicism. It is hypothesized that persons who feel socially distant from the great majority of Jamaicans who compose the lower socio-economic-racial groups are more likely to be politically cynical, in the sense meant here, than are persons who feel less socially distant from them.

I use the term, "socio-economic-racial," to specify these groups in order to give due recognition to the correlations between social, economic, and racial subordination in Jamaica which I discussed earlier in Chapter I. The argument over the "real" basis of social stratification and of intergroup hostility and antagonism in Jamaica—whether racial or socioeconomic—is relatively fruitless. I am referring to social distance from the "black lower classes," even though on the one hand members of such classes were not always black or even brown by the standards of physical anthropometry and although on the other hand racial, rather than socioeconomic, characteristics predominated in local conceptualizations of the social distance between superordinate and subordinate groups. "Quashee," originally an Ashanti name for a person born on Sunday, was a common term in Jamaica used to designate a member of the lower socioeconomic classes, but its connotation appeared to be largely racial, referring to a black or a Negro.

Among elites in Jamaica, social distance from the lower socioeconomic-racial groups was accompanied by the lack of identification with these lower groups, and by haughtiness, alienation, disaffection, and aversion. Hostility, antagonism, and even ill-will were also associated with the sense of social distance. In addition, people who felt great social distance from "Quashee" viewed him as a threat to the established order and feared him and the violence he might do if aroused.[10] Thus, it is not surprising to find that elites whose sense of social distance from the black lower classes was high were also politically cynical. In fact such elites were not only cynical about the electorate, but also were cynical about the elected political leaders. They opposed political democracy based on universal adult suffrage in Jamaica and they opposed self-government and political independence as well.

It would be a mistake to think of the lack of social unity between higher and lower classes in Jamaica and of the political cynicism of elites as something unique to Jamaica, to new nations, to economically under-developed areas, or to plural societies. Jamaica was in the throes of politi-cal, economic, and social transformations that began in Western societies in the eighteenth century with "the industrial revolution in England, the political revolutions in the United States and France, and the development of centralized government and national citizenship." [11] A "democratic revolution," which was spreading around the world, was taking place in Jamaica during the last two decades. Jamaica's problems of social unity, social distance, and political cynicism appear to be characteristic of the democratic revolution and are reminiscent of the same problems faced ear-lier by other nations. The spread of ". . . egalitarian ideas at a time when society was still sharply divided into clearly distinguishable social ranks with their separate immunities and autonomous jurisdictions . . ." [12] re-sulted, as a general rule, in a preoccupation with the lower-class "threat" to the established order. The political integration of the masses previously excluded from participation has invariably been greeted with repugnance and opposition on the part of most members of the previously privileged groups. It was fashionable, as Jamaica approached independence, for Jamai-can intellectuals to emphasize the problems of social unity in Jamaica and to imply that, if not unique to Jamaica and other plural societies, they were especially acute in Jamaica compared to the milder forms similar problems took in the older nations. On the contrary, the problems seem to be general ones, typical of all countries at a certain stage in the demo-cratic revolution. I doubt if the situation in Jamaica, even though it in-volved the additional factor of race, was really any worse than it was in England at an earlier time. Discussions of present-day Jamaican social stratification often echo Disraeli's earlier description of the English working and ruling classes: "two nations between whom there is no intercourse and no sympathy; who are as ignorant of each other's habits, thoughts and feelings, as if they were dwellers in different zones, or inhabitants of dif-ferent planets, who are formed by a different breeding, are fed by a dif-ferent food, are ordered by different manners, and are not governed by the same laws." [13]

The hypothesis that feelings of social distance from the lower classes produce political cynicism among elites can be most directly tested by relating the Index of Political Cynicism to the responses to an item on the questionnaire asking whether the respondent felt that he had more in common with civic, government, or business leaders in countries outside the West Indies Federation (not yet defunct in 1958) or with the general public in Jamaica. Although in Jamaica the level of identification with the public was generally high, revealing the dominance of nationalist over social-class loyalties among Jamaican elites, a comparison of subgroups does support the hypothesis. Of the elites who said that they had more in common with the average Jamaican, 45 per cent were politically cynical compared to 65 per cent who were cynical among the elites who said that they had more in common with leaders in other countries or who said that it's six of one and a half-a-dozen of the other.

Also, this hypothesis may help to explain the high level of cynicism among persons born in the non-British Caribbean and in the Far East, Middle East, and other places as shown in Table 19. In general, such persons were socially distant from the black lower classes in the extreme. Although education increasingly was becoming an avenue for the deliberate creation of increased opportunities for persons with relatively humble social origins, it retained, in 1958, its function of crystallizing, validating, and institutionalizing social differences. Thus, some of the variation in political cynicism by educational level may be explained by the hypothesis of social distance. At least through graduation from college or university, increasing education made some people, in fact and feeling, more socially distant from the black lower classes, and as a result, more politically cynical. But, as will be pointed out below, there is additional evidence that leads one to conclude that the third hypothesis, rather than the social-distance hypothesis, was more likely to underlie the correlation between cynicism and education.[14]

Cosmopolitanism may measure in part social distance from the average Jamaican, so the social-distance hypothesis may help to explain the relationship between political cynicism and the number of foreign countries lived in for at least one year. When compared to leaders who prefer the JLP, the leaders preferring the PNP and the leaders with no political party preference were relatively high on cynicism. The PNP level of cynicism was to be explained by the third hypothesis given below and perhaps to some extent by the powerlessness hypothesis, but not by the hypothesis of social distance. The latter, however, may explain the cynicism of leaders with no political party preference. Such leaders remained above "wrestling with the rabble" for political power.

Additionally, the social-distance hypothesis may explain some of the variation in cynicism among the different types of governmental elites. In the most general sense, the "clients" of elected political leaders and nominated officials, civil servants, and legal elites alike were *all* the people of Jamaica. The manifest functions of the elected political leaders and nominated officials put the welfare of the country and the people in their hands;

civil servants were charged with the proper implementation of policies directed by the representatives of the people; and barristers and solicitors, particularly judges, were bound to administer the law with due consideration to the abstract purpose of justice for all. Given the nature of the political system in Jamaica, however, the differentiation of functions between these types of elites resulted in different pressures upon them to minimize or maximize, as the case might be, their social distance from the public, which in Jamaica means predominantly the lower classes. The politicians were inclined to minimize social distance and maximize personal, pseudo-personal, and symbolic ties to the "people," [15] while the legal elites were inclined to maximize social distance from the people and to emphasize the impersonal and impartial functioning of the judicial system. In pursuing their primary purpose of taking actions for the welfare of the people, the politicians were constantly resorting to empathy for, and identification with, the lower classes, and secondarily concerning themselves with the legal propriety of their proposed actions. That is, the decrees to be passed were foremost and the framework of rules within which decrees were passed was secondary. To the contrary, legal elites primarily pursued the task of determining the legal propriety of actions and the meaning and applications of the framework of laws itself. Concern for the welfare of the people may have ultimately underlay the performance and nature of their function according to political theory, but the highest priority should be given by them, not to the immediate and apparent needs and welfare of the people *in general,* but to the one need and single welfare that was embodied in the "correct" interpretation of the law. In this regard, civil servants occupied an intermediate position.

Finally, the feeling of social distance appears to be quite congenial to those elites who felt that they were relatively powerless or had lost power with recent political developments in Jamaica; thus, these two things, social distance and powerlessness, generally worked together in producing political cynicism.

Hypothesis 3: intolerance of recalcitrance. Among elites who favor progress, intolerance of recalcitrance that is perceived to interfere with progress produces political cynicism. This hypothesis accounts for the fact that political cynicism developed not only among elites who opposed the political, economic, and social emergence of the lower classes that accompanied independence, but also among elites who favored, and even agitated for, the changes that resulted in such an emergence. In Chapter II, I tried to show how social change in Jamaica can be viewed as including long-term trends characterized by the rising status of the lower classes, that is by rising minimums of human rights for all Jamaicans. Economic advancement, distributional and social reforms, and civil and political equality are what is meant by "progress" in the above hypothesis.

The new, national, change-leading elites, prominently including elected political leaders but also including differentially some persons from nearly all of the elite groups shown in Table 20, were persons who were committed to the rise of Jamaican (and/or West Indian) nationalism, to political independence from the United Kingdom, as will be discussed in Chapter VI, and to progress as defined above. Generally, they identified with and had considerable empathy for the lower classes; they did not feel socially distant from the black lower classes. Nor did they feel that they had lost power as a result of recent political, economic, and social developments. On the contrary, most of them were brown, and a few were black-skinned, Jamaicans, and they felt that they were ascendant. In some cases, as pointed out in Chapter III, especially among the politicians and civil servants, they would not have been where they were if it had not been for the transition to self-government. Nonetheless, some of them were becoming politically cynical, and *if there is any threat to democracy in Jamaica in the near future, it is not so much because of the cynical leaders whose cynicism results from feelings of powerlessness or social distance from the lower classes as because of cynical leaders among the change-leading elites.*

It is not because elites hope and work for the progress of the lower classes that they become cynical. Actually, the most optimistic and idealistic elites were to be found among the change-leading elites. But when change-leading elites were also intolerant of the inevitable obstacles to progress which they met in the form of recalcitrance to coöperate with their efforts to develop Jamaica, they became cynical in the extreme. This process of intolerant reaction to the recalcitrance of other Jamaicans regarding directed social change took several forms, but the most obvious was when members of the lower classes themselves were perceived to be the obstacles to their own progress. The impatience that a change-leading elite expressed when the very people he was trying to help failed to coöperate in his efforts knew no bounds.

Sometimes this occurred even though the members of the lower classes involved might be making, under the circumstances, a reasonably adequate and rational adjustment not only from their point of view but also from an objective point of view. For example, a government scheme to destroy temporary shacks in a Kingston slum located on government land and to replace them with modern one- and two-story blocks of apartments was opposed by a slum dweller. Although understanding the situation thoroughly when it was explained to him by an agricultural extension officer, a farmer refused to plant grass that would prevent erosion on the hills surrounding his farm. A second farmer, although needing capital badly for adequate utilization of his land, would not take advantage of a government scheme offering loans with small interest payments. Such things made change-leading elites tear their hair and made some of them politically cynical, because it was these same "unreasonable and irrational" people who had the vote. But in these situations and others like them, many elites did not become politically cynical, but began an often successful search for the *rationality* in the view of the "recalcitrant tool of action" and a probe into the assumptions underlying the scheme itself and its implementation. Thus, the slum dweller preferred to stay in the slum, because there he paid no or very little rent, because he was a member of an informal yard organization that acted as a mutual aid society and that would probably be destroyed given the ecology of the new housing, because the design of the new housing made difficult certain desired patterns of family organization especially involving the outdoor play and supervision of the children, and because his slum shack represented an investment for which no one was planning to compensate him. The first farmer refused to act in order to prevent soil erosion in the manner prescribed because if he did a mongoose could easily creep up in the grass and attack his chickens. The second farmer would not borrow money because he would have to put up his land as security and under the risky and uncertain conditions of Jamaican small farming he was unwilling to face the very *real possibility* of losing his land.[16]

In the cases cited above it was not so much the actions of the people that needed to be called into question, but the actions of the change-leading elites and their agents themselves. Most of the change-leading elites and many members of their subordinate staffs who helped to implement programs of various types were aware of this. They tried to encourage feed-back and to create flexible programs of implementation. Unfortunately, not all of the "subversions of progress" created by the people can be thus solved. Sometimes the members of the lower classes were in fact short-sighted and highly selfish. In many cases, this conclusion had to be reached even after extensive and sympathetic efforts to understand them. Some members of the lower classes did make excessive or unreasonable demands that flowed from exaggerated conceptions of their rights, distorted notions of resources available, and vague and unclear ideas concerning their own duties and obligations in the development of their country. But their power at the polls and their potential for violent demonstration meant that their demands could not be ignored. Change-leading elites, if intolerant of these foibles, felt that their own sacrifices and efforts to help the people were unappreciated, they were deeply hurt and resentful, and they became politically cynical.

Recalcitrance was not limited to lower-class persons, but occurred in the middle and upper classes as well. When opposition to progress occurred among the upper classes, who may be cynical themselves because of feelings of losing power and social distance, change-leading elites did not, as a result, become politically cynical. It was regarded as natural and normal for upper-class persons to oppose progress in Jamaica; they were not, after all, among the persons in the name of whom change was being directed and for whom benefits were intended. But when recalcitrance occurred among the middle classes—especially among civil servants, barristers and solicitors, educators, social welfare elites and workers, doctors, religious leaders, and other persons expected to be a part of the change-leading elite or its staff [17]—then change-leading elites became politically cynical. The middle classes in Jamaica were growing in size during the developments of the last twenty years and they were perceived to be an articulate and important part of the electorate even though they were relatively small in numbers compared to the lower classes. But the onus of carrying the burdens and sacrifices associated with political, economic, and social developments fell upon them to a large extent. Because they were educated, they were expected to understand the meaning of independence and to acknowledge their duties to their country. Because they were better off than the mass of Jamaicans, they were expected not to demand too much of the limited, but growing, wealth of Jamaica until after the level of living of the lower classes had been significantly raised. But they did not always, or even often, live up to these expectations. Instead, doctors in government hospitals, postal clerks, engineers and architects in government departments, agricultural extension officers, social welfare workers, and others went on strike or otherwise pressed their demands for narrowly selfish interests; they made special pleas for concessions of one kind or another; and in a variety of other ways they often disregarded the heroic roles expected of them and violated, in some cases, their own illusions about their contributions to progress in Jamaica. As one political leader told me, these people knew that social changes had resulted in a premium being placed on their skills and professions and they knew that they were essential to future developments. With that knowledge, they could "blackmail" government and business concerns into higher salaries, increased benefits, and more allowances for themselves even though in order to satisfy their demands, resources had to be used that were sorely needed to alleviate unemployment, poverty, and other grave conditions among the lower classes. From this view it was a short step to political cynicism. Some change-leading elites took it in the last few years. However, others were able to tolerate even the obstacles to progress created by some members of the middle classes, and they did not become politically cynical.

What was it that underlay this intolerance of such recalcitrance? It was in part simply the fact that even after eighteen years of tutelary democracy, Jamaican leaders were still relatively inexperienced with democratic realities and did not yet fully appreciate the distinction between ideal purposes and real achievements. They hadn't yet really understood that a real democracy falls short of the ideals that inspire it, but that *it is these ideals that do in fact inspire it.*

Also, it was in part a more subtle fact. Among some Jamaican elites, there was a belief that rapid economic progress could occur only by "grinding the faces of the poor." Among them, there was fairly general agreement that the best conditions for economic progress were when the distribution of economic benefits to the mass of Jamaicans was restricted, when investment in consumer goods was relatively low, when capital formation was high, when investment in plant and equipment was high, and when the new wealth of the society was generally plowed back into the production of more wealth rather than consumed in any way. For them, social welfare, unemployment benefits, poor relief, and so forth, were wasted expenditures, except in so far as they represented an "ambulance service" that ameliorated the worst discontents of the masses, which resulted from the *necessities* of economic growth, and except in so far as they kept the masses from out-and-out rebellion that, of course, would completely disrupt economic growth. Although this view is clearly oversimplified, it was supported by some professional economists in advice given to government and business in Jamaica, it affected the formulation of some private and public policies, and it encouraged intolerance. It did the latter because it knocked the props out from under the legitimacy of the lower-class claims and demands for a larger share of the economic benefits of the society, and for that matter from under the demands of the middle classes as well—who "would only use the additional money for more consumption." Thus, if economic growth was desired, as it was by the change-leading elites, then "scientific knowledge" could be used against any group that demanded a larger share of the economic pie, except investors and entrepreneurs and persons advocating projects of governmental economic development. Economic theory was used to show that such demands were "excessive," "unreasonable," and "contrary to the interests of the nation as a total economy." Thus, a firm belief in this theory of economic growth brought with it a "scientific" justification for intolerance of recalcitrance that was perceived to interfere with progress. Of course, it also specified some of the acts that were to be regarded as recalcitrant.[18]

There is insufficient space here to evaluate the validity of this theory of economic growth. It seems clear that many economists, although stating it in more complex and more qualified terms, would support it. But not all economists would subscribe to it, and some, such as Gunnar Myrdal, who was cited earlier, would contradict it and would argue instead for a circular theory of causation between redistributional reforms and economic progress.[19] Thus, the latter economists would deny that economic progress can occur only by "grinding the faces of the poor" and would state further that the increasing welfare of the poor may be an important spur to economic development. If this is true, and it may well be, then the intolerance of the change-leading elites that derives from the contrary theory of economic growth is indeed ironic.

Unfortunately, very little of the data from the 1958 survey can be brought to bear directly on the intolerance hypothesis. The main reason for this appears to be that the importance of this cause of cynicism has increased greatly in recent years and the importance of social distance and especially powerlessness has declined. In 1956 during the pilot study on which the 1958 questionnaire was largely based, cynicism due to feelings of powerlessness and social distance dominated the scene. Though in 1958 there was evidence of developing intolerance among the change-leading elites, it was not until 1960 that it became more widespread, having become so sometime between August, 1958, and September, 1960. This timing is undoubtedly related to the continued transfer of political power and the achievement of complete internal self-government on July 4, 1959. It remains to be seen whether or not full independence will increase political cynicism due to intolerance of recalcitrance that is perceived to interfere with progress. It might, because many of the change-leading elites can no longer convincingly blame the British, the old upper classes, or imperialism in general for holding Jamaica back, but increasingly they look to the people, and to each other, when it comes to blaming someone for failure to achieve their goals of progress.

The correlation between educational level and political cynicism in Table 19 may be explained in part by the intolerance hypothesis. We know that favorable attitudes toward the spread of economic and social equality, an important part of the concept of progress, were positively correlated with educational level. Commitment to progress increased as education increased. However, it is quite likely that intolerance, as defined here, increases with education as well—at least through graduation from college. As the welfare of the lower classes increasingly becomes a genuine moral issue for educated people, the more intolerant of the lower classes the same educated people are likely to become if the lower classes don't behave "the way they should" according to the theories of their educated benefactors. Thus, educated persons may become politically cynical. This phenomenon is closely akin to what Karl Marx must have felt when he used the "myth of progress" to explain away the evidence that was slowly accumulating that showed that the economic and social conditions of the working classes in England and elsewhere in Europe were generally improving under capitalism. But he was unable, by these pronouncements, to stem the tide of workers who were deserting what to *him* was their "historical role" and who instead were eagerly seeking their share of the increasing material benefits of a capitalistic and industrializing world.

Cynicism was less frequent among persons who had gone beyond graduation from college than it was among any other educational category except for those who had no more than an elementary school education. This may be because, barring the possibility of an unrelenting commitment to a theory of social change such as Marx had, they became more tolerant as a result of a better understanding of the complexities, subtleties, and uncertainties of human knowledge, while being no less committed to the goal of progress.

From their inception the two major political parties in Jamaica differed in ideology. The PNP was originally socialistic. It was a social reform party with a definite set of plans for development which reflected a sense of mission, theories of socialism, and idealism. During the last ten years it backed away from socialism, but in 1958 the PNP was still more elaborate, deliberate, and doctrinaire in its "planning for progress" than was the more pragmatic JLP.[20] This commitment to progress, combined with the fact that they had been the party in power since 1955, contributed to intolerance of recalcitrance among members and supporters of the PNP. As the party in power, the PNP faced the reality of the recalcitrant masses in a way it never did when it was the opposition party from 1944 to 1955, and its morality of progress permitted righteous indignation. Development schemes met with resistance among the people they were designed to benefit, and petty and unenlightened self-interest clearly motivated some persons who should have been making sacrifices for the modernization of the country —even, of course, among PNP supporters themselves. Thus, the intolerance hypothesis may explain much of the difference in amount of cynicism between the PNP and the JLP shown in Table 19.

The intolerance hypothesis also accounts for much of the cynicism shown among some of the elites in Table 20, but this cannot be demonstrated by variations in cynicism between elites because of the confounding and differential effects of the powerlessness and social-distance factors. The intolerance hypothesis, however, probably explains all of the cynicism among the elected political leaders and much of it among the civil servants and social welfare elites. It was also prominent as a cause of cynicism among nominated officials, educational and religious elites. Additionally, it may explain a small amount of the cynicism among the legal elites, medical elites, and economic elites in both commercial and agricultural activities. The 1958 survey data, unfortunately, in no way test this proposition.

Conclusion

Whether or not Jamaicans can make democracy work depends on many things. Important among them is the degree of commitment to democratic ideals among Jamaican leaders. Such ideals inspire men's actions and help to make real-life democracies, as imperfect as they may be, work as well as they do. Widespread rejection of such ideals, the spread of political cynicism, undermines the foundations of democracy by raising the question of its legitimacy.

In this chapter, the amount of political cynicism, as measured by disrespectful and contemptuous attitudes concerning the political competence of the average Jamaican voter among Jamaican leaders, was examined. By this measure, we found that political cynicism was fairly widespread; half of the leaders were at least moderately cynical and a fifth of them were cynical in the extreme.

Contemplation of the 1958 questionnaire data as well as of additional materials based upon interviews, informants, and personal observation led to the formulation and detailed discussion of three hypotheses which specify the causes of political cynicism among elites in Jamaica. These are:

(1) Feelings of powerlessness and the sense of losing relative power with respect to public affairs produce political cynicism.

(2) Feelings of social distance from the subordinate socio-economic-racial groups within the society produce political cynicism.

(3) Among elites who favor progress, intolerance of recalcitrance (on the part of persons whom such progress is supposed to benefit) that is perceived to interfere with progress produces political cynicism.

In Jamaica, as in many other new nations, the drive toward self-government and independence was defined as being consistent with democratic theory, in fact it was conceived to be a logical necessity according to democratic notions. Other things being equal, politically cynical leaders (nondemocrats) tended to oppose independence and politically idealistic leaders (democrats) tended to favor it, as will be discussed in the following chapter. Tutelary democracy was not simply imposed by the United Kingdom onto Jamaica, but a democratic political system was an important part of the nationalists' image of Jamaica's future. Furthermore, the configuration of attitudes which linked antidemocratic sentiments (political cynicism) with feelings of powerlessness and the sense of losing relative power with respect to public affairs, and with feelings of social distance from the subordinate socio-economic-racial groups, was increasingly unpopular from 1944 to 1962 both from the *official* British point of view and from the standpoint of Jamaican nationalist ideology. Such a pattern was then fading, it could not be safely expressed, and it was not considered legitimate when viewed from the perspective of the political future most Jamaicans thought that Jamaica should and would have. Threats to Jamaica's new democracy probably will not come from this quarter.

There is a real danger to the continuation of democratic forms in Jamaica, however. It comes not so much from those leaders who opposed independence and progress, as from those who wanted independence and who want progress. It comes from among the change-leaders themselves who are trying to move the people of Jamaica into a better future but who sometimes become impatient with the democratic process when it appears to them to impede the progress they hope to achieve. This particular kind of antidemocratic or politically cynical attitude carries with it its own legitimation and can be expressed freely, since it is antidemocracy in the name of the people's welfare, in the name of economic and social progress. The irony is, as I have tried to point out, that the assumption underlying this view may be fallacious. No one has proved that progress toward economic and social goals is more easily made under a nondemocratic than under a democratic political system; in fact there is some evidence to the contrary.[21] If the attitudes of the politically cynical change-leading elites win out in the struggle for the image of Jamaica's future, the Jamaican people might lose some of their newly won political rights without being any closer to their economic and social goals than they would have been anyway.

Chapter VI

Should Jamaica Be
Politically Independent?

OF THE BIG DECISIONS of nationhood, one has priority over all others. That is, of course, the decision to seek political independence or not, to strive for nationhood or to remain a colonial dependent of another nation. It is beyond the scope of this book to give an account of the details of the nationalist struggle for independence in Jamaica or of the obviously relevant world-wide events, external pressures, and internal forces that shaped British colonial policy after World War II. However, attitudes of Jamaican leaders toward the political changes that were leading to independence are described and analyzed here. Such attitudes were among a few key variables that carried Jamaica across the wide gulf that separated a politically dependent colony from a politically independent nation.

As Jamaica approached political independence, as the people faced the removal of their citizenship in the United Kingdom and the colonies and the acquisition of new *Jamaican* citizenship, not all "Jamaicans" favored political change. Some were antinationalist and opposed Jamaica's transition to independence. Many were indifferent. And others were extremely nationalist in their views, seeing in political independence a precondition for a variety of benefits ranging from self-respect to economic development. Such persons "decided" that Jamaica's future would be a better one if Jamaica became independent, and some of them began working to bring about independence. This chapter is an attempt to understand these different attitudes. Specifically: How widespread were nationalist attitudes among Jamaican leaders? What reasons did leaders give to support such attitudes? What social characteristics were correlated with nationalist attitudes? What caused some leaders to say, "Yes, Jamaica should be politically independent!" And what caused others to say with equal fervor, "No, Jamaica should remain a British colony!"

The Distribution of Nationalist Attitudes

Nationalist attitudes are here defined as favorable attitudes toward political independence, favorable sentiments toward the transition of Jamaica from a colony to an independent nation. Specifically, a respondent who said that Jamaica had more to gain than to lose as a result of political independence was classified as a "nationalist," and one who said the opposite was designated an "antinationalist." Not all aspects of nationalism as defined by other writers are included in this definition, but it is precise with a clear empirical referent, and it is consistent with the common core of most definitions as they apply to nascent nations. For example, James S. Coleman says that a ". . . colonial nationalist movement normally has two main objectives. The first is to terminate imperial rule; the second is to create a modern nation-state." [1] Furthermore, he defines nationalism in those cases where the reference group is not a *de facto* nation largely in terms of ". . . sentiment and activity directed toward the creation of a nation and the attainment of independent statehood." [2]

By this definition, not all Jamaican elites were nationalist as can be seen from their responses to the following question: "Does *Jamaica* have more to gain or lose as a result of political independence from the United Kingdom?"

Jamaica has more to gain	66%
Political independence will make no difference	7
Jamaica has more to lose	26
Jamaica gains in some ways and loses in others	1
Total	100%
Number of cases	(234)
No answers	(4)

Even among the nationalists, the viewpoints were not generally emotional nor extreme in 1958. There was relatively little bitterness expressed against the United Kingdom, there was a general recognition of the worth of the British tutelage in democratic self-government, and there was hope of continued material assistance, advice, and sympathy from the United Kingdom. As an example, the British Governor was kept on as Governor-General by the nationalist elite for a time even after independence. Additionally, an awareness that independence was not a panacea for the problems facing Jamaica and a realization that economic and other problems confronted an independent Jamaica were clearly expressed. This temperate, even cautious, attitude seems quite different from the demands for immediate or early independence expressed by the leaders of some of the other emergent nations, and reflects the general satisfaction among Jamaicans who favored independence with the tempo of the political transition that culminated in independence. Finally, nearly as many Jamaican elites, 58 per cent, thought that the *United Kingdom* had more to gain than to lose as a result of Jamaica's independence as thought that *Jamaica* had more to gain. Fewer, 18 per cent, thought that the *U.K.* had more to lose when compared with the 26 per cent who thought that *Jamaica* had more to lose than to gain by independence.

When they were asked to explain their attitudes, however, the nationalists were nonetheless definite about their desire for independence and their beliefs that independence would accelerate economic, political, social, cultural, and spiritual progress for Jamaica. The progress envisaged by the nationalists can be conveniently divided into two broad categories. First are the intangible, subjective, or psychological benefits. Independence was viewed as conferring equality of status in relation to other peoples of the world. It was seen as eliminating inferior status, as transforming "subjects" of the British empire into "citizens" of Jamaica, as giving new rights and new dignity to Jamaicans including a direct influence in the decisions that would affect their own welfare, as promoting the respect among Jamaicans for fellow Jamaicans, and as increasing the respect of other countries for Jamaica and Jamaicans. The language used to discuss this benefit of independence often contained references to "freedom" or "a free people" and frequently included the explicit statement that new rights and responsibilities would result in the increased development of national spirit, enthusiasm, and consciousness; in a greater sense of achievement; in the cultivation of local talents and initiative; in greater efforts on the part of Jamaicans to work for themselves; and generally in the maturation and improvement of the personal characters of Jamaicans. Fifty-six per cent of the 154 elites who thought that Jamaica had more to gain by independence gave such explanations for their attitudes.

Second are the material, especially economic, benefits that were expected to derive from the freedom to plan Jamaican affairs with the interest of Jamaica foremost in mind. Although colonial rule was observed to be beneficial in a variety of ways, the convenience and interest of Britain were thought in the long run to have had priority over the welfare of Jamaica. Thus, *Jamaican* leaders acting in *Jamaica* in the interest of the *Jamaican* people with no allegiance overriding their loyalty to *Jamaica* were thought to maximize *Jamaica's* economic progress. Many of the same leaders who said this also pointed out that independence had its economic dangers in that the United Kingdom would no longer be obligated in quite the same way to consider the welfare of Jamaica, that Colonial Development and Welfare grants might be lost, and that British preferences on Jamaican products might be endangered. Despite these considerations, 51 per cent of the nationalists thought that economic benefits on the balance would result from independence. They saw freedom to expand trade in markets other than the United Kingdom; for example, Canada and the United States. They saw new opportunities to seek financial assistance and loans from other nations and from international agencies; they saw changes in the pattern of internal economic development based upon what will be best for Jamaica; they saw Jamaica in a better bargaining position in the world economy; and they saw more rapid action and decision-making on matters pertaining to the national economy when such action was necessary after they were "no longer hog-tied to the U.K."

About 8 per cent of the nationalists gave other explanations for their favorable attitudes toward independence, sometimes in addition to the two major factors. The most frequently mentioned additional explanation was that independence would contribute toward social stability, the prevention of political unrest, and the integration of the various racial elements. That is, if new rights and freedoms had not been acquired by the Jamaican people through the peaceful and orderly transfer of political power, then the desire for such rights and freedoms might have become the basis of conflict within the society. Independence was thought to be a symbol of progress for most racial and class levels in Jamaica, and without it discontents, especially lower-class discontents, might have become organized in extreme ways leading to excesses of interracial-class hostility, conflict, and disunity.

Of the 62 antinationalists, the persons who thought that Jamaica had more to lose than to gain as a result of Jamaica's political independence, 68 per cent believed that Jamaica would lose economically. They said that England would no longer be responsible for Jamaica's economic situation, that preferences, loans, grants, and subsidies would be lost, that new expenses of defense and foreign affairs would have to be locally paid for, and that Jamaica could not compete without aid in the world economy.

Some of the elites who thought that Jamaica would lose economically as a result of independence appeared to be only mildly antinationalist and they noted that Jamaica might nonetheless gain in self-respect. However, 19 persons or 31 per cent of the antinationalists were adamant and extreme in their antinationalism in giving as their explanation for their attitudes that Jamaicans—leaders and common people alike—were simply not capable of governing themselves. They said, often with considerable hostility, that the people were too illiterate; that the working classes were interested only in money; that graft and corruption would come; that Jamaicans lacked the background and character, if not the brains, to run their own country; that Jamaican politicians were inexperienced; that as the expatriate leaders left the country, so would high intellectual, educational, and moral qualifications, as well as truth, honesty, and patriotism; that without the British, unrest would threaten internal security; that thinking would become parochial; and that there would be no mature minds to spearhead progressive ventures. A few persons giving such explanations went so far as to predict that Jamaica would develop into a republic such as Haiti or other Latin American dictatorships.

A few miscellaneous responses were given by nine elites. These included a belief that Jamaica was too small for independence; an appeal to English nationalism and the assertion that Jamaica's background, traditions, and language were English; the ironic thought that the island's politicians could no longer blame "the imperial power" for all that was sure to go wrong in the future; the statement that the U.K. could in the future deport undesirable *Jamaican* citizens; and the observations that Jamaica would have no adequate defense forces and that independence was political fragmentation and, as such, resulted in a loss of strength.

Political Independence and Economic Relations

One of the things established by the above explanations of attitudes toward independence is the importance of economic considerations—anticipated economic benefits among the nationalists and anticipated economic losses among the antinationalists. The pattern of elite opinion on this point is further delineated by the responses to the following question: "In your opinion should Jamaica now strive to establish very close economic relations with the United Kingdom, establish moderately close economic ties, or strive to lessen such relations?"

Establish very close economic relations	56%
Establish moderately close economic relations	36
Lessen economic relations	8
Total	100%
Number of cases	(237)
No answers	(1)

There is a small correlation between attitude toward political independence and attitude toward the closeness of economic ties to the U.K., with elites who favored the lessening of economic relations being somewhat more likely to be nationalists than elites who favored establishing very close economic relations with the U.K. The remarkable fact is, however, that such a small percentage of the Jamaican elites recommended lessening economic relations with the U.K. Thus, favorable attitudes toward political independence were not motivated to any large extent by the desire to break with the U.K. economically. Over half of the Jamaican elites recommended that economic relations should be very close. Independence might be conceived as bringing more freedom for Jamaica to extend her economic sphere to a wider arena than before, but the United Kingdom remained very much within that arena in the minds of most Jamaican elites.

The Scale of Nationalism

Another of the big decisions that every emergent nation must make—or must have made for it—is "What should the boundaries of the new nation be?" As it turned out, the island of Jamaica became the geographical unit that defined the territorial boundaries of the new nation. In 1958 when these data were collected, however, Jamaica was part of the West Indies Federation, which included nine other units: Antigua, Barbados, Dominica, Grenada, Montserrat, St. Kitts–Nevis–Anguilla, St. Lucia, St. Vincent, and Trinidad; and Jamaica was slated to achieve political independence, not as a separate nation, but as part of a larger nation whose territory would include the territory composing the 1958 Federation. As noted in Chapter I, a referendum held in Jamaica in September, 1961, resulted in a decision for Jamaica to withdraw from the Federation and to seek independence separately. It is beyond the scope of this book to discuss the details of the rise of *Jamaican* versus *West Indian* nationalism, but the 1958 survey clearly shows that independence had more support among Jamaican elites (66 per cent thought that Jamaica would gain) than did federation. For example, note the answers to the following question: "Does Jamaica have more to gain or lose as a result of being part of the Federation?"

Jamaica has more to gain	41%
Federation makes no difference	4
Jamaica has more to lose	51
Gain in some ways, lose in others	4
Total	100%
Number of cases	(232)
No answers	(6)

There is a positive correlation between favorable attitudes toward independence and favorable attitudes toward federation (from data not given here), but a sizable minority, one-fourth of all Jamaican elites, said that Jamaica would gain by independence but would lose by federation.

The major factor underlying the antifederation feeling among elites was the fairly general belief that Jamaica had more to lose economically by being independent as part of the Federation than she did by being independent on her own—and as the responses discussed earlier show, economic problems already weighed heavily on the minds of many Jamaican elites. Added to the economic problems of independence per se were the costs of the Federal government itself (Jamaica was to provide 43 per cent of the general revenue) and particularly the economic liabilities of the smaller, less developed islands with which Jamaica was saddled in federation. Other reasons for opposing federation were given including the geographical isolation of Jamaica from the other units and the assertion that the self-government and independence of Jamaica would not be fully complete—either *vis-à-vis* the United Kingdom or *vis-à-vis* the other islands—within the Federation.[3]

The Correlates of Nationalism

Attitudes toward political independence are given in Table 22 by selected social characteristics. There was little variation in favorable attitudes toward political independence by age. However, on another question, the one concerning closeness of economic relations, 70 per cent of the oldest group, 57 per cent of the middle-aged group, and 37 per cent of the youngest group favored very close economic relations with the U.K. Thus, although favorable attitudes toward *political* independence are found to about the same degree in the different age groups, there were wide differences by age when attitudes toward *economic* independence from the U.K. are considered. Younger elites may have been more rabid, thorough-going, and intense in their nationalist attitudes than older elites.

Men were somewhat more nationalist than women, but the women who did favor political independence were more likely to favor economic independence than were the men who favored political independence.

The elites who rated lowest according to their occupations (see Appendix I) were more likely to believe that Jamaica would gain as a result of political independence than were elites who had higher occupational ratings. The reason for this may be that independence was perceived by some as being beneficial for one's personal career (as distinct from the welfare of Jamaica as a whole). The transition to self-government was accompanied by a large increase in governmental functions and the expansion of the governmental bureaucracy. Thus, new jobs—clean, respectable, and desirable—were created for Jamaicans. Also, existing political offices and civil service positions were "Jamaicanized" as the result of the deliberate policy of replacing British by Jamaican personnel, as pointed out earlier. Some elites visualized new occupational opportunities for themselves in the private sector as well. One-fourth of the Jamaican elites felt that self-government within Jamaica or the Federation had beneficially affected their own careers, and elites who felt this were overrepresented among the persons with lower-rated occupations.

The variations in attitudes toward independence by annual income and respondent's perception of his financial mobility were generally consistent with this explanation. The lower income elites were somewhat more likely to think that political change had affected their careers beneficially than the higher income elites, and so did the "upwardly mobile," as defined by self-perceived financial mobility, compared to the financially stable elites. Oddly enough, the downwardly mobile elites, by this measure, also were more likely than the stable elites to say that political change had affected their careers beneficially. The latter combination of responses is in part due to several elected political leaders and others involved in governmental or quasi-governmental activities who said that they had been financially downwardly mobile even though self-government had *generally* benefited their careers. They said that if they had remained in, or entered, business or some other profession than politics, they would have been much better off financially by 1958. Nonetheless, such persons were generally nationalists.

Eighty per cent of the members and supporters of the People's National Party (PNP) among the elites thought that Jamaica had more to gain than to lose as a result of political independence compared to only 51 per cent of the members and supporters of the Jamaica Labour Party (JLP) and 61 per cent of the elites with no political party preference. Since its inception, the PNP had constitutional reform leading to self-government and independence as one of its major goals, and its name, of course, symbolized the importance of nationalism to its purposes. In 1940, the PNP additionally declared its adherence to socialist principles and thereby linked its antiimperialism to the achievement of a more equalitarian society.[4] On the other hand, the JLP, founded a few years after the PNP, was much less concerned with the achievement of self-government, and at least until 1959 it was more pragmatic than the PNP in concentrating on bread-and-butter issues of the workers' welfare rather than on abstract nationalist or socialist

TABLE 22. *Percentage of Jamaican Leaders Who Say That Jamaica Has More to Gain as a Result of Political Independence by Selected Social Characteristics*

Selected social characteristics	Per cent who say Jamaica has more to gain	Number of cases on which the per cent is based
Age:		
55 and over	67	(69)
40–54	63	(115)
25–39	70	(50)
Sex:		
Men	67	(216)
Women	56	(18)
Occupational rating:		
1 (highest)	64	(135)
2	63	(84)
3 and 4 (lowest)	93	(15)
Education:		
Graduate school	67	(49)
Completed college	68	(44)
Some college	57	(35)
Secondary or training school	63	(90)
Elementary only or less	87	(15)
Annual income:		
£3,000 and over	53	(49)
£2,000–£2,999	72	(50)
£1,999 and less	69	(114)
R's perception of his financial mobility:		
R. better off than father	69	(170)
R. same as father	55	(33)
R. worse off than father	63	(24)
Religious preference:		
None	82	(11)
Catholic	72	(25)
Protestant	68	(177)
Jewish	33	(12)
Political party preference:		
People's National Party	80	(102)
None	61	(64)
Jamaica Labour Party	51	(63)
Country of birth:		
Other Caribbean	80	(5)

Selected social characteristics	Per cent who say Jamaica has more to gain	Number of cases on which the per cent is based
Jamaica	71	(168)
Canada and the U.S.	69	(13)
British Caribbean other than Jamaica	55	(11)
British Isles	43	(30)
Other (including Middle East, Far East, USSR)	43	(7)
Number of foreign countries lived in for at least one year (Jamaican-born only):		
2 or more	65	(48)
1	71	(49)
None	76	(70)
Type of elite position:		
Educational leaders	80	(15)
Elected political leaders	79	(19)
Civil servants	75	(67)
Legal elites	73	(11)
Appointed officials	69	(13)
Religious leaders	60	(10)
Economic elites, agricultural	58	(12)
Medical elites	57	(23)
Economic elites, commercial	54	(58)
Social welfare elites	50	(4)

ideologies. Furthermore, the JLP explicitly offered loyalty to the Crown and rejected socialism while giving more encouragement than the PNP to private enterprise. Thus, it is not surprising that fewer nationalists and fewer equalitarians, as we shall see below, preferred the JLP to the PNP.

Other correlates of nationalist attitudes shown in Table 22 are as follows: education, the some-college group being less nationalist than either the less or more highly educated groups; religious preference, the Agnostics, Atheists, and Independents being most nationalist in their attitudes followed by the Catholics, Protestants, and finally the Jews; country of birth, elites born in the non-British Caribbean being most nationalist followed by those born in Jamaica, Canada and the United States, the British Caribbean other than Jamaica, and finally the British Isles and elsewhere; the number of foreign countries lived in for at least one year, a measure of cosmopolitanism, the less cosmopolitan elites being slightly more nationalist than the more cosmopolitan elites; type of elite position, educational leaders being most nationalist followed in order by elected political leaders, civil servants, legal elites (judges, barristers, and solicitors), appointed officials, religious leaders, economic elites in agriculture, medical elites, economic elites in commerce and other nonagricultural activities, and social welfare elites. Interpretations of these correlations are discussed below.

The Causes of Nationalism

Three hypotheses, each specifying a cause of nationalist attitudes, are suggested by these correlations and by other information.[5] In some cases the causes that are specified below, as in the discussion of political cynicism, appear to cut across the variables shown in Table 22, and as a result, confound the relationships between such variables and attitudes toward independence. Additional relevant data from the 1958 survey are given in support of each of the hypotheses, although it should be kept in mind that such data do not constitute adequate tests of the hypotheses because of the *ex post facto* nature of the formulations.

THE EQUALITY HYPOTHESIS.—*The desire for civil, political, economic, social, and cultural equality produces nationalist attitudes.*

A strong streak of equalitarianism was at the roots of Jamaican nationalism; and the converse appears true too, there was a strong streak of antiequalitarianism at the roots of antinationalist sentiments. This was noted among the "intangible, subjective, or psychological" explanations for nationalist attitudes and was present to some extent in the explanations that cited economic benefits deriving from independence which were discussed earlier. The explanations prominently included civil and political parity with the citizens of other nations of the world and the desire for freedom in the world economy of nations. But these things were only part of the Jamaican nationalists' equalitarianism as expressed in their open-ended responses. The desire for internal progress and reform was stressed as well. It included, for example, the seemingly divergent goals of eliminating the superiority of the white English "foreigners" over light-brown members of the Jamaican middle classes as well as establishing reforms that would reduce civil, political, economic, social, and cultural inequalities between the black lower classes and the Jamaican middle and upper classes.

In Chapter II I tried to show that much of the history of Jamaica can be understood in terms of a trend toward equality and that independence can be viewed as another significant step in the continuation of this trend. Striking support for the validity of this analysis is found in the beliefs and attitudes of Jamaican leaders themselves. Independence was perceived to be another milestone on the road to equality, on the road from slavery to citizenship and leadership. Thus, the desire for political independence reflected in part a commitment to the ideal of equality and a hope that the trend toward equality would continue; the desire to remain a colony was conversely an expression of antiequalitarianism.

Equalitarianism as a cause of nationalism is not limited to Jamaican nationalism. It can be seen in the humanitarian nationalism of the eighteenth century; in the diatribes against inequalities and injustices, against tyranny and arbitrariness; in the hopes for human progress and guaranteed individual rights.[6] It is less apparent in the writings of the aristocratic Englishman, Henry St. John, Viscount Bolingbroke, for all of his humanitarianism, than in the writings of Jean Jacques Rousseau and Johann Gottfried von Herder, other major contributors to the philosophy of humanitarian nationalism. The doctrine of equality is perhaps most apparent in the Jacobin nationalism that arose during the French Revolution. The slogan, *liberté, égalité, fraternité,* linked equalitarianism with nationalism and referred to individual liberty, social *equality,* and *national* fraternity. In France, Jacobin nationalism became an intolerant, militaristic, and fanatical movement with liberty eventually becoming the slave of national patriotism, but a desire for equality remained a strong national purpose. Napoleon Bonaparte ". . . asserted that the French people cared more for equality than for liberty and most of all for national glory." [7]

The rise of American nationalism differs somewhat from recent nationalisms in that it did not involve a struggle against "foreign" rulers. "The war of the thirteen colonies against Britain was not a war of natives against alien rulers but a British civil war for the interpretation, the maintenance, the broadening of the British constitution, a struggle between Whigs and Tories, both in the thirteen colonies and in Great Britain." [8] A new nation was born as a result of the revolutionaries' victory, but the ". . . tie which united it—and separated it at the same time from other nations—was not founded on the common attributes of nationhood—language, cultural tradition, historical territory or common descent—but on an *idea* which singled out the new nation among the nations of the earth." [9] As Hans Kohn points out, the idea, expressed in the Constitution and the Bill of Rights declared for the *equality of all men.* Equal and impartial liberty, the dignity of *every* individual was proclaimed. Civil, political, economic, and social rights were stressed, although "equality" of economic rights was largely thought of in terms of property rights, liberty included the settlers' rights to expand at the expense of the American Indians, and black men were excepted at first. Nevertheless, equalitarianism was an important part of the conception of the American nation, and the American

Revolution and its aftermath set the stage for developments in Great Britain and in other British colonies which resulted in the *equal and kindred partnership of the independent nations* of the British Commonwealth, a political association not available to the 13 American colonies.[10]

Equalitarianism can be seen in the nineteenth century welding of liberalism, romanticism, and nationalism, within which it became part of an evolutionary conception of progress. From England it spread to Germany, Portugal, and Spain, and there is evidence of liberal nationalism in a series of constitutions that were ". . . framed in southern Europe and in South America and . . . were characterized by the union of nationalism with liberalism." [11] The philosophers of the gospel of liberal nationalism assumed that ". . . the broadest practicable exercise of personal liberty, political, economic, religious, and educational . . ." would result from nationalism, from each nationality being ". . . a political unit under an independent constitutional government which would put an end to despotism, aristocracy, and ecclesiastical influence . . ." [12] The peace-loving philosophy of liberal nationalism ironically led to violence and wars for liberation, freedom, and national unity. After World War I, the map of Europe was largely redrawn in conformity with the notions of liberal nationalism, but in achieving its goal liberal nationalism, as Hayes points out, ". . . suffered a transformation. Its liberalism waned as its nationalism waxed." [13]

Equalitarianism, then, may underlie the rise of nationalism at many different times and places. Although equalitarianism may be sufficient to produce nationalist sentiments, it does not appear to be necessary. For example, traditional nationalism, although generally humanitarian, was basically antiequalitarian and proaristocratic as it was expressed in the writings of Edmund Burke, the Vicomte de Bonald, Friedrich von Schlegel, and others. Also, neither separatist nor unifying nationalist movements are necessarily equalitarian. For example, Southern nationalism at the time of the unsuccessful secession of the Southern states from the United States did not stand for progressive principles, and Bismarck's successful unification of Germany was based upon an antiliberal form of nationalism. Furthermore, integral nationalism, such as represented by Italian Fascism and German Nazism, appears anti-humanitarian and illiberal. Integral nationalism made the nation not a means to humanity but an end in itself, and it subordinated personal liberties to its own purpose. It stressed mobilization of effort and national power at the expense of freedom and the maintenance of human rights. Civil and political rights for most persons in such nations were restricted and economic and social rights for minorities of various kinds were often restricted as well, although economic advancement and the raising of minimums of economic rights for "citizens in good standing" are reasons that were given to justify such actions, along with the achievement of internal and external security.[14]

As in Jamaica, equalitarianism appeared to loom large in the development of nationalist attitudes within the former and remaining colonial areas, in the new and emergent nations. This was especially true during the period prior to the actual achievement of independence. However, developments in some of the new nations, such as Ghana for example, indicated that after independence, even though lip service to equality continued, restriction of civil and political rights in fact took place. The old dilemma of the balance between freedom and power confronted the new elites of the newly independent nations. Freedom, liberty, and equality were stressed before independence. But after responsibility for the achievement of progress was placed in the hands of the nationalist elite, then national power assumed greater priority. Too much freedom often appeared to the new national elite to result in anarchy and to prevent the achievement of national goals. The subservience of the individual to the state appeared necessary to achieve national unity and order, mobilization, coördination of effort, and organization of human resources, so that the nation would have the power to progress.[15] Thus, liberal nationalism was most characteristic of the national movements in the new states before independence, but after independence the nationalism began to shift in character and sometimes with startling rapidity, and became more like integral nationalism. No such shift had yet been made in Jamaica, and such a shift may be unlikely given the spread of democratic and equalitarian ideals and the relatively long and orderly transition to independence during the period of tutelary democracy. Yet intellectual seeds, reminiscent of the philosophy of integral nationalism, were present among some of the younger Jamaican intellectuals and other elites, and were apparent in some of the views expressed during the national debate concerning the entrenchment of a "Bill of Rights" in the new Jamaican Constitution which began during the latter part of 1961.

Some data from the 1958 survey in Jamaica can be brought to bear on the equality hypothesis. The equalitarians, according to the Index of Equalitarianism given in Chapter IV, can be compared to the nonequalitarians with respect to their attitudes toward political independence. The findings support the hypothesis. Seventy-four per cent of the equalitarians thought that Jamaica had more to gain than to lose as a result of political independence compared to 57 per cent of the nonequalitarians. This is an incomplete analysis, however, since the Index of Equalitarianism used measures only attitudes toward economic and social equality.

Controlling for each of the variables shown in Table 22, one finds that the relationship between equalitarianism and nationalist attitudes does not disappear, but remains for almost all of the subgroup comparisons. In fact, although there are two or three exceptions and some refinements of the original relationship, for most subgroup comparisons the correlation between equalitarianism and nationalist attitudes is larger than the zero-order correlation. Generally, when each structural variable shown in Table 22 is considered simultaneously along with equalitarian attitudes as a cause of nationalist sentiments, the combined explanatory power exceeds that of either the structural variable or attitude toward equality alone.

A leader's higher income made him opposed to independence only if he was a nonequalitarian, and equalitarianism did not affect the likelihood of nationalist sentiments among leaders with low incomes; downwardly mobile leaders opposed independence if they were nonequalitarians but supported it if they were equalitarians; Catholics tended to support independence whether or not they were equalitarians, but equalitarianism affected the nationalist sentiments of Jews greatly, the nonequalitarian Jews being antinationalist in the extreme; PNP supporters were nationalists even if they were nonequalitarians, but JLP supporters were nationalists depending on whether or not they were equalitarians (85 per cent of the JLP equalitarians were nationalists—slightly more than PNP equalitarians even —compared to 26 per cent of the JLP nonequalitarians); all but one of the educational leaders were equalitarians, and that one was an antinationalist; elected political leaders were generally nationalists even if they were nonequalitarians; and Jamaicans who had never lived in another country for as long as a year tended to be nationalists without regard to their equalitarianism.

Thus, the relationships between the structural variables and nationalist attitudes and the relationship between equalitarianism and nationalist attitudes generally hold up with a simultaneous analysis of both. But there are a few exceptions and refinements with the structural variable sometimes overriding the equalitarian attitude, such as in the case of PNP party preference, and the equalitarian attitude sometimes overriding the structural variable, such as in the case of JLP party preference.[16]

THE POLITICAL IDEALISM HYPOTHESIS.—*Idealism regarding political democracy produces nationalist attitudes.*

In this case it is perhaps the converse that invites explanation: cynicism regarding political democracy produces antinationalist attitudes. By political cynicism, I refer to negative and unfavorable attitudes toward the electorate, as specified in Chapter V.

Some of the intangible, subjective, or psychological benefits suggested by the Jamaican elites who favored independence contain sentiments that are aspects of political idealism. They included the rights and abilities of Jamaicans to govern themselves and occasionally included specific mention of democratic principles as underlying nationalist desires. But the factor of idealism-cynicism regarding political democracy seems most apparent as cynicism and was strongly present in the sentiments of the adamant and extreme antinationalists.

Comparing the cynics with the idealists as classified according to the Index of Political Cynicism, one finds that the data support the hypothesis. Fifty-seven per cent of the politically cynical elites expressed nationalist sentiments compared to 75 per cent of the noncynical or politically idealistic elites.[17]

This negative relationship between political cynicism and nationalist sentiments remained with few exceptions even after each of the variables shown in Table 22 was introduced simultaneously into the analysis. However, nationalist attitudes among leaders aged 39 and under were not affected by variations in cynicism; only about 40 per cent of the leaders born in the British Isles were nationalists no matter whether they were cynics or idealists; and there was little variation in nationalist sentiments by cynicism among elected political leaders, who were quite likely to be nationalists, nor among economic-commercial and social welfare elites, about 50 per cent of whom, respectively, were nationalists.

Additionally, equalitarianism and idealism concerning political democracy each contributed something toward nationalist attitudes independently of the other, as can be seen from Table 23. Eighty-four per cent of the elites who were both equalitarian and politically idealistic thought that Jamaica had more to gain than to lose as a result of political independence, com-

TABLE 23. *Percentage of Jamaican Leaders Who Say That Jamaica Has More to Gain as a Result of Political Independence by Equalitarianism and Political Idealism*

Equalitarianism and political idealism	Per cent who say Jamaica has more to gain	Number of cases on which the per cent is based
Equalitarian and idealistic	84	(57)
Equalitarian and cynical	67	(63)
Nonequalitarian and idealistic	66	(53)
Nonequalitarian and cynical	46	(52)

pared to 46 per cent of the elites who were both nonequalitarian and politically cynical. Nearly two-thirds of both the equalitarian cynics and the
nonequalitarian idealists were nationalists.

Three major factors that appear to account for political cynicism, and
therefore which were at the base of antinationalist sentiments as well were
given in Chapter V.

THE SELF-INTEREST HYPOTHESIS.—*The perception of political independence as being beneficial to one's personal career produces nationalist
attitudes.*

Unlike the equality and the political idealism hypotheses, which refer
to broad ideologies and to the interests of all humanity, the entire people
of a country, or at least a social section, class, or group, the self-interest
hypothesis refers specifically to narrow and individual interests, to the perceived benefits of independence for a person's own career. The converse is,
of course, that the perception of independence as being harmful to one's
personal career produces antinationalist attitudes, but it is not usually true
among equalitarians and political idealists. Thus the converse of the self-
interest hypothesis is applicable only to nonequalitarians or political cynics.

This hypothesis was discussed earlier where it was pointed out that the
transition to independence was accompanied by increased opportunities for
Jamaicans to achieve desirable occupational positions, because of the replacement of (primarily British) expatriates and especially because of the
expansion of governmental and quasi-governmental services. It was suggested that this hypothesis helped to explain the variations in nationalist
attitudes by occupational rating, annual income, and perception of financial
mobility. Also, it may help to explain the nationalist sentiments of the
legal elites (who were very cynical politically), the elected political leaders
(who were relatively nonequalitarian but also politically idealistic) and particularly of the civil servants (who were both relatively nonequalitarian
and politically cynical). Additionally, this hypothesis may help to explain
the relatively low incidence of nationalist attitudes among the people born
in the British Isles, among whom were persons who knew that their personal careers were deleteriously affected, and people born in "Other"
places (see Table 22) and Jews, whose minority status led to anxiety concerning their fate in the new nation. In the case of people born in "Other"
places, however, the political cynicism hypothesis, especially from the
standpoint of social distance, entered into the picture in producing antinationalist attitudes.

In Table 24, data are brought to bear upon the self-interest hypothesis
more directly. The percentage of Jamaican elites who thought that Ja-

maica had more to gain than to lose as a result of independence is given by whether or not the elites thought that self-government within Jamaica or the Federation had affected their careers in any way. Consistent with the hypothesis, the largest percentage having nationalist attitudes were persons who said that self-government or the Federation had affected their careers beneficially. Elites who said, "yes, unspecified as to beneficially or deleteriously," "yes, deleteriously in every way," or "no" were less likely to express nationalist sentiments. Elites who said "not yet, but it will" were least likely to favor independence.

TABLE 24. *Percentage of Jamaican Leaders Who Say That Jamaica Has More to Gain as a Result of Political Independence by Elites' Perceptions of the Effect of Political Changes on Their Careers*

Has federation or self-government within Jamaica affected your career in any way?	Per cent who say Jamaica has more to gain	Number of cases on which the percentages are based
Yes, beneficially	78	(59)
Yes, unspecified	60	(10)
Yes, deleteriously in every way	61	(18)
Not yet, but it will	33	(9)
No	64	(135)

Unfortunately, the perceived effects on one's personal career of federation and self-government within Jamaica are confounded in the question that was asked in the questionnaire, and the small number of cases do not permit a meaningful breakdown of nationalist attitudes by equalitarianism, political cynicism, and perceived career effects simultaneously.

Conclusion

In this chapter, I have described the nature, distribution, and social correlates of nationalist attitudes among elites in Jamaica, and I have formulated three major hypotheses concerning the causes of these attitudes which appear consistent with the Jamaican experience and which may be fairly general factors, although not universal, in the rise of nationalism at other times and places.

The conclusions can be summarized as follows:

1. The desirability of political independence was not agreed to by all

elites, but was rather a matter of fundamental differences of opinion among them. Although about two-thirds of the Jamaican elites were definitely nationalist, about one-fourth were antinationalist.

2. Nationalist attitudes for the most part did not reflect a great deal of bitterness toward the imperial power, nor was independence generally viewed as a panacea for the problems confronting the new nation.

3. Nevertheless, the reason usually given to support the nationalist attitudes can be conveniently summarized as "independence will promote progress for Jamaica." The kinds of progress visualized were, first, subjective or psychological (e.g., elimination of feelings of inferiority *vis-à-vis* other peoples of the world), and second, material, especially economic.

4. The reasons given to support the antinationalist attitudes in general were, first, that Jamaica will lose economically by political independence, and second, that Jamaicans—leaders and common people alike—were simply not capable of self-government.

5. Generally, favorable attitudes toward political independence were not motivated by any desire to lessen economic relations with the United Kingdom. Nationalists saw political independence as bringing economic benefits and a wider arena of economic activity than before, but for the most part the United Kingdom remained very much within that arena.

6. The territorial scale of nationalist attitudes among elites in Jamaica was more favorable to the formation of a new nation of Jamaica alone than a new nation that included Jamaica along with other British territories in the Caribbean. Subsequent to the 1958 mail questionnaire study, Jamaica withdrew from the West Indies Federation and requested independence as a separate and distinct nation.

The consideration of the data presented in this book and of other observations made in Jamaica at different times from 1956 to 1962 led to the formulation of the following hypotheses concerning the causes of nationalism:

Hypothesis 1. The desire for civil, political, economic, social and cultural equality produces nationalist attitudes.

Hypothesis 2. Idealism regarding political democracy produces nationalist attitudes.

Hypothesis 3. The perception of political independence as being beneficial to one's personal career produces nationalist attitudes.

The converse of each of these hypotheses is also considered in each case a plausible and reasonable formulation given the data available on the Jamaican experience, with the exception that the converse of hypothesis 3, the self-interest hypothesis, is applicable only to nonequalitarians or political cynics.[18]

Chapter VII

What Should Jamaica's Global Alignments Be?

BEFORE INDEPENDENCE, the new nations had little or no control over their foreign affairs. These were matters for the imperial power, the European metropole, to decide. With the rise of nationalism and the drive toward independence, however, the question of the most desirable and beneficial international relations for the new nation to have from the point of view of its own welfare was raised. The new nations stepped into a new world where they were able to decide for themselves what their external affairs would be, although they were often tied by many bonds of sentiment and tradition, and of economics and culture, to the European country that had dominated them during the years of colonial rule. The new nations also stepped into a world that since World War II was global in scale and offered only two real alternatives for alignment, the Western or the Communist bloc, with the possibility of the neutralist role of nonalignment being a third alternative.

No other nations, except possibly China in recent years, come as near to symbolizing the current world conflict over the shape of the future as do the United States and the Soviet Union. The answer to the question, "What should the new nation's global alignments be?", may depend in large part on the relative moral rightness and differential effectiveness of these two major powers as perceived and evaluated by the new national elites. Furthermore, since the new national elites are in the process of consciously shaping their emerging political, economic, and social institutions, the outcome of each of the big decisions facing new nations, including "How large a role should the government play in the affairs of the society—especially in the economy?" "What should the social and cultural history of the new nation be?" "What kind of a social structure should the new nation have?" and "Should the new nation have a democratic political system?" may be influenced to some degree by the new national leaders' views of the major existing alternative models, Russia and the United States, especially with reference to the differential performance of these two countries in the achievement of their major goals and to the relative power of the different ethical principles or theories which each use to justify them.

The purpose of this chapter is to describe and analyze images of the United States and the Soviet Union which were held by Jamaican leaders as Jamaica approached independence. As they viewed the world situation, did Jamaican leaders believe that the United States was more often morally right in its actions than the Soviet Union? Which country did they think was acting more effectively in dealing with the underdeveloped countries of the world? What reasons did they give for their opinions? In what ways was the social differentiation of Jamaican leaders correlated with images of the two major powers? What global alignments would Jamaica make?

Overall Comparison: Moral Rightness

The Jamaican elites overwhelmingly favored the United States over the Soviet Union as an actor on the world scene. This can be seen from their responses to the question: "As you understand the general positions taken by the Soviet Union and the United States with respect to the world situation, which do you feel has been morally right more often in recent years?" [1]

The Soviet Union has been right more often	1%
Both about the same	16
The United States has been right more often	83
Total	100%
Number of cases	(227)
No answers	(11)

Of the 188 Jamaican leaders who said that the United States has been morally right more often than has the Soviet Union, 47 per cent emphasized a commitment to the principles of democracy, 32 per cent a fear and hatred of Soviet methods, and 22 per cent a suspicion of Soviet motives.[2] This was determined from an analysis of the respondents' replies to an open-ended question that asked them to explain their answers to the above check-question.

Those respondents classified as emphasizing a commitment to the principles of democracy specifically mentioned the maintenance of public liberties and representative government within the United States and the lack of it within the Soviet Union; or they mentioned the United States' democratic ways contrasted with the undemocratic ways of the Soviet Union as a participant in the world community of nations. With respect to democracy they said:

The USA recognizes as a policy the freedom of the individual to do what he thinks that he ought to do, and the USSR's policy is just to the contrary in that persons must do only what suits the political party in power.

What the USA and democracy stand for is the only right answer.

The code of ethics of the USSR is completely removed from our way of thinking.

The USA is one of the champions of the rights of the individual.

The United Nations more or less expresses the essence of world opinion, and USA decisions have been more in accord with United Nations findings.

The USA is a democracy; the USSR is a dictatorship. The USA's views represent the will of the people more than the USSR's views.

The USA allows free expression of the views and ideas of people.

The people can't be wrong as often as a ruling few can.

The USA is for freedom of speech, religion, and politics, and is against enslavement of weaker and smaller nations.

Don't be silly, we do not wish to be slaves again.

This is not to say that there were no "except for's" or "in spite of's." There were. Domestic racial prejudice was seen as a blemish on American democracy, and the picture of the United States as dealing with other countries democratically was considered to be marred by stubbornness and stupidity in refusing to recognize Red China.

A second set of responses seems enough different from the set on democracy to warrant a separate category. These responses referred specifically to the lack of humanity of Soviet methods when compared with those of the United States. They differed from the above replies in that they referred to means or methods of exercising control. Disapproval of Soviet methods at home and abroad felt by the respondents was expressed in the following statements:

The USSR's blood purges of individuals who voice any form of disagreement could not happen in the USA.

The Soviet Union has resorted to violence and executions in order to maintain its point of view in other countries.

Brain-washing is immoral.

The USSR feels that its way of life is the only way, and it uses all means to enforce that way whether people wish it or not.

The Soviet Union has been more coldly calculating, accepting the view that any behavior *vis-à-vis* capitalist states is justified.

Soviet methods are based on expediency rather than on moral standards.

It is interesting to note in passing that twenty of the respondents mentioned Soviet actions in Hungary and six cited Russia's obstructionist actions in the United Nations to support their contentions that Soviet methods are not based upon humanitarian principles.

Related to both democratic principles and inhumane methods are the comments about Soviet and American motives and goals. These comments reveal a picture of the Soviet Union as trying to dominate the world scene, to impose its ideology on others, and to extend its power and influence, contrasted with a picture of the United States as seeking to preserve the integrity of other peoples and to aid them economically for primarily altruistic reasons rather than out of self-interest. For example:

Russia has a lust for world power.

The Soviet Union wants to dominate the world.

The USA does not have territorial aspirations.

The motive behind the actions of the USA has not been a selfish motive, except so far as preservation of world peace is beneficial to the citizens of the USA, and this is equally beneficial to everybody.

Actions leading to domination and suppression of weaker nations seem to be mainly the work of the USSR.

Five respondents thought the United States has been morally right more often than the USSR because America is a Christian country, while Soviet leaders do not believe in God. One mentioned the recent American effort toward desegregating the races as a point in favor of the United States.

The reasons given by the three persons who said that the Soviet Union has been morally right more than the United States were:

Racial prejudice in the United States; the Soviet Union does not have it. [Mentioned twice.]

The USSR's socialistic policy is humane.

The USA has been aggressive rather than defensive on the world scene, but the Russian attitude has been conciliatory throughout—*prima facie* at least; whether the Russians are fundamentally sincere about it is a much deeper question.

The respondents who believed America and Russia to be about the same when it came to moral rightness were inclined to fall into one of two groups: (1) The "plague on both your houses" type, which is exemplified by the respondent who said, "The USA's McCarran Acts and McCarthyism have been almost as odious as Russia's negative policy at world conferences!" And (2) the "everything is relative" type, which included five respondents who agreed that "it all depends on what you are taught to believe." There was also some pairing of reasons already cited in the earlier categories.

Moral Rightness by the Dates Questionnaires Were Returned

From Table 25 one can see that those respondents to the 1958 survey who returned their questionnaires during the earliest period possible had the smallest relative number who said that the United States has been morally right more often than the Soviet Union, 70 per cent so reporting. This percentage increased to 89 for the questionnaires returned between July 17 and August 26, stayed relatively high through October 9 and then lowered to 75. One explanation for these variations may be that they reflect changes in the world scene and then-current actions of the United States and the Soviet Union. With this in mind, I constructed a day-by-day record of events that I hypothesized would affect attitudes toward the United States and the Soviet Union. I selected the dates shown in Table 25 as cutting points, because particularly important and relevant events occurred then, or were then reported in Jamaica, and it appeared to me that shifts in attitudes would be correlated with them. A word of caution must be given here. There is no way of telling for certain from these data what effect international events, as they were reported in news sources available in Jamaica, were having on the attitudes of Jamaican elites; thus the time-series analysis is largely speculative. It is offered as a possible explanation by one who was in Jamaica during much of the period under consideration and who was deeply involved at work and socially with Jamaican elites.

In local newspapers, on Radio Jamaica, in magazines, and elsewhere (there was no television in Jamaica), many items of information relevant to attitudes toward the United States and the Soviet Union appeared during May. American and Canadian business concerns made definite commitments to bring new industries to Jamaica. Russia's demonstration of its lead in the space race by the successful launching of its "Sputniks" while American rockets were still earthbound remained in the news. The Lebanon

TABLE 25. *Percentage of Jamaican Leaders Who Said That the United States Has Been Morally Right More Often than the Soviet Union, by Dates Questionnaires Were Returned, 1958*

Dates returned	Per cent who said that U.S. is right	Number of cases on which per cent is based
May 31 to June 17	70	(47)
June 18 to July 16	87	(76)
July 17 to August 26	89	(47)
August 27 to October 9	85	(45)
October 10 to December 22	75	(12)

crisis was building up; it was announced that the Miami Weather Bureau had been ordered to keep secret its long-range hurricane forecasts; and a colored Jamaican cleric who claimed to have been subject to an illegal and unprovoked assault by a white passenger on a bus in Florida because he would not sit in the "colored section" had his complaint rejected by a Florida judge (an example of a type of story that is often highlighted in Jamaican newspapers). Of these and other items in the news during May and early June, two, more than any others, may have accounted for the *relatively* unfavorable attitudes toward the United States from May 31 to June 17. One was the strain in American relations with the West Indies Federation caused by a dispute about the location of the West Indies federal capital in Trinidad, and the other was then Vice-President Richard M. Nixon's tour of Latin America and subsequent related events.

The then newly formed, but now defunct, West Indies Federation selected for its ultimate capital site a United States naval base located at Chaguaramas in Trinidad. The United States had received the base during World War II as part of the lend-lease agreements with Britain, and fifty American destroyers were given to the British government in return. (The latter were often described in Jamaican and British news sources as being of "doubtful strategic value.") The details of the case will not be given here, but one can understand that the United States was put in the difficult position of having to choose between giving up a naval base that represented a considerable investment and that was of possible strategic importance or hurting the prestige of the newest emergent nation in the Western Hemisphere. After consulation with the United Kingdom, the United States chose the latter course. The government in Jamaica put up a howl, and was further embarrassed some weeks later when it became clear that the American decision on Chaguaramas was final (at least for the immediate future). Opinion was divided, but many members of the Jamaican elites resented the way that the United States handled this situation.[3]

Also in the news during this period was the Latin American tour of Vice-President Nixon. Referring to the tour in the *Sunday Gleaner,* Gordon K. Lewis wrote: "The 'good neighbour' policy could hardly have received a more humiliating rebuff; and this is of first class importance for West Indian foreign policy in the years to come. For if the new Federation identifies itself too closely with American ideology it runs the risk of being regarded in Latin America as a Yankee instrument." [4] In general, Jamaican leaders were more amused than upset by Latin American rejection of American political leadership and the criticism of the State Department and the Pentagon implied in the hostility directed at Nixon. However, the fact that Eisenhower sent a contingent of U.S. Marines to the Caribbean in the middle of May, "to be held there in readiness for possible aid to the Venezuelan government in protecting U.S. Vice-Pres. Richard M. Nixon and his party," [5] did not go unnoticed in Jamaica, and, for some, amusement turned to derision.

On the other hand, Imre Nagy's execution on June 16 after a secret trial was a grim reminder of Russian brutality in Hungary in 1956 that may have resulted in the increase in responses favorable to the United States by June 18. The favorable responses continued at a very high level through the last half of July and August after the U.S. Marines had landed in Lebanon, and through September after the 7th Fleet sailed into China seas in a clear indication of American determination to support policy with action, to honor commitments with deeds. This was serious business, and, however ill advised it may have seemed to the Jamaicans, it was a far cry from the image of the United States as a "big bully" in Latin America. The Chaguaramas and Nixon incidents were not forgotten, but they assumed a less important place.

The respondents who returned questionnaires after October 9 were somewhat less likely to feel that the United States was morally right than were those who had returned them between June 18 and October 9. The reasons for this shift are not entirely clear, but by October 9 the Lebanon and Quemoy crises were over, and in the eyes of many Jamaican leaders the United States was primarily interested in executing a tactical withdrawal from both Lebanon and Formosa. By October 24 the Soviet intention to lend money to Egypt to finance the Aswan Dam project was announced, and it followed closely on West Indian–USA talks on possible American aid to the West Indies, about which one participant was reported to have quipped, "If only we could uncover a Communist nest!" [6] Presumably, American aid then would have been forthcoming in ample quantities to "fight a bogey." The talks ended with no commitments being made.

Moral Rightness by Selected Social Characteristics

In Table 26 attitudes toward the United States are shown by a number of social characteristics of the respondents. There was little difference in attitudes by age, but the youngest—those under age 40—were least favorable to the United States.[7] Women were less favorable than men. Occupational rank made no difference. Highly educated respondents were less favorable than were those with little education. Low incomes made for somewhat less favorable attitudes. Agnostics, Atheists, and Independents had the least favorable attitudes to the United States, followed by Jews, and then by Protestants. Catholics had the most favorable attitudes to the United States.

TABLE 26. *Percentage of Jamaican Leaders Who Said That the United States Has Been Morally Right More Often than the Soviet Union, by Selected Social Characteristics*

Selected social characteristics	Per cent who said that U.S. is right	Number of cases on which per cent is based
Age:		
55 and over	81	(68)
40–54	86	(109)
25–39	78	(50)
Sex:		
Men	85	(211)
Women	62	(16)
Occupational rating:		
1 (highest)	84	(130)
2	80	(81)
3 and 4 (lowest)	81	(16)
Education:		
Graduate school	75	(47)
Completed college	83	(42)
Some college	85	(34)
Secondary or training school	84	(88)
Elementary only	100	(15)

Selected social characteristics	Per cent who said that U.S. is right	Number of cases on which per cent is based
Annual income:		
£2,000 and more	86	(96)
£1,999 and less	77	(111)
Religion:		
None	55	(11)
Catholic	96	(24)
Jewish	69	(13)
Protestant	85	(171)
Political party preference:		
None	86	(67)
People's National Party	75	(102)
Jamaica Labour Party	91	(64)
R's perception of his financial mobility:		
R. better off than father	83	(164)
R. same as father	91	(33)
R. worse off than father	81	(26)
Type of elite position:		
Economic elites, agricultural	92	(13)
Appointed officials	92	(12)
Economic elites, commercial	91	(55)
Legal elites	91	(11)
Religious elites	90	(10)
Elected political leaders	89	(19)
Medical elites	77	(22)
Civil servants	76	(63)
Social welfare elites	75	(4)
Educational leaders	53	(15)
Foreign countries lived in for at least one year:		
2 or more	78	(95)
1	82	(62)
None	90	(69)

Respondents who preferred the People's National Party (PNP), the party in power in Jamaica at the time the study was made and therefore the one that received the severest blow to its prestige as a result of the Chaguaramas episode, were less favorable to the United States than were those who preferred the Jamaica Labour Party (JLP).[8]

Those persons who thought that they were either better off or worse off financially than their fathers were during their youth were somewhat less favorable to the United States than were persons who thought their financial status was the same as that of their fathers.

Ranked from least favorable to most favorable attitudes toward the United States, the different types of elites were: educational leaders; social welfare elites, civil servants, and medical elites; and elected political leaders, religious elites, legal elites, economic-commercial elites, appointed officials, and economic-agricultural elites.

Finally, Table 26 reveals that living abroad for extended periods resulted in less favorable attitudes toward the United States on the part of the Jamaican elites.[9]

Although the differences shown in Table 26 for the most part are not large, they reveal that the United States was least favored by the leaders who were *young; women; highly educated; supporters of the PNP; educational leaders, social welfare elites, civil servants,* or *medical elites; cosmopolitan* (as measured by foreign residence); *Jews, agnostics, atheists,* or *independents; financially mobile* (mostly upward); or *of relatively low incomes.*

None of these subgroups was pro-Russian, in that none contained a majority of persons who said that the USSR is morally right more often than the United States. They were simply somewhat less favorable to the United States than were other subgroups, who overwhelmingly favored the United States. Yet these variations may be clues that can be profitably regarded by Jamaicans and Americans as warning signals.

In general, it appears that some of the segments of the leadership in Jamaica which were particularly committed to rapid social, economic, and political change were least likely to favor the United States. These were among the persons who felt that they had a mission to perform for their country, who were pushing for ordered, rationalistic plans of economic development, education and social welfare for the common people, Jamaican and/or West Indian nationalism, modernization, materialism, and socialism, and who were deeply dedicated to the welfare of the common people, to representative government, and to the maintenance of public liberties. Thus, according to the Indexes of Equalitarianism and Political Cynicism, we find that leaders with favorable attitudes toward economic and social equality and with idealistic beliefs about political democracy were least likely to think that the United States was morally right. The differences were not large, but it is ironic to find that the Jamaican elites who were most committed to that ideology which is professed by the people of the United States and which remains at the core of the meaning and character of the American nation were among the least favorable to the United States. This appears to be a contradiction, but it is explained by the fact that some Jamaican leaders, particularly among those most oriented toward change, did not regard the United States as the land of the free. In other words, they did not reject American ideology, but they did reject the failure of the United States to live up to it more fully both at home and abroad. This was a minority view, but it again reminds Americans that they must guard against preaching democracy and equality to others without constantly striving for the acheivement of genuine democracy and more equality within their own nation, in their relations with others, and within those nations they call their friends. Otherwise, the "progressives," that is, the most forward-looking and most change-oriented elites, within the developing areas may look upon the United States increasingly as a conservative and reactionary force that is dedicated to opposing social change and maintaining the *status quo,* despite words to the contrary.

Overall Comparison: Effectiveness

In spite of the fact that the respondents generally thought that the United States has been morally right more often than has the Soviet Union, they generally believed (usually with some regret) that the Soviet Union was more efficacious in dealing with the peoples of underdeveloped countries than was the United States. The question specifically asked for an evaluation of relative effectiveness *within the underdeveloped countries,* because such countries have become the major arenas of competition between the United States and the Soviet Union. For example, the significance of the underdeveloped countries for the relative world influence of the United States and Russia is indicated by these figures: in 1950, 54 per cent of the world's land area, 63 per cent of the world's population, and 70 per cent of the world's national political entities were contained in the underdeveloped areas.[10] The Jamaican leaders' responses to the question ". . . which one is more effective in winning over to its point of view the people living in the so-called underdeveloped countries of the world?" were as follows:

The Soviet Union is more effective	56%
Both about the same	20
The United States is more effective	24
Total	100%
Number of cases	(222)
No answers	(16)

The answers to the open-ended probe, "Please explain why you think so," clearly reveal a conflict in the minds of many of the respondents between democratic processes and efficient, lasting, and rapid economic advancement. They said that, for the so-called "backward" nations, democratic institutions and large-scale economic reforms are to some degree mutually exclusive. Of the respondents hung up on this dilemma, some gave priority to political democracy (and were more likely to say that the United States was more effective) and others gave priority to economic advancement (and were more likely to say that the USSR was more effective).

Of the 125 persons who said that the Soviet Union has been more effective than the United States, the largest percentage, 42 per cent, held that communism offers greater material benefits and opportunities for economic advancement to the peoples of underdeveloped areas than does the United States, but they often added that these peoples in all probability must be willing to sacrifice some degree of individual freedom in order to achieve economic reforms. For example:

The Soviet Union offers a better way of life via socialism to the suffering people in underdeveloped areas.

Communism seems attractive to the peoples of underdeveloped areas for material gains, but they may have to sacrifice freedom for better economic conditions.

I am scared that a poverty-stricken people prefer a regime that levels everybody to one that enables only some to get rich.

The USSR flatters, holds out promises, rouses passions against the democracies, and then steps in with economic improvements in quick order to convince a conditioned elite that the country is improving.

In the Soviet Union there is no capitalist interest. Benefits are shared among the people. This is not the case with the USA.

The majority of countries are "have nots" and as such are more easily influenced by appeals to passion and for radical change by fraud or force, if necessary.

In underdeveloped countries there is illiteracy, unemployment, hunger, and starvation. To share and share alike by taking from the rich has tremendous psychological effect.

Because of the peoples' despair in underdeveloped countries, they respond to the alleged [economic] advantages of communism.

Thirty-four per cent of the respondents who believed the Soviet Union to be more effective than the United States referred to the superior propaganda operations of the Soviet Union with the assertion or implication that the Communist claims are false. Mention of propaganda as a factor making for effectiveness was often accompanied by comments about the uneducated (and thus gullible) and poverty-stricken masses in these countries:

The propaganda machine of the USSR holds out false promises of utopia.

The people are ignorant and susceptible to specious arguments and deceitful promises.

The Soviet propaganda is effective initially, but after that domination, fear, and ruthless policing succeed in keeping them subjected.

The illiterate and poverty-stricken people accept Russia's teachings readily and are less mindful of America's positive contributions to development.

Because people in underdeveloped countries fall easily to propaganda and usually feel that their poverty is due to lack of opportunities or to the efforts of people higher placed who deny them what should come to them.

Because Soviet propaganda is very forceful and well directed.

Fourteen per cent of the respondents who said that the Soviet Union has been more effective than the United States believed that the actions of the Soviet Union toward the underdeveloped countries have been unrestrained by moral considerations, and that the Soviet Union has been completely expedient in the matter of extending Soviet power. Although such actions were considered effective, they were highly disapproved by these respondents.

Other reasons were also given. Twelve per cent of the respondents who felt the USSR has been more effective said that there was no color prejudice in the Soviet Union as there was in the United States (Little Rock was mentioned as an example), and that since most of the underdeveloped countries are populated by colored peoples, they will not listen to America. Ten per cent referred to American reliance on dollars which have been doled out with such an air of patronage that the recipients end up hating the United States. Among the miscellaneous responses were four praising the achievement of the USSR—including the Soviet supremacy in the space race.

Thirty-five per cent of the respondents who said that the United States has been more effective than the Soviet Union showed an appreciation of American aid and its ability to win friends in the underdeveloped countries. Respondents who said this often added that United States aid, whether given directly in dollars or indirectly in research, education, or health services, has been seldom used for gaining internal control of a country but has been given democratically, while Soviet aid often has been used for purposes of political intrigue in an attempt to foster a new "Soviet colonialism."

The majority of the other reasons cited dealt with American democratic ways with references to Puerto Rico and the Philippines, or with Soviet undemocratic and totalitarian ways with references to Hungary, Czechoslovakia, and East Germany. These comments generally were similar to those given in justification for choosing the United States in answer to the "morally right" question that was discussed earlier.

For the most part, the explanations of the respondents who maintained that the United States and the Soviet Union have been the same in effectiveness were combinations of the reasons already discussed, paired so as to offset each other. Six of the respondents, however, pointed out that the degree of effectiveness varies by area, owing to differential intensity of effort and the different histories and backgrounds of the people involved. They felt that the Soviet Union is generally more effective in the East and the United States in the West.

Effectiveness by the Dates Questionnaires Were Returned

Table 27 shows that there is some variation in opinions concerning the relative effectiveness of the United States and the USSR in underdeveloped countries by the dates on which questionnaires were returned. Thus, if my earlier reasoning is correct, there should be some variation by international events as they were reported in sources available in Jamaica. The percentage of respondents who thought the USSR has been more effective than the United States was 50 or more at each time period. The smallest percentage impressed with Russia's effectiveness occurred between June 18 and July 16, however, just after the reminder of the Russians' barbarous treatment of the Hungarians (the announcement of Nagy's execution), and the largest percentage occurred between July 17 and August 26, just after the U.S. Marines had landed in Lebanon. It is curious that in the

TABLE 27. *Percentage of Jamaican Leaders Who Said That the Soviet Union Has Been More Effective than the United States, by the Dates Questionnaires Were Returned*

Dates returned	Per cent who said that USSR is more effective	Number of cases on which per cent is based
May 31 to June 17	57	(44)
June 18 to July 16	50	(74)
July 17 to August 26	64	(47)
August 27 to October 9	58	(45)
October 10 to December 22	58	(12)

view of the Jamaican elites the high point of Russian effectiveness occurred at the same time as the high point of moral rightness of the United States (see Table 25). From the responses to the open-ended probes, it appears that the United States was thought to be morally right in its action in Lebanon by many Jamaicans, but that the effectiveness of Soviet propaganda was considered to have been thereby strengthened in many underdeveloped countries where the American side of the situation might not be fully reported.

Effectiveness by Selected Social Characteristics

Table 28 shows that the younger leaders were a little more likely than were those over 40 to think the USSR has been effective; women were more likely to think so than were men, as were the lowest compared with the highest occupationally ranked respondents, and low-income compared with high-income persons.

TABLE 28. *Percentage of Jamaican Leaders Who Said That the Soviet Union Has Been More Effective than the United States, by Selected Characteristics*

Selected social characteristics	Per cent who said that USSR is more effective	Number of cases on which per cent is based
Age:		
55 and over	55	(65)
40–54	54	(108)
25–39	64	(49)
Sex:		
Men	55	(206)
Women	75	(16)
Occupational rating:		
1 (highest)	48	(127)
2	65	(79)
3 and 4 (lowest)	81	(16)
Education:		
Graduate school	62	(47)
Completed college	56	(41)
Some college	56	(32)
Secondary or training school	52	(86)
Elementary only	60	(15)

TABLE 28. *Percentage of Jamaican Leaders Who Said That the Soviet Union Has Been More Effective than the United States, by Selected Characteristics* (continued)

Selected social characteristics	Per cent who said that USSR is more effective	Number of cases on which per cent is based
Annual income:		
£2,000 and more	48	(96)
£1,999 and less	61	(106)
Religion:		
None	20	(10)
Catholic	68	(24)
Jewish	55	(11)
Protestant	56	(169)
Political party preference:		
None	52	(61)
People's National Party	60	(95)
Jamaica Labour Party	56	(62)
R's perception of his financial mobility:		
R. better off than father	57	(163)
R. same as father	42	(31)
R. worse off than father	63	(24)
Type of elite position:		
Educational leaders	80	(15)
Medical elites	65	(23)
Economic elites, agricultural	62	(13)
Elected political leaders	58	(19)
Civil servants	55	(62)
Economic elites, commercial	52	(54)
Social welfare elites	50	(4)
Religious elites	44	(9)
Legal elites	44	(9)
Appointed officials	42	(12)
Foreign countries lived in for at least one year:		
2 or more	54	(92)
1	54	(63)
None	61	(66)

Catholics were most impressed with Soviet effectiveness, followed by Protestants and Jews, with Agnostics, Atheists, and Independents being least impressed.

Differences in perception of relative effectiveness by political party are not great, but adherents of the People's National Party were most likely to think that the USSR has been effective, followed by adherents of the Jamaica Labour Party and those with no political party preference, in that order.

Respondents who saw themselves as being worse off financially than their fathers were somewhat more likely than those who thought they were better off to have said that the Soviet Union has been more effective than the United States. Those who saw themselves as having about the same financial position as their fathers were least likely to take this view.

There is considerable variation in the perception of the relative effectiveness of the Soviet Union and the United States among the different types of elites. In order of their likelihood of viewing Russia as more effective than the United States, the different types of elites were: educational leaders, medical elites, economic-agricultural elites, elected political leaders, civil servants, economic-commercial elites, social welfare elites, religious and legal elites (tied), and appointed officials.

Lack of foreign residence is correlated with saying Russia has been more effective than the United States, but the differences shown in Table 28 are small.

The very highest and the very lowest educational groups have the largest percentages who thought the USSR has been more effective than the United States when compared with the intermediate educational groups, but again the differences are slight.

Summarizing Table 28, one can observe that the Jamaican leaders who were most likely to believe that the USSR has been more effective in under-developed countries than the United States include *the younger persons; women; relatively low-prestige elite occupations; the highest and the lowest educational groups; elite members with relatively low incomes; Catholics; the PNP; the financially mobile; educational leaders, medical elites, economic-agricultural elites, and elected political leaders;* and *the noncosmopolitan elite members.*

Note that the "progressives," as defined earlier, are well represented. They were least likely to select the United States in the "morally right" question and they were most likely to select the USSR in the "effective" question (compare Tables 26 and 28). This pattern of correlation with the two effect variables can be seen for age, sex, income, political party preference, the respondent's perception of his financial mobility, and—to some extent—type of elite position, the educational leaders being a striking example. It would also be true for education, if it were not for the fact that such a large percentage of the persons with only an elementary education regarded the Soviet Union as more effective than the United States. It is not true of foreign residence, and this is contrary to the other findings if cosmopolitanism is a valid measure of "progressivism," but then other factors specific to foreign residence may account for this.

A striking exception to this pattern of correlation is found in the case of religious preference. Ninety-six per cent of the Catholics said that the United States has been morally right more often than the Soviet Union, but 68 per cent of them also thought that the Soviet Union has been more effective than the United States. This corroborates what many writers have suggested: active, noncomplacent anti-Communists have been found among the Catholics more often than among any other subgroup.

Conclusion

In this chapter, images of the United States and the Soviet Union held by Jamaican leaders, important factors determining Jamaica's global alignments, were described and analyzed. Two questions were used to define such images, one that concerned the relative moral rightness of the general positions taken by the United States and the USSR in the world situation and another that concerned their differential effectiveness in winning over to their point of view the people living in underdeveloped countries.

The results were that the leaders overwhelmingly viewed the United States as being morally right more often than the Soviet Union. Thus, from these data one must conclude that the climate of opinion among Jamaican leaders was much more favorable to reaching a decision to align with the United States and the Western powers than to reaching a decision either to remain neutral or to align with the Communist countries. Furthermore, events which occurred since 1958 represent the consequences of these images as they were expressed in concrete action. On February 28, 1963, Jamaican Senator Hugh Shearer proclaimed before the Jamaican Senate the official governmental policy that Jamaica was opposed to communism, was not neutral, and was firmly aligned with the nations of the West, a fact which had become increasingly clear during the Cuban crisis.[11] Of course, the decision to join the British Commonwealth had been the first foreign policy decision that Jamaica had made and the foregone decision to join the United Nations had been the second. By 1963, the Jamaican government had gone so far as to begin arrangements for the advice and aid of Canada and the United States in the military defense of Jamaica. Thus, despite Jamaica's somewhat independent voting record in the United Nations, Jamaica exchanged military personnel with the United States and

Canada, and the United States government appointed a military attaché to its embassy in Jamaica.

It was clear from the open-ended responses that for some Jamaican leaders, political democracy was a powerful, motivating force. It was far from a dead issue. It was a live and important value. Liberty, social justice, and equality were symbolized by the United States. The image of the Soviet Union was also clear, but it was a contrary one. For most leaders it was a picture of inhumanity in the methods used to maintain order and control at home and abroad, of a leadership that was coldly calculating, expedient, and void of moral restraints in the achievement of ends in which it "religiously" believed. It was a picture of dedication to the extension of power, influence, and ideology, of domination without the consideration for the integrity of other peoples. No such stigma attached to the activities of the United States in the views of these leaders.

These were not the complete images, however. Only about a fourth of the Jamaican leaders believed that the United States has been more effective than the Soviet Union in dealing with the people living in underdeveloped countries, and over half of them thought the opposite, that the Soviet Union has been more effective than the United States. They generally believed that the large-scale economic reforms so necessary in underdeveloped countries may be difficult, if not impossible, to achieve under a system of political democracy, given the economic and social conditions which prevail in underdeveloped areas including the lack of an informed, educated citizenry. Communism, some of the Jamaican leaders said, offered greater material benefits and opportunities for economic advancement to underdeveloped countries than did the United States, although at the probable cost of sacrificing representative government and public liberties. Furthermore, some said that the USSR has been more effective than the United States, because Soviet propaganda often was false (thus more seductive and persuasive) and usually forceful and well directed, and because in acting to achieve control and domination, the Soviet Union was relatively unrestrained by moral consideration and could be completely expedient.

To the detriment of the image of the United States were the comments of some respondents concerning racial prejudice, refusal to recognize Red China, McCarthyism, dollar diplomacy, and the air of patronage and superiority which the United States often displayed toward relatively poor countries. Yet these comments were in the minority.

Although the attitudes of the Jamaican leaders were generally pro-American, they did vary with respect to certain social characteristics, with elites defined as "progressives" being somewhat less pro-American than the others. This fact is theoretically interesting, because such elites were among those who were particularly committed to rapid political, economic, and social change. Further study should be directed to the conditions that produce progressives in the developing and underdeveloped nations, and the generality of the concept as well as its analytic utility as an explanatory frame should be investigated beyond what was possible in this book.

This fact is of practical significance, because progressive elites may be particularly sensitive weather vanes in determining the direction of pro- or anti-American feeling in new and developing nations. Their attitudes concerning global alignments may be most contingent upon the changing realities of their countries' situation in the world. And progressives may be most willing to sacrifice political democracy, if they believe that they must, in order to achieve rapid economic growth and distributional and social reforms within their own countries. For example, the rise of Castro in nearby Cuba could not go unnoticed in Jamaica, and by 1962 a few of the younger Jamaican elites who were among those most committed to economic and social change and to the welfare of the lower socio-economic-racial groups were beginning to wonder whether or not a Communist dictatorship didn't offer a better way to achieve economic and social progress than a liberal, welfare-capitalistic, democracy based on a two-party system. Additionally, there was as early as 1962 some evidence, despite the pro-Western global alignment proclamation of 1963, that there was increasing support among Jamaican leaders for a neutralist's role in international affairs compared to 1958, although those favoring neutralism by no means were as yet in the majority.[12]

Chapter **VIII**

Conclusion: Jamaica's Precarious Future

IT WAS DECIDED in 1963 that Jamaica would stand by the side of the Western democracies, and this decision obviously will affect the shape of Jamaica's future in significant ways. Of course, such a decision is contingent and subject to reconsideration. What exactly Jamaica will become internally and what impact, if any, Jamaica will eventually have on the other nations of the world are problematic. Some persons might point out the many limitations to future developments in Jamaica. They might say that it is too much to expect a great deal from such a small, poor, and unimportant nation. After all, they might ask, what is Jamaica? And they might answer, it is less than two million people living on a tropical island 146 miles long; who are newly united in a national state; whose origins can be traced to far-flung areas of the world; and who include mostly the descendants of Negro slaves, but also many other racial and ethnic types including descendants of people from England, Ireland, Wales, Scotland, France, Portugal, Germany, India, China, and Syria; many of whom are uneducated, underemployed, poorly housed, underfed, and badly clothed; whose economy is still largely agricultural; some of whom are alienated from and cynical about their political, economic, and social institutions—in fact about their new nation itself; and more than a few of whom are estranged from the realities of their own past and who have little or no faith in the possibilities of their own future. Reviewing such considerations, such persons would probably make dire predictions concerning Jamaica's future, perhaps resorting to that old fear of the established Jamaican elites —that Jamaica might become another Haiti, or perhaps calling on the new specter of Communist Cuba for another, although for some less

171

disquieting (because order and progress, if not freedom would be thought to be included), image of Jamaica's future.

I would answer such persons by saying that my observations in Jamaica over a period of years support the contention that there is as much chance, in fact more, of Jamaica progressing still more, perhaps even of taking the lead among the new nations in seeking the welfare of humanity as a whole. There is a chance for Jamaica to transcend its present limitations and to achieve more fully the moral ambitions of Western Civilization—perhaps especially to achieve the values of the Enlightenment. Across every land today, voices can be heard speaking in the name of politically, economically, or socially submerged groups, groups which are underprivileged compared to others within their own countries as well as entire peoples who are underprivileged compared to the peoples of other countries. There is a disturbing similarity to the refrain whether it comes from the new nations of Africa or Asia; from the *fellahin* of the Middle East or from the peasants of South America; from the slums of London, Rome, Rio de Janeiro, New York, or Chicago; from the Negro in the American south or from the lower classes in the Caribbean. To put it in much overused words, it is a vision of the oneness of humanity, of a better life for more people in *this* world.

It is possible that Jamaica can become a symbol to the world, to the developed and underdeveloped, to the committed and uncommitted nations alike. One future that Jamaicans might create would continue the sets of trends which already characterize Jamaica and which have been specified in this book: increases in the scale of society and the trend toward equality. Jamaica could prove to the world that economic and social progress can occur in a relatively poor country while maintaining a representative political system and public liberties; that the creation of a truly inclusive society where there is no arbitrary prejudice and discrimination of any kind is possible; that opportunities for all people can be increased; that equal access to all facilities and institutions can be achieved; that civil and political equality can be realized in fact; that minimums of economic, social, and cultural rights can be raised; that the people, under democracy, can become more mobilized, efficient, and coördinated so that the power to achieve the society's collective goals will be increased; that the people individually, like the society itself, can be developed and their self-realization attained; that a nation can be concerned not just with its own welfare, but with the welfare of all people everywhere; and that a nation can put humanity even above its own newly won national sovereignty. In sum, Jamaica could prove that some key ideas underlying Western thought still have vigor and meaning, that a belief in progress, reason, and the perfectibility of man carries with it a force that can help make the vision of a "better world" come true.[1]

This is not to predict what Jamaica's future *will be,* but to say what it *could be,* to say what is *possible.* Such a future is perfectly consistent with past trends in Jamaica, and it is compatible with the attitudes and hopes, the images of the future, held by important segments of the new Jamaican elite.

It would be unrealistic, however, not to stress again what these data have revealed as a major threat to such a hope for Jamaica's future: *that the equalitarian and democratic promise of Jamaican nationalism may not be fulfilled.* Although less of a threat today than a few years ago, the inequalitarians, authoritarians, and antinationalists must still be contended with. Their generally antiprogressive views could still upset the nationalist drive to a new future. Also, a danger is apparent among some of the more moderate political leaders whose change-leading propensities are becoming less pronounced while their satisfaction with the present realities of economic and social life is growing. Finally, another danger lies in the possibility of the spread of cynicism concerning political democracy among the Jamaican leaders, and the greatest danger may be found among the nationalists themselves. As they have come into power and responsibility, some Jamaican leaders who are dedicated to changing Jamaica into a more equalitarian society, to raising minimums of economic and social rights, become impatient with the democratic process. Usually committed to the ideals of democracy during the transition to independence, such leaders begin to view democracy as an obstacle to economic development and social reform, to further desired economic and social changes. Of course, if Jamaica adopted an authoritarian and undemocratic system, a reduction of civil and political rights for some sections of the population would immediately occur, reversing some of the trends specified in this book. It would be of little comfort to those whose rights were restricted that the symbols and vocabulary of democracy would probably be maintained while the substance of democracy was eroded.

Generally, the new national leaders of Jamaica seem to have avoided corruption and opportunism, the twin evils of unworthy leaders in most societies. The questions remain, "Can they also avoid the characteristic failing of the present-day leaders of new nations, namely cynicism concerning political democracy?" and "Can they effectively lead the way to a more equalitarian society?" Somewhere within the genius of the Jamaican people and the wisdom, restraint, and faith of the Jamaican leaders, affirmative answers may be found.

Appendixes

Occu-pational rating	Professionals	Proprietors	Businessmen
1 (Highest)	Doctor; dentist; engineer; judge; lawyer; clergyman; professor; school superintendent; headmaster of secondary school; architect; statistician; etc.	Investment of $75–100,000 in business or industry—varies by community size.	"Top management" president; manager; executives of corporations; public utilities; banks; etc.
2	High school teacher; headmaster of elementary school; trained nurse (RN); chiropodist; chiropractor; mortician; clergyman (no college); engineer (no college); veterinarian.	Reputed value of $20–70,000—"A very good business, but not the largest kind."	Assistant, department, and office managers or supervisors; managers of large branches; manufacturer's agents.
3	Grade school teacher; optician; assistant to undertaker; city veterinarian; pharmacist; (any unionized profession); land surveyor.	Value or equity reputed $5–20,000 in a "good" but rather "small" business, etc.	Managers of branch stores and business (no office staff); buyers and salesmen with "connections" (office and "secretary").

Occupational Ratings

White collar workers *	Landowners, farmers, et al.†	Service personnel	Manual workers
Executive secretary of status organizations; certified public accountant; editor of reputed newspapers, magazines; executive level of government, Permanent Secretary, Director of Government Department, Undersecretary, Principal Assistant Secretary; Chairman, Parish Council; Member of House of Representatives.	"Gentlemen farmers," landowners not directly supervising operations; the "patrons" of community activities.	Commissioner of Police.	
Secretary, Parish Council; senior education officer; accountant, insurance, stock and bond, real estate men in reputed firms; columnist, editorial writer, etc.; assistant secretary; organizing secretary of youth organization.	Landowners, operators, and managers of large properties who have an active urban life.	Assistant Commissioner of Police; Deputy Commissioner of Police.	
Clerk of court; education officer; bank broker's clerk; secretary; senior postal clerk; railroad agent; supervisor in public utilities; county and civil officials; newspaper reporters; executive officers; etc.	Owners and operators of good mechanized farms with "hired hands."	Commercial pilot; Superintendent of Police.	Small contractor who works with his men.

Occupational rating	*Professionals*	*Proprietors*	*Businessmen*
4		Value or equity in business of $2–5,000 —few if any employees.	
5		Value or equity $500– 2,000—no employees.	
6		Less than $500 equity.	
7			

(Lowest)

SOURCE: Adapted from W. Lloyd Warner, Marchia Meeker, Kenneth Eels, *Social Class in America,* Chicago: Science Research Associates, Inc., 1949, pp. 140–141, and Carson McGuire, "Social Status, Peer Status, and Social Mobility," a mimeographed memorandum for research workers based upon procedures used in studies for the Committee on Human Development, University of Chicago, Chicago, Ill., 1948.

White collar workers *	Landowners, farmers, et al.†	Service personnel	Manual workers
Bailiff; cashier; deputy clerk of court; stenographer; bookkeeper; typist; mail clerk; ticket agent; auto, book, clothing, dry goods salesman, etc.; government clerks; office employees; administrative assistant; clerical officer.	Small landowners and the "forgotten farmer" who owns a "decent place"; operators of good leased property employing hired help.	Deputy superintendent of police; butcher; tailor; local dry cleaner; railroad and Pullman conductors; assistant superintendent of prison.	Construction, factory or mine foreman; carpenter, electrician, plumber, master mechanic; railroad engineer or trainman; printer; etc.
Field timekeeper, sugar estate; office boy; drugstore, hardware, grocery, five and ten clerks, etc.; telephone and beauty operator; dressmaker, practical nurse, etc.	Tenants on good farms; owners of farms who just manage to eke out a living, some by "working out"; others by working in plants, etc., supplement income from crops.	Policeman; barber; gas station operator; butcher's apprentice; bartender; headwaiter; laundry agent; butler; etc.	Apprentice to skilled trades; timekeeper; railroad fireman or brakeman; telephone and telegraph lineman; medium-skilled factory workers; etc.
	Sharecroppers; established farm laborers; subsistence farmers who work out at unskilled jobs—e.g., "cottagers."	Taxi and truck drivers; baggage men; delivery men; gas station attendant; waitress; chauffeur; etc.	Semiskilled factory and production workers; warehouseman; janitor; watchman; cook (unless reputed).
	Migrant worker, unestablished and does not want to be—moves with the seasons; "unemployed— no occupation."	Domestic servant (but not butler, housekeeper); busboys, etc.; reputed lawbreakers.	Laborer; unskilled miners and mill hands; section hands; migrant workers; scrub women; laundress.

* When in doubt about government officers, compare salaries in *The Handbook of Jamaica*.

† Sizes of some estates listed in *The Handbook of Jamaica*.

Note: Actors, authors, musicians, artists, etc. may be rated from "1" to "5" (according to the reputation of their work and degree of acceptance). . . . This occupational rating scale worked fairly well in Jamaica for the classification of leaders, but I think that it should be modified before being used again in the developing areas.

Appendix II

The 1958 Jamaican Elite:
Who's Who Analysis and
Questionnaire Study

THE *Who's Who* ANALYSIS and the mail questionnaire study done in 1958 are discussed together, since the same basic sampling procedure applies to both. A total of 803 Jamaican elites were selected by the methods described below, and they constituted the basic list of Jamaican elites studied. Seven hundred and forty-four of them were listed in *Who's Who, Jamaica,* and became the basis of the "social characteristics" data for 1958 reported in Chapter III. Of the 803, there were 238 who properly filled out questionnaires and returned them, and these 238 respondents became the basis of the analysis of elites' beliefs, attitudes, and ideologies analyzed in several chapters throughout the book. In addition to the method of sample selection, a discussion of the reasons for nonresponse and an evaluation of the mail questionnaire survey are given below.

The 1958 Who's Who *Analysis*

The first step in constructing a basic list of names to constitute an adequate sample of the 1958 Jamaican elite was to select a 25 per cent sample of names from *Who's Who, Jamaica, 1957.*[1] This was done in May, 1958 by selecting every fourth name after a random start from 1 to 4 using page proofs from the *Who's Who,* which was then in press. The page proofs were made available through the courtesy of Clifton Neita, editor of *Who's Who,* and Easton Neita, Director and Secretary of Who's Who (Jamaica),

Ltd. In this manner, 598 persons were selected. Of these, seven persons were eliminated from the analysis, because it was later learned that they had died, were critically ill, or had left the island permanently. Because the 1957 *Who's Who* was still being compiled and revised in 1958, these data were accepted as 1958 information and were so designated throughout the book where reference is made to them.

The second step was to add to the 591 persons selected as part of the random sample from the *Who's Who*. The additions were made by select-ing other persons, who had not fallen in the random sample, but who were selected from the King's House Invitation List, which was a ranking of persons in Jamaica according to their official status, be they elected politi-cal leaders, civil servants, religious leaders, bank officials, foreign trade commissioners, or what. Other lists were used to check the up-to-dateness of the Invitation List, such as the Civil Service Seniority List; the list of members in the House of Representatives and the Legislative Council; and the list of Chairmen of Parish Councils and Mayors. However, the King's House Invitation List was the basic frame of reference for the sup-plementary sample. For some groups (appointed officials and *higher* civil servants) the sample selected equaled the universe from which it was drawn. Lesser civil servants, however, were sampled by means of the *Who's Who* random sample. For elected political leaders, the sample approached the universe, but parish councilors were included only if they occupied the office of Chairman or fell into the random sample. In this manner 212 additional names were added to the *Who's Who* sample of 1958 Jamaican leaders making a total of 803 persons who comprised the complete sam-ple. Thus, the King's House Invitation List was used to obtain a more complete sampling of top leaders and to compensate for any omissions of top leaders in the *Who's Who*.

As described in the preface:

WHO'S WHO JAMAICA aims to give brief, accurate, biographical data of Jamaicans, and other persons connected with the island, whose positions or achievements make them of general interest. In this volume are recorded life-sketches of officials, members of the professions, educators, writers, artists, politicians, successful businessmen and women and others engaged in sports, social welfare and philanthropic work.

The standards of admission to WHO'S WHO JAMAICA divide the eligible into two classes, (a) those selected because of special prominence in creditable lines of achievement, as agreed by consensus, or substantiated by actual evidence of work accomplished; (b) those arbitrarily included on account of official positions. . . .

The sketches have been edited from an impartial point of view; no particular opinion, political or otherwise, has in any way influenced the policy under which the work has been compiled. . . .[2]

In general, the *Who's Who* seemed to be fairly valid and reliable. I was able to observe the compilers' methods and their records in order to satisfy myself that the work was conscientiously and honestly done. Nonetheless, there was undoubtedly error, especially at the lower echelons of the elite. Some persons failed to fill out and return the forms sent them by Who's Who, Ltd., although top-ranked persons were generally included whether or not they filled out their own forms. Also, a few errors occurred in the publishing process itself, and more than fifteen persons did not get into *Who's Who* even though copy had been prepared for them which should have been included.

In addition, of the 212 persons selected from the King's House Invitation List, 59 were not listed in *Who's Who*. Thus, the analysis that is based upon these data rests upon 744 of 803 persons constituting the basic sample of 1958 Jamaican elites, or 93 per cent.

The Mail Questionnaire Study

The 803 elites whose selection is described above were each mailed a questionnaire which they were asked to fill out and return.[3] The questionnaires with a covering letter were first posted in Jamaica from May 27 through June 1, 1958; follow-up letters were mailed on June 21; a second wave of questionnaires was mailed to all nonrespondents on July 15 and 16; and starting at the end of August and running through most of September, 1958, a final plea for responses was made by personal telegram. By December 22, 1958, when the last properly filled-out questionnaire was returned, 238 useable questionnaires had been returned for a response rate of 29.6 per cent. All but five of the respondents had returned their questionnaires before October 25.

Seventy-one of the nonrespondents wrote giving their reasons for not filling out the questionnaire. The percentage distribution of these is as follows:

Reason	Per Cent
Off the island temporarily	26
Not in Jamaica long enough to know the answers	21
No time to answer	11
Worried that identity would be known	9
Not interested in the subject of the study	7

Reason	Per Cent
Questionnaire too long	6
Questionnaire asks for confidential material	6
Respondent thinks he is too old to be helpful	6
Respondent thinks the questionnaire too personal	3
Respondent suffering from short-term illness	3
For the same reasons Morris Cargill gave	1
Respondent says he has no scientific evidence on which to base his answers	1
Total	100
Number of cases	(71)

It is by no means suggested that the above percentage distribution of reasons was the same as the distribution in the total group of nonrespondents. Bias undoubtedly entered into the self-selection of the seventy-one persons who wrote giving their reasons for their unwillingness to fill out the questionnaire. From a consideration of these reasons and especially from information obtained in personal interviews, however, some assessment of the factors that contributed to the nonresponse can be made which might be a guide to other researchers.

1. For this sample, the questionnaire was undoubtedly too long and complicated, given the fact that there were a considerable number of persons with less than a college education among the Jamaican elites. Note from Table A2 that the nonrespondents were more likely to have only a secondary school education than were the respondents.

2. The number of persons who were off the island during all or some of the time of the survey was probably less than the 26 per cent giving this as a reason for not answering the questionnaire and this reason was in part a rationalization for not responding, but this factor was clearly important even so. Elites are generally more mobile geographically in the course of their routine activities than are nonelites, but this may be particularly so in places like Jamaica where so many of the organizations in most institutional spheres are heteronomous and heterocephalous.

3. Another factor entering into the nonresponse was the number of Jamaican elites who had not been in Jamaica long enough "to know the answers" to many of the questions in the questionnaires. This also may be characteristic of underdeveloped countries entering a period of rapid political, economic, and social change. There is a continuing need for expertise of various kinds which in the early periods of development can only be fully supplied by relying on expatriates. Thus, for the purposes of this study, "Jamaican elites" were defined with respect to their performance of elite functions and with respect to the consequences of the performance of

these functions for Jamaican society. It was not necessary for an elite to be born in Jamaica to be considered a "Jamaican elite." A British-born director of a Jamaican government department, an American-born engineer employed by a sugar estate in Jamaica, and a Trinidadian-born professor at the University College of the West Indies, for example, would be included by this definition of Jamaican elites. Many of these people, especially if recent arrivals, may not have formed definite opinions about the Jamaican situation. Some of them take little interest in Jamaican affairs even after relatively long residence and think of their stay in Jamaica as only temporary. A few are insecure in their positions because they are expatriates and want to do nothing, even—or perhaps especially—filling out a questionnaire dealing with important and controversial issues of Jamaican and West Indian affairs, that would in any way jeopardize their positions. Others found this a convenient excuse for not taking the time to answer the questionnaire.

4. Given the Jamaican situation, certain questions on the questionnaire also contributed to the nonresponse. Question 9 was the worst (see Appendix III) from the point of view of the response rate. It called for the complete names of ten persons with whom the respondents discussed certain important issues or problems facing Jamaica. It was not answered by enough of the respondents to perform the sociometric analysis that was planned, and it probably accounted for more of the total nonresponses than any other question. There was a fear among many of the Jamaican elites—especially among those who were Jamaican born—that some kind of guilt-by-association would result that would somehow compromise them. Clearly, a concern with the anonymity of their responses was involved here as well.

5. Another contributing factor to the nonresponse was the "personal data" section of the questionnaire given in questions 38 through 53. The questions for the personal data section were formulated in such a manner that all of the detailed information that was needed about the respondents for the data analysis that was planned would be obtained. Making this section so complete and detailed was a serious mistake as far as the response rate was concerned. Although I had given the usual guarantees of anonymity, many respondents—probably a larger percentage than the 9 per cent shown above—thought that by giving the information requested, they would be pinpointing themselves. They thought that anyone who wanted to do so could discover their identity. The scale on which this response occurred is probably a reflection of the fact that Jamaica is a small society, most of the leaders know each other or about each other and their family connections, and the notion of impersonal analysis of anonymous data seems remote from the experience of some, if not many,

of the Jamaican leaders—at least when the data analyzed is about *them* and not about some dependent population such as the lower classes, prison inmates, school children, and so on.

6. Another difficulty occurred with respect to civil servants. Before posting any questionnaires, I tried to receive from the Governor and the Chief Minister official sanction for the study to the extent of having the national government ask the civil servants to coöperate. But such direction to the civil servants was not forthcoming, and although the civil servants were directed by letter from the Chief Secretary to each of the Permanent Secretaries of the Ministries that they and other civil servants were free to coöperate as they wished, some general resistance developed among the civil servants in some of the Ministries. The grounds for the resistance were in some cases a concern with giving information that was considered confidential, but it was mostly that some civil servants objected to the questions about their political party preference and activity (Questions 52, 52a, and 52b) and feared some reprisals from either the PNP or the JLP depending on which party the civil servants said they preferred. Also, the civil service was supposed to be nonpolitical, and generally was as far as political action was concerned—although it had been accused of being otherwise; some civil servants believed that their responses would violate their officially neutral role.

What apparently happened was this: The Chief Minister and his PNP advisers thought that I would document their belief that the civil servants generally disagreed with PNP policies, the PNP being in power at the time of the study. They believed this in part because the federal equivalent of the PNP, the FLP, had just lost the federal elections to the federal equivalent of the JLP, the DLP. This resulted in my losing the full coöperation of the government in my attempt to obtain data from the civil servants. Ironically, the civil servants turned out to be overwhelmingly in favor of the PNP and in favor of PNP policies, notwithstanding minor disagreements. Additionally, many such civil servants feared filling out the questionnaires precisely because they were PNP supporters and viewed the federal elections that had just been held as an omen of a JLP victory in the next Jamaican elections which were to be held in 1959. Thus, they did not want to compromise themselves with the JLP politicians who they thought might soon be in control of the government. As it turned out, everyone's fears were groundless (the PNP won the 1959 elections), but they still deleteriously affected the response rate.

I attempted to combat the resistance among some of the civil servants by asking the Chief Secretary again to communicate the official position (that Jamaica was a free country and that civil servants were free to answer) to the Permanent Secretaries; I talked personally to as many Permanent Secretaries and Principal Assistant Secretaries as I could; I talked to officers of the Civil Service Association; and I tried more informally to get personal contacts among the civil servants which I used to urge particular civil servants to fill out the questionnaires themselves and to ask others who had received them to fill them out. In addition, I enclosed with the follow-up letter (see Appendix III) to every civil servant the following mimeographed note:

GOVERNMENT OFFICERS PLEASE NOTE

Before any questionnaires were mailed to civil servants in Jamaica, official approval to do so was sought from the Chief Minister and His Excellency, The Governor. We were advised that no official direction could be given the civil servants, but that we were free to send our questionnaires to them and that they were free to answer at their own choice. A letter to this effect was sent by the Chief Secretary to each of the Permanent Secretaries.

WENDELL BELL

In the end, civil servants were not underrepresented among the respondents to the questionnaires (see Table A1), although it is not clear what particular measures to increase their responses were in fact effective.

7. On June 21, 1958, a descriptive article explaining the questionnaire survey appeared in the *Daily Gleaner* which I assume helped increase the number of responses, but on August 7, 1958, an elected member of the then newly formed Federal Parliament, Morris Cargill, who was among other things a columnist for the *Daily Gleaner,* chose to parody my questionnaire in his column. Needless to say, I was worried at the thought of what such a parody of my study by such a socially prominent and politically active person might do to my response rate, which was already disappointingly low. My reply, neither as witty nor as amusing as the original letter despite my efforts, appeared in the *Gleaner* some time later. It seems as if the exchange, parody and reply, actually had little effect on the response rate. I know for certain that I lost one respondent (see the percentage distribution of reasons given above), and I know for certain that I gained one I wouldn't have otherwise obtained. In any event, the weekly response rate continued its steady descent with no evidence of fluctuation due to the exchange.

8. Finally, various categories of postal clerks decided to go on strike on June 30, 1958, and again from July 21 through July 24, 1958. Although these were relatively brief periods, they occurred at crucial times in the questionnaire survey—when the follow-up letters and the second wave of questionnaires should have been having most effect. During the later period,

some of the post boxes became so full that in many places it was impossible to mail anything. I know for a fact that this contributed to a reduction of the response rate.

Considering the above difficulties and problems, it is perhaps fortunate that the response rate for the questionnaire study was as high as 29.6 per cent. The question remains, however, as to how biased the respondents are when compared to the nonrespondents. What are the systematic differences, if any, between the respondents and the nonrespondents? The linkage between the selection of the samples for the *Who's Who* study and the questionnaire survey permit a tentative answer to this question for a number of variables. Of the 238 respondents to the questionnaire survey, 218 were listed in *Who's Who*. Of the 565 nonrespondents, 526 were listed. Thus, the comparison of most of the respondents with most of the nonrespondents to the questionnaire survey is possible with respect to a series of variables that are given in the biographies in *Who's Who*.

Table A1 compares the respondents to the nonrespondents with respect to type of elite position.[4] Note that all types of elites are represented in the respondents to about the same degree as they are among the nonrespondents. There are no significant differences between the two groups.

TABLE A1. *Comparison of Respondents with Nonrespondents According to Type of Elite Position from among Persons Listed in* Who's Who, *1957*

Type of elite position	Respondents per cent	Nonrespondents per cent
Elected political leaders	6	7
Appointed officials	5	4
Civil servants	27	25
Economic elites	34	37
Labor leaders	−0.1	0
Religious leaders	4	5
Educational leaders	6	4
Judges	1	1
Medical elites	11	9
Barristers and solicitors	4	5
Social welfare elites	1	1
Other elites	1	2
Total	100	100
Number of cases	(218)	(526)

$X^2 = 6.7$, 10 d.f., p > .75 (Labor leaders were grouped with "other").

The comparison between respondents and nonrespondents is extended in Table A2 by using twelve additional variables. On ten of them there are no differences between the respondents and the nonrespondents. These are: the nature of the sample, whether random or special; age; sex; country of birth; urban-rural residence; occupational rating; marital status; religion; total number of memberships in formal associations; and total number of officerships held in formal associations. The chi-square approaches significance in the case of religion, however, with the Anglicans and Roman Catholics being slightly underrepresented among the respondents, and the Methodists, Other Christians, and Jews being slightly overrepresented.

There are significant differences between the respondents and nonrespondents with respect to two of the twelve comparisons given in Table A2. One of these occurs with the comparison of educational levels in which elites with some university or more are overrepresented among the respondents and those with only a secondary or training school education are underrepresented. There is little difference in the case of persons with only an elementary school education. Nonetheless, all educational levels are included among the respondents.

The second significant difference occurs in the case of occupational mobility. There is no difference among the downwardly mobile elites, but the stable elites are underrepresented among the respondents, and the upwardly mobile—steps 2 and 3—are overrepresented. Again, however, all mobility categories are included among the respondents.

TABLE A2. *Comparison of Respondents with Nonrespondents According to Selected Characteristics from among Persons Listed in Who's Who, 1957*

Selected characteristics	Respondents per cent	Non-respondents per cent	Chi-square
Nature of sample:			.93, d.f. = 1, p > .30
Random	82	79	
Special	18	21	
Total	100	100	
Number of cases	(218)	(526)	
Age:			9.83, d.f. = 8, p > .25
65 or over	9	9	
60–64	9	6	

Selected characteristics	Respondents per cent	Non-respondents per cent	Chi-square
55–59	11	12	
50–54	12	18	
45–49	21	18	
40–44	16	18	
35–39	12	9	
30–34	7	7	
25–29	3	3	
Total	100	100	
Number of cases	(216)	(469)	
Sex:			.094, d.f. $= 1$, $p > .75$
Men	93	94	
Women	7	6	
Total	100	100	
Number of cases	(218)	(526)	
Country of birth:			5.20, d.f. $= 9$, $p > .80$ *
Jamaica	73	75	
British Caribbean (other than Jamaica)	4	4	
Caribbean (other than Br. Caribbean)	2	1	
England	10	9	
British Isles (other than England)	2	3	
Canada	3	1	
United States	4	3	
Middle East	−0.1	0	
Far East	1	1	
Europe other than the U.K.	1	2	
Other	−0.1	1	
Total	100	100	
Number of cases	(217)	(516)	
Urban-rural residence:			.91, d.f. $= 2$, $p > .50$
Kingston metropolitan area	68	70	
Spanish Town and Montego Bay	6	4	
Small town or rural	26	26	
Total	100	100	

Table A2. *Comparison of Respondents with Nonrespondents According to Selected Characteristics from among Persons Listed in* Who's Who, *1957* (*continued*)

Selected characteristics	Respondents per cent	Non-respondents per cent	Chi-square
Number of cases	(217)	(526)	
Occupational Rating:			.77, d.f. = 2, p > .50
1 (highest)	69	72	
2	22	20	
3 and 4 (lowest)	9	8	
Total	100	100	
Number of cases	(217)	(522)	
Education:			13.31, d.f. = 4, p < .01
Graduate school	21	19	
Completed university	20	13	
Some university	13	11	
Secondary or training	39	51	
Elementary only	7	6	
Total	100	100	
Number of cases	(217)	(499)	
Occupational mobility:			11.83, d.f. = 5, p < .05
Up 4 or more	3	2	
Up 3	15	15	
Up 2	30	24	
Up 1	21	17	
None	29	40	
Down 1	2	2	
Total	100	100	
Number of cases	(211)	(445)	
Marital status:			
Married	85	82	
Divorced	2	†	
Widowed	2	2	
Single	11	16	
Total	100	100	
Number of cases	(218)	(526)	

Selected characteristics	Respondents per cent	Non-respondents per cent	Chi-square
Religion:			12.61, d.f. = 7, p > .08
Anglican	48	54	
Baptist	4	4	
Methodist	11	8	
Presbyterian	6	5	
Roman Catholic	11	16	
Other Christian	13	9	
Jewish	6	3	
Other	1	1	
Total	100	100	
Number of cases	(204)	(440)	
Total number of memberships in formal associations:			7.47, d.f. = 6, p > .25
6 or more	14	12	
5	5	5	
4	9	8	
3	15	12	
2	9	16	
1	18	20	
None	30	27	
Total	100	100	
Number of cases	(218)	(526)	
Total number of officerships in formal associations:			1.89, d.f. = 5, p > .80
5 or more	3	3	
4	4	2	
3	4	4	
2	9	6	
1	18	16	
None	62	69	
Total	100	100	
Number of members of formal associations	(153)	(386)	

* Middle East grouped with "other" for computation of chi-square.
† "Divorced" for nonrespondents could not be determined.

In sum, of the 13 possible comparisons between respondents and non-respondents (including both Tables A1 and A2), 11 show no significant differences. However, two do: education and occupational mobility. Thus, in handling the data analysis for the questionnaire survey, I have tried to be cautious in those cases where two variables are related to each other when both are related to either education and mobility and when education and mobility have not been controlled. Mobility is not much of a problem, because it does not correlate with many other variables in this study, but education is since it is often correlated with the variables being considered. Often there is not much one can do except to point out the danger, since the number of cases available seldom permit the control of education in exploring the relationships of various other variables. The reader is hereby warned of this limitation in the analysis.

Finally, my use of the questionnaire data has been more in the spirit of exploration and discovery than in the spirit of proof. That is, I have used the data analysis as an aid in thinking about what might be true of Jamaican leaders rather than trying to *test* hypotheses formulated prior to the data collection. Thus, I have looked at the data this way and that, and I have drawn on much other information, my own observations from different trips to Jamaica from 1956 to 1962 as well as the views of many informants in addition to published sources. Additionally, I have drawn on the informal communications of many social scientists who know Jamaica, including the UCLA graduate students who returned to the West Indies with me in 1961–1962 to carry out a larger series of studies on elites and nationalism. I have taken as my chief task the formulation of hypotheses which are consistent with data presently available.

The Questionnaire and Letters

STUDY OF JAMAICAN LEADERS

Strictly Confidential

We would appreciate your co-operation in completing this questionnaire. From your answers we hope to learn a great deal about the nature of leadership and administration in countries undergoing political, economic, and social changes. Some of the questions are easier to answer than others, but please answer them all as they have been carefully selected and many have been included to yield information comparable to that available or being obtained among the leaders of other countries. Please be frank. *This questionnaire is anonymous and the names of persons which you may give will not be identified in any way.*

FACTS AND OPINIONS CONCERNING POLITICAL, ECONOMIC, AND SOCIAL CONDITIONS

1. In your opinion should Jamaica now strive to establish very close economic relations with the United Kingdom, establish moderately close economic ties, or strive to lessen such relations?

    .... Establish very close economic relations.

    .... Establish moderately close economic relations.

    .... Lessen economic relations.

    1a. Please explain your answer. ------------------------------------

    ----

    ----

2. Does the *United Kingdom* have more to gain or lose as a result of Jamiaca's political independence?

    .... The United Kingdom has more to gain.

_____ Political independence makes no difference one way or the other.

_____ The United Kingdom has more to lose.

2a. Please explain your answer. _____

_____

_____

_____

_____

_____

_____

3. Does *Jamaica* have more to gain or lose as a result of political independence from the United Kingdom?

_____ Jamaica has more to gain.

_____ Political independence makes no difference one way or the other.

_____ Jamaica has more to lose.

3a. Please explain your answer. _____

_____

_____

_____

_____

_____

_____

_____

4. Does *Jamaica* have more to gain or lose as a result of being part of the Federation?

_____ Jamaica has more to gain.

_____ Being part of the Federation makes no difference one way or the other.

_____ Jamaica has more to lose.

4a. Please explain your answer. _____

_____

_____

_____

_____

_____

_____

_____

5. All in all, would you say you are very interested, fairly interested, or not interested in things that happen outside the Caribbean—that is, world affairs?

        _____ Very   _____ Fairly   _____ Not

   5a. . . . in things that happen within the Federation—that is, West Indian affairs?

        _____ Very   _____ Fairly   _____ Not

   5b. . . . and how interested are you in things that happen right here in Jamaica—that is, Jamaican affairs?

        _____ Very   _____ Fairly   _____ Not

6. Has Federation or self-government within Jamiaca affected your career in any way, even indirectly?

        _____ Yes   _____ No

(IF YES)

6a. In exactly what way? _____

_____

_____

_____

_____

_____

_____

_____

7. In general, do you feel that you have more in common with civic, government, or business leaders in countries *outside* the Federation than you have with the general public in Jamaica, about the same, or less?

        _____ I have more in common with leaders in other countries than with the general public in Jamaica.

        _____ About the same.

        _____ I have more in common with the general public in Jamaica than with the leaders in other countires.

8. In your opinion what are the three most important issues or problems facing Jamaica at the moment?

(PLEASE LIST THEM IN ORDER OF THEIR IMPORTANCE)

   (1st) _____

   (2nd) _____

               _____

               _____

   (3rd) _____

               _____

9. With what individuals have you most seriously discussed these and other important issues or problems facing Jamaica, regardless of whether you agree with them or not? (PLEASE GIVE COMPLETE NAMES OF 10 PERSONS)

(1) ------------------------------   (6) ------------------------------

(2) ------------------------------   (7) ------------------------------

(3) ------------------------------   (8) ------------------------------

(4) ------------------------------   (9) ------------------------------

(5) ------------------------------   (10) ------------------------------

10. Here are some considerations of *political campaign strategy* which are often discussed. Thinking specifically of Jamaican voters, which of the following ideas would you feel were good strategy or poor strategy?

(1) In campaigning, the thing to do is to lash out at the opposition's record and program instead of calmly presenting your own side's records and plans. Thinking of Jamaican voters, is that good strategy or poor strategy?

-------- Good   -------- Fair   -------- Poor

(2) In campaigning, the thing to do is to point out how different issues affect the voter's pocketbook instead of how issues affect the whole society and economy. Thinking of Jamaican voters, is that good strategy or poor strategy?

-------- Good   -------- Fair   -------- Poor

(3) In campaigning, the thing to do is to stir up strong emotions, hates and fears instead of presenting a careful discussion of complex problems facing the country. Thinking of Jamaican voters, is that good strategy or poor strategy?

-------- Good   -------- Fair   -------- Poor

(4) In campaigning, the thing to do when the other side makes a smear attack is to level fresh charges against them instead of making a reasoned explanation of the facts. Again, thinking of Jamaican voters, is that good strategy or poor strategy?

-------- Good   -------- Fair   -------- Poor

11. What five Jamaican civic, political, or business leaders appeal most to the general public and have the largest following?

(1) ------------------------------   (3) ------------------------------

(2) ------------------------------   (4) ------------------------------

(5) ------------------------------

11a. What do you think is the basis for their popularity? --------------

----

----

12. The following is a list of things which are said to influence the way some people vote. In your opinion how important is each of these factors in influencing the average Jamaican voter?

	Very Important	Somewhat Important	Not Very Important
(1) Visits or phone calls from active party workers			
(2) The people around a candidate or closely associated with him			
(3) Loyalty to a political party			
(4) The personality of a candidate			
(5) The way a person's friends plan to vote			
(6) Campaign speeches and publicity			
(7) Serious consideration of the issues involved			

13. Generally, how much of a personal voice do you feel you have in the decisions which affect important aspects of political, economic, or social life in Jamaica?

.... No more than the average Jamaican.

.... A little more than the average Jamaican.

.... A great deal more than the average Jamaican.

.... More than all but a few other persons in Jamaica.

14. Considering all aspects of Jamaican life, who would you say are the most influential *individauls* on the entire island? That is, who are the people who can really get things done and who are really most important in influencing major economic and political decisions which affect all of Jamaica? In each case, does the person usually stay behind the scenes or is he in the forefront of affairs?

(PLEASE LIST 10 INDIVIDUALS IN ORDER OF THEIR IMPORTANCE)

	NAME	Check Only One Behind the Scenes	Forefront of Affairs
(1st)			
(2nd)			
(3rd)			

	Check Only One	
NAME	Behind the Scenes	Forefront of Affairs

(4th) --- ------------ ----------
(5th) --- ------------ ----------
(6th) --- ------------ ----------
(7th) --- ------------ ----------
(8th) --- ------------ ----------
(9th) --- ------------ ----------
(10th) -- ------------ ----------

15. Which *organizations* or *clubs* do you think most influence the economic and political life of Jamaica?

(PLEASE LIST 5 IN ORDER OF THEIR IMPORTANCE)
   (1st) ------------------------- (3rd) -------------------------
   (2nd) ------------------------- (4th) -------------------------
                 (5th) -------------------------

16. Considering the present political, economic, and social conditions in Jamaica, what type of leader do you think Jamaica needs most? -------------

----

----

17. Here is a list of 14 posts and occupations which the general public ranks highly compared to others. *Comparing just those listed here with each other,* which posts and occupations in general rank *very high, high* or *just medium* in the prestige or respect given to them by persons having social positions similar to your own?

	Very High	High	Just Medium
Physician and Surgeon	----------	------	----------
Owner of a large department store . . .	----------	------	--------
Principal Assistant Secretary in a Ministry	----------	------	--------
Attorney General	----------	------	--------
Owner of a large sugar plantation . . .	----------	------	----------
Planter and Penkeeper	----------	------	----------

	Very High	High	Just Medium
Head of a Ministry	---------	-----	--------
Deputy Director of a Government Department	---------	------	---------
Managing Director of a large company .	---------	------	---------
Professor at UCWI	---------	------	---------
Colonial Secretary	---------	-----	--------
Member of the House of Representatives	---------	------	---------
Permanent Secretary in a Ministry . .	---------	------	---------
Solicitor	---------	------	---------

The next 6 items are factual statements about important aspects of Jamaican life. Please circle the appropriate letter in response to each question to indicate the answer you feel is most correct:

"T" means that you are pretty sure the statement is true.
"t" means that you guess the statement is true.
"?" means that you have no idea about the truth of the statement.
"f" means that you guess the statement is false.
"F" means that you are pretty sure the statement is false.

Circle One

18. It is more difficult now than ever before in Jamaica to move out of the lowest social and economic positions . . T t ? f F

19. The amount of contact individuals in the higher social and economic brackets have with those in the lower brackets in Jamaica is very small if contacts with domestic help are excluded . . . . T t ? f F

20. In Jamiaca there is very little real understanding between individuals in different racial or religious groups . . . T t ? f F

21. People in Jamaica make definite social distinctions based upon income and occupation . . . . T t ? f F

22. There is less and less room at the top of the social and economic structure in Jamaica as time goes on . . . . T t ? f F

23. The concentration of wealth in the upper brackets in Jamaica is increasing . . . . T t ? f F

The 9 items which follow are statements about your own attitudes and opinions. There are no right or wrong answers. You are simply expressing your own opinion on each statement after each item. Please circle the appropriate letter:

"A" means you *definitely* or *strongly agree.*
"a" means you *agree somewhat* or *tend to agree.*

"?" means you are *undecided* or *in between*.
"d" means you *disagree somewhat* or *tend to disagree*.
"D" means you *definitely* or *strongly disagree*.

Circle One

24. Differences in rank among people are acceptable since they are chiefly the result of the way individuals have made use of the opportunity open to them . . . . A a ? d D

25. Social clubs which restrict membership on a racial basis ought to be considered as being against Jamaican principles . . . . A a ? d D

26. Differences in rank within an organization should be kept clearly before the members to increase their incentive to do good work and rise within the organization . . . A a ? d D

27. High social or economic position in Jamaica is a pretty good sign of an individual's superior ability or efforts A a ? d D

28. Differences in prestige among the various occupations in Jamaica should be reduced . . . . A a ? d D

29. People of about the same social or economic position ought to pretty much mingle with their own kind . . A a ? d D

30. It is unwise to try to run a business on a completely democratic basis where all members have an equal voice in the making of decisions . . . . A a ? d D

31. The incomes of most people are a fair measure of their contribution to human welfare . . . . . . A a ? d D

32. We should not be too concerned if there are many people in low positions in Jamaica since most of them do not want the responsibility of higher positions . . . A a ? d D

THE NEXT FEW QUESTIONS CONCERN COMPLETELY HYPOTHETICAL SITUATIONS. PLEASE READ THE FOLLOWING IMAGINARY STORY OF THE ECONOMIST AND THEN ANSWER THE QUESTIONS ABOUT IT.

STORY OF THE ECONOMIST

A department head in the civil service asks one of his staff members, an economist, to prepare a memorandum in support of a certain policy that has been followed for some time. In studying the matter, the economist finds that he can defend this policy only if he presents arguments that differ with what is generally accepted among most economists in and outside of the government.

33. Can the department head expect this civil servant to prepare such a memorandum?

-------- Yes   -------- No

34. What do you think this civil servant ought to do in view of his obligation to the government and his obligation as a professional economist? Should he prepare the report, or should he refuse to prepare it?

       _____ Should prepare   _____ Refuse

       Why do you think so? _____

_____

_____

_____

_____

_____

_____

35. If this civil servant prepared such a memorandum, following his chief's wishes, and it became known that he did, what do you think his colleagues among the economists would think of him?

_____

_____

_____

_____

_____

_____

_____

_____

_____

ONE ADDITIONAL HYPOTHETICAL QUESTION

36. Assuming that the elected political leaders completely agreed among themselves that they were right on some important policy decision, what do you think these leaders *would* actually do if the Governor of Jamaica should exercise his reserve powers and overrule them on the decision? _____

_____

_____

_____

_____

_____

_____

_____

     36a. In your opinion is that what they *should* do?

       _____ Yes   _____ No

(IF NO)

36b. What do you think they *should* do in such a circumstance?

THE NEXT FEW QUESTIONS HAVE A DIFFERENT FRAME OF REF-
ERENCE. THEY CONCERN YOUR OPINIONS REGARDING THE
WORLD SITUATION.

37. As you understand the general positions taken by the Soviet Union and
the United States with respect to the world situation, which do you feel
has been morally right more often in recent years?

_____ The Soviet Union has been right more often.

_____ Both about the same.

_____ The United States has been right more often.

37a. Please explain why you think so. ---------------------------------

----

37b. . . . which one is more effective in winning over to their point of
view the people living in the so-called underdeveloped countries
of the world?

_____ The Soviet Union is more effective.

_____ Both about the same.

_____ The United States is more effective.

37c. Please explain why you think so. ---------------------------------

----

IN ORDER TO ANALYZE IN A MEANINGFUL WAY, THE INFORMA-
TION YOU HAVE GIVEN, WE NEED TO KNOW SOME FACTS ABOUT
YOURSELF.

38. What is your age? _____   39. Sex: _____ Male
                                              _____ Female

40. In what country were you born?

41. Were you born in a large city, middle-sized city, small town or village,
    or in the country? (CIRCLE WHICH ONE)

42. Are you married, single, divorced, separated, or widowed? (CIRCLE
    WHICH ONE)

    (IF OTHER THAN SINGLE)

    42a. Do you have any children? _____ Yes   _____ No
    (IF YES)
    42b. How many? _____
    42c. What are their ages? _____

43. What is your regular occupation? (IF YOU HAVE MORE THAN ONE
    OCCUPATION GIVE YOUR PRIMARY OR MAIN OCCUPATION)

    _____(PLEASE GIVE DETAILED ANSWER)_____
    43a. In what kind of a business or organization are you employed?

    _____
    (IF YOU ARE A GOVERNMENT OFFICIAL OR POLITICAL
    LEADER)
    43b. Are you a civil servant, an elected politician, or a nominated officer?

        _____ Civil servant

        _____ Elected

        _____ Nominated

    (IF YOU WORK FOR YOURSELF, OR IF YOU ARE A MANAGER
    OR AN OFFICIAL)
    43c. Usually, how many people are under your supervision? _____

    (IF YOU HAVE ANY OTHER OCCUPATIONS)
    43d. What are your other occupations? _____

    _____
44. What was your father's primary occupation during your youth?

    _____(PLEASE GIVE DETAILED ANSWER)_____
45. How many years of formal education have you had? _____

    (IF YOU ATTENDED A SECONDARY SCHOOL)
    45a. What secondary school did you attend? _____
    45b. Where is it located? _____

(IF YOU ATTENDED A COLLEGE OR UNIVERSITY)
45c. What college or university did you attend? ----------------------------
45d. Where is it located? ---
45e. What college or university degrees do you have? --------- ----------

46. Approximately, what was your gross income for the year 1957 before taxes?

----

47. Generally are you now *better off, about the same,* or *worse off financially* than your father was during your youth?

-------- I'm better off than my father was.

-------- I'm about the same as my father was.

-------- I'm worse off than my father was.

48. What was your first regular, full-time occupation?

-----------------------(PLEASE GIVE DETAILED ANSWER)----------------

49. What is your religious preference?

-------- None

-------- Catholic

-------- Jewish

-------- Protestant, PLEASE SPECIFY DENOMINATION ------------

-------- Other, PLEASE SPECIFY -------------------------------------

50. Are you a member of a church? -------- Yes   -------- No

(IF YES)
50a. To what particular church do you belong? ------------------------
50b. In what town or neighborhood is it located? ------------------------

51. Have you ever lived in any country outside of Jamaica for as long as a year?
-------- Yes   ------- No
(IF YES)

51a. In what other countries have you lived? --------------------------

----

52. Generally, what is your political party preference in Jamaica?

-------- None.

-------- People's National Party.

-------- Jamaica Labour Party.

-------- Other, PLEASE SPECIFY

(IF YOU HAVE A POLITICAL PARTY PREFERENCE)
52a. Are you a member of the party of your preference?
-------- Yes   No --------

(IF YES)

52b. Compared to the average member of your political party are you *more active, about average* or *less active* in the affairs of the party?

-------- I'm more active than most.

-------- About average.

-------- I'm less active than most.

53. Have you had any books, articles, or pamphlets published during the last 10 years?

-------- Yes   No --------

(IF YES)

53a. How many books? --------
53b. How many articles? --------
53c. How many pamphlets? --------

ONE CONCLUDING QUESTION CONCERNING YOUR OPINIONS.

54. What important changes do you think will occur in Jamaica during the next 10 years? --

----

Any other comments you think might be useful would be appreciated.

THANK YOU FOR YOUR COOPERATION

Covering Letter for First Mailing

UNIVERSITY OF CALIFORNIA

Department of   MAY 12, 1958
Anthropology and Sociology   or
Los Angeles 24, California   MAY 22, 1958
                                       (Actually posted on May 27th
                                       through June 1, 1958)

DEAR SIR:

As part of a study of political change and leadership, we are conducting a survey of opinions among certain types of leaders in Jamaica. The study is supported financially by the Social Science Research Council, the American Philosophical Society, and the University of California. The general purpose of the study is to learn about the problems which face countries undergoing rapid change and to analyze the opinions of various leaders concerning these problems. Your answers will be compared with those given by other leaders in different countries.

Using careful scientific methods, we have selected a sample of business, government, and civic leaders in Jamaica. You have been selected as part of this sample. In a study such as this one, it is essential that we have the same questions answered by all those whom we include in our sample. For a proper statistical analysis we need rather complete descriptions of the personal backgrounds as well as the opinions of leaders. Please answer freely—no individual will be identified in any way.

In order to insure your anonymity, place your completed questionnaire in the envelope provided. Do not put any identifying mark on the questionnaire or on the first envelope into which you place it. Seal the envelope containing your questionnaire and then place it in the stamped, addressed envelope. The number on the outside of this envelope is for our clerical use in keeping a record of who has or has not returned his questionnaire. However, the envelopes are opened at different times and no identifying mark is placed either on the inside envelope or your questionnaire.

The information in the questionnaires will be coded and placed on IBM punch cards. The statistical analysis will be performed by an electronic computer (IBM 709) located at the Western Data Processing Center, University of California, Los Angeles. The book which will be published reporting the findings of this questionnaire study will contain no information which will identify any particular individual.

Your coöperation is greatly appreciated.

Very truly yours,

(signed) WENDELL BELL
Wendell Bell
Associate Professor

Local address:
INSTITUTE OF SOCIAL AND ECONOMIC RESEARCH
UNIVERSITY COLLEGE OF THE WEST INDIES
MONA, JAMAICA

Follow-up Letter

UNIVERSITY OF CALIFORNIA

Department of   JUNE 5, 1958
Anthropology and Sociology   (Actually posted on
Los Angeles 24, California   June 21, 1958)

DEAR SIR:

Some time ago we sent you a questionnaire in connection with our study of prominent persons living in Jamaica. May we remind you to return it to us in the self-addressed stamped envelope provided for the purpose at your earliest convenience.

Several persons have written or called us and enquired about our methods for protecting their identity. The following information is provided in case you have been concerned about the anonymity of your answers:

(1) The number on the return envelope is used by us to determine which persons have returned their questionnaires. Once we have checked the number against our lists, the envelope is discarded. This is done *before the next envelope which contains the questionnaire is opened.*

(2) Some persons have said that after answering the personal data questions they have described themselves so fully that they could be identified by some people. *We can assure you that no such an identification can be made.* In the tables and figures presented in the report, *no tabulations will be made in such a way that a given individual can be identified.*

(3) May we remind you that the envelopes are not opened in Jamaica, but are sent directly to the staff coders at the University of California where the questionnaires are processed for machine tabulation.

If you have already returned your questionnaire, please disregard this letter.

Very truly yours,

(signed) WENDELL BELL
Wendell Bell
Associate Professor

Local Address:
INSTITUTE OF SOCIAL AND ECONOMIC RESEARCH
UNIVERSITY COLLEGE OF THE WEST INDIES
MONA, JAMAICA

Covering Letter for Second Wave of Questionnaires

UNIVERSITY OF CALIFORNIA

Department of
Anthropology and Sociology
Los Angeles 24, California

JUNE 10, 1958
(Actually posted on July
15th and 16th, 1958)

DEAR SIR:

Several persons have written or called in connection with the Jamaican Leadership Study saying that they had misplaced the questionnaires which we sent them. In the event that this is true in your case, we are enclosing another questionnaire for you. Please fill it out and return it at your earliest convenience. (According to our records, we have not yet received a questionnaire from you.)

Thank you again for your coöperation.

Very truly yours,

(signed) WENDELL BELL
Wendell Bell
Associate Professor

Local address:
INSTITUTE OF SOCIAL AND ECONOMIC RESEARCH
UNIVERSITY COLLEGE OF THE WEST INDIES
MONA, JAMAICA

Notes

NOTES

NOTES TO CHAPTER I: JAMAICA

[1] Frank Cundall, "The Aborigines of Jamaica," pamphlet reprinted from the *Handbook of Jamaica for 1933–34,* Kingston, Jamaica: Institute of Jamaica, 1934; Philip M. Sherlock, "The Aborigines of Jamaica," Kingston, Jamaica: Institute of Jamaica, 1939; Sven Lovén, *Origins of the Tainan Culture, West Indies,* Göteborg: Elanders Bokfryckeri Akfiebolag, 1935.

[2] Philip Ainsworth Means, *The Spanish Main, Focus of Envy, 1492–1700,* New York: Charles Scribner's Sons, 1935, p. 47.

[3] W. Adolphe Roberts, *Jamaica, The Portrait of an Island,* New York: Coward-McCann, Inc., 1955, p. 11.

[4] Roberts, *ibid.,* p. 13.

[5] Arthur Percival Newton, *The European Nations in the West Indies, 1493–1688,* London: A. and C. Black, Ltd., 1933, p. 63.

[6] Frank Cundall and Joseph L. Pietersz, *Jamaica under the Spaniards,* Kingston, Jamaica: Institute of Jamaica, 1919, p. 34.

[7] F. R. Augier, S. C. Gordon, D. G. Hall, and M. Reckord, *The Making of the West Indies,* London: Longmans, 1960; Lewis Hanke, *Aristotle and the American Indians,* London: Hollis and Carter, 1959; Salvador de Madariaga, *The Rise of the Spanish American Empire,* London: Hollis and Carter, 1947; Lesley Byrd Simpson, *The Encomienda in New Spain,* Berkeley and Los Angeles: University of California Press, 1950.

[8] J. H. Parry and P. M. Sherlock, *A Short History of the West Indies,* London: Macmillan & Co., Ltd., 1956, p. 24. (Quoted here and elsewhere by permission of authors and publisher.)

[9] R. B. Le Page and David De Camp, *Jamaican Creole,* London: Macmillan & Co., Ltd., 1960, p. 5.

[10] Le Page and De Camp, *ibid.,* p. 17.

[11] Le Page and De Camp, *ibid.,* p. 74.

[12] Melville J. Herskovits, *The Myth of the Negro Past,* New York: Harper and Brothers, 1941; K. Onuwuka Dike, *Trade and Politics in the Niger Delta, 1830–1885,* Oxford: Clarendon Press, 1956; and J. D. Fage, *An Introduction to the History of West Africa,* Cambridge: University Press, 1955.

[13] This discussion of immigration and racial composition follows Le Page and De Camp, *op. cit.,* pp. 85–96; Leonard Broom, "The Social Differentiation of Jamaica," *American Sociological Review,* 19 (April, 1954), pp. 115–125; and George W. Roberts, *The Population of Jamaica,* Cambridge: University Press, 1957, pp. 64–70. Also

211

see Andrew W. Lind, "Adjustment Patterns Among the Jamaican Chinese," *Social and Economic Studies,* 7 (June, 1958), pp. 144–164.

[14] *West Indies Population Census, 1960* (provisional), Bulletin No. 14 (Jamaica), Kingston, Jamaica, W.I.: Department of Statistics, 1962, p. 1.

[15] R. B. Davison, *West Indian Migrants,* London: Oxford University Press, 1962.

[16] Broom, *op. cit.,* p. 118. (Quoted here and elsewhere by permission of author and publisher.)

[17] M. G. Smith, "The Plural Framework of Jamaican Society," *The British Journal of Sociology,* 12 (September, 1961), pp. 249–262.

[18] These data are from the *Eighth Census of Jamaica and Its Dependencies, 1943 as* adapted by James T. Duke, "Equalitarianism among Emergent Elites in a New Nation," unpublished Ph.D. dissertation, University of California, Los Angeles, 1963. (Quoted by permission of author.)

[19] Smith, *op. cit.*

[20] W. J. Gardner, *A History of Jamaica,* London: T. Fisher Unwin, 2nd edition, 1909, p. 471.

[21] Hume Wrong, *Government of the West Indies,* Oxford: Clarendon Press, 1923, p. 43. (Quoted here and elsewhere by permission of the publisher.)

[22] Wrong, *ibid.,* p. 41.

[23] Wrong, *ibid.,* p. 38.

[24] Sir Alan Burns, *History of Nigeria,* London: George Allen and Unwin, Ltd., 1929; and Sir Harry H. Johnston, *A History of the Colonization of Africa by Alien Races,* Cambridge: University Press, 1930.

[25] Augier, Gordon, Hall, and Reckord, *op. cit.,* p. 157. (Quoted here and elsewhere by permission of authors and publisher.)

[26] Wrong, *op. cit.,* p. 58.

[27] Gardner, *op. cit.,* p. 275. Also see Wrong, *ibid.*

[28] Wrong, *op. cit.,* p. 130.

[29] George E. Eaton, "Trade Union Development and Labour Policy in Jamaica," unpublished paper, p. 9. Also, George E. Eaton, "Trade Union Development in Jamaica in the Perspective of the Role of Trade Unions in Underdeveloped Countries," unpublished dissertation, McGill University, Montreal, Canada, 1960.

[30] Wrong, *ibid.*

[31] O. W. Phelps, "Rise of the Labour Movement in Jamaica," *Social and Economic Studies,* 9 (December, 1960), p. 429.

[32] Eaton, "Trade Union Development and Labour Policy in Jamaica," *op. cit.,* p. 8.

[33] C. Paul Bradley, "Mass Parties in Jamaica: Structure and Organization," *Social and Economic Studies,* 9 (December, 1960), pp. 395–396. (Quoted here and elsewhere by permission of author and publisher.)

[34] M. G. Smith, "The Political Implications of Jamaican Social Structure," unpublished paper, pp. 5–6. (Quoted by permission of the author.)

[35] Bradley, *op. cit.,* p. 396.

[36] Smith, "The Political Implications of Jamaican Social Structure," *op. cit.,* p. 9.

[37] Bradley, *op. cit.,* p. 393.

[38] *West India Royal Commission Report,* London: His Majesty's Stationery Office, Cmd. 6607, 1945.

[39] *Handbook of Jamaica, 1961,* Jamaica: The Government Printing Office, 1961, pp. 47–48.

[40] *Handbook of Jamaica, 1961, ibid.,* p. 48.

[41] *The Daily Gleaner,* Kingston, Jamaica, October 4, 1961.

[42] *General Election, 1962,* Report of the Chief Electoral Officer, Kingston, Jamaica: The Government Printer, 1962, p. 4.

[43] Douglas Hall, *Free Jamaica, 1838–1865,* New Haven: Yale University Press, 1959, pp. viii–ix. (Quoted by permission of author and publisher.)

[44] *West India Royal Commission Report, op. cit.,* pp. 4–5.

[45] Augier *et al., op. cit.,* pp. 263–265.

[46] Augier *et al., ibid.,* p. 265.

[47] Augier *et al., ibid.,* p. 264.

[48] Augier *et al., ibid.,* p. 262.

[49] *West India Royal Commission Report, op. cit.,* p. 8.

[50] Augier *et al., op. cit.,* p. 283.

[51] Augier, *et al., ibid.,* p. 289.

[52] David Lowenthal (editor), *The West Indies Federation,* New York: Columbia University Press, 1961, Table III.

[53] *Economic Survey, Jamaica, 1961,* Central Planning Unit, Government of Jamaica, 1962, pp. 43–46.

[54] *Economic Survey, Jamaica, 1961, ibid.,* p. 55.

[55] *Economic Survey, Jamaica, 1961, ibid.,* pp. 26–27.

[56] G. E. Cumper, "The Development of the West Indies," in G. E. Cumper (editor), *The Economy of the West Indies,* Kingston: University College of the West Indies, 1960, pp. 22–23. (Quoted here and elsewhere by permission of author and publisher.)

[57] G. E. Cumper, "Employment and Unemployment in the West Indies," in Cumper (editor), *ibid.,* pp. 171–172. (Quoted here and elsewhere by permission of author and publisher.)

[58] *Economic Survey, Jamaica, 1961, op. cit.,* pp. 15–22.

[59] C. O'Loughlin, "Economic Structure in the West Indies," in G. E. Cumper (editor), *The Economy of the West Indies, op. cit.,* p. 105.

[60] Arthur Brown, "Economic Development and the Private Sector," *Social and Economic Studies,* 7 (September, 1958), pp. 103–113.

[61] W. Arthur Lewis, "Competition and Regulation in the West Indies," in Calvin B. Hoover (editor), *Economic Systems of the Commonwealth,* Durham, N.C.: Duke University Press, 1962, p. 507.

[62] Lewis, *ibid.,* p. 508.

[63] Brown, *op. cit.,* p. 105.

[64] Cumper, "The Development of the West Indies," *op. cit.,* p. 23.

NOTES TO CHAPTER II: GENERALIZING JAMAICA'S DEVELOPMENT

[1] Edward Hallett Carr, *What Is History?* New York: Alfred A. Knopf, 1962, pp. 30–31.

[2] Carr, *ibid.,* pp. 173–176.

[3] Elsa V. Goveia, *A Study on the Historiography of the British West Indies to the End of the Nineteenth Century,* Mexico: Instituto Panamericano de Geografía e Historia, 1956.

[4] I use "society" in a generic sense here to include all social relations whether political, economic, educational, religious, or whatever.

[5] For my discussion of scale, I am indebted to Godfrey and Monica Wilson, *The Analysis of Social Change,* Cambridge: University Press, 1954; and to Eshref Shevky,

see Eshref Shevky and Wendell Bell, *Social Area Analysis,* Stanford University Press, 1955, Chapter II, pp. 3–19.

⁶ J. H. Parry and P. M. Sherlock, *A Short History of the West Indies,* London: Macmillan & Co., Ltd., 1956, p. 1.

⁷ A chapter devoted to interclass hostility in Jamaica is given in James A. Mau, "Social Change and Belief in Progress: A Study of Images of the Future in Jamaica," unpublished Ph.D. dissertation, University of California, Los Angeles, 1963.

⁸ M. G. Smith, "The Plural Framework of Jamaican Society," *The British Journal of Sociology,* 12 (September, 1961), pp. 249–262.

⁹ Melville J. Herskovits, *The Myth of the Negro Past,* New York: Harper and Brothers, 1941, p. 62.

¹⁰ Freda Wolfson, *Pageant of Ghana,* London: Oxford University Press, 1958, pp. 146–147.

¹¹ M. G. Smith, "Slavery and Emancipation in Two Societies," *Social and Economic Studies,* 3 (December, 1954), pp. 269–270. (Quoted by permission of author and publisher.)

¹² Herskovits, *op. cit.,* p. 109 *et passim.*

¹³ For example, see George Francis Dow, *Slave Ships and Slaving,* Salem, Mass.: Marine Research Society, 1927; and J. D. Fage, *An Introduction to the History of West Africa,* Cambridge: University Press, 1955.

¹⁴ F. R. Augier, S. C. Gordon, D. G. Hall, and M. Reckord, *The Making of the West Indies,* London: Longmans, 1960, p. 74.

¹⁵ W. L. Burn, *Emancipation and Apprenticeship in the British West Indies,* London: Jonathan Cape, 1937; W. J. Gardner, *A History of Jamaica,* London: T. Fisher Unwin, 2nd edition, 1909; and Robert Worthington Smith, "The Conflict between Planter and Parliament over the Slave Laws of Jamaica," unpublished Ph.D. dissertation, University of California, Los Angeles, 1942.

¹⁶ Philip D. Curtin, *Two Jamaicas,* Cambridge: Harvard University Press, 1955, p. 81. (Quoted by permission of author and publisher.)

¹⁷ In Trinidad and British Guiana, the link to Asia through the East Indian population is also of significance.

¹⁸ From the autobiography of Captain Richard Drake, as given in Dow, *op. cit.,* p. 191.

¹⁹ See Goveia, *op. cit.;* and Curtin, *op. cit.*

²⁰ Reinhard Bendix, "National Citizenship of the Lower Classes: A Comparative Perspective," unpublished paper, pp. 2–3. (Quoted here and elsewhere by permission of the author.) I am greatly indebted to Professor Bendix for the conception of social change as including rising minimums of human rights. See his "Social Stratification and the Political Community," *Archives Européenes de Sociologie,* I (1960), pp. 181–210; and "The Lower Classes and the 'Democratic Revolution,'" *Industrial Relations,* 1 (October, 1961), pp. 91–116.

²¹ R. H. Tawney, *Equality,* London: George Allen and Unwin, Ltd., 1952, pp. 97–98.

NOTES TO CHAPTER III: WHO ARE JAMAICA'S LEADERS?

¹ Harold D. Lasswell, Daniel Lerner, and C. Easton Rothwell, *The Comparative Study of Elites,* Stanford: Stanford University Press, 1952.

² See S. F. Nadel, "The Concept of Social Elites," *International Social Science Bulletin,* 8 (No. 3, 1956), pp. 413–424.

³ Morely Ayearst, *The British West Indies, The Search for Self Government,* Wash-

ington Square: New York University Press, 1960; Charles Henry Kunsman, Jr., *Recent Developments in Representative Government in Jamaica, 1938–1953,* unpublished M.A. thesis, University of California, Berkeley, 1955; C. M. MacInnes, "Constitutional Developments of the British West Indies," in *Developments Towards Self-Government in the Caribbean,* The Hague, Bandun: W. van Hoeve, Ltd., 1955; Hume Wrong, *Government of the West Indies,* Oxford: Clarendon Press, 1923.

⁴ It should be noted that Jamaica moved slower and more carefully toward independence than most other new nations. There is no question but that this was beneficial in many ways. A large cadre of Jamaicans were trained for leadership in politics and the civil service and to a lesser extent in commerce and industry. One negative effect, however, was that the average person in Jamaica faced full independence in 1962 with less thrill and challenge than if independence had come rapidly rather than in gradual increments from 1944 to 1962. The drama of the political transformation was somewhat diffused by too many little events rather than a single climax. Some members of the Jamaican masses felt that they had been told they were getting freedom from colonialism so many times since 1944 that they were a bit cynical when independence finally came. As a result, the psychological impact of independence, although considerable, was less than it might have been.

⁵ *The Handbook of Jamaica for 1939,* Kingston, Jamaica: The Government Printing Office, 1939; *The Handbook of Jamaica for 1954,* Kingston, Jamaica: The Government Printing Office, 1954; *Who's Who and Why in Jamaica 1939–40,* Second Edition, compiled and published by L. A. Thoywell Henry, Kingston, Jamaica: The Gleaner Co., Ltd.; *Who's Who, Jamaica, 1954,* edited by Clifton Neita, Kingston, Jamaica: The Gleaner Co., Ltd., 1954.

⁶ Of course from the point of view of non-Jamaicans, the top governmental elites became more exclusive rather than less so, since Jamaican nationality status, although in a sense being achieved by Jamaicans through political change, was emergent as an ascriptive criteria for membership in the governmental elite group. At the same time, the need for persons possessing certain specialized and differentiated skills in connection with economic and social development (e.g., in the bauxite industry and the University College of the West Indies) increased the number of non-Jamaicans among some types of elite groups.

⁷ The facts are somewhat more complicated than this statement suggests in that for about two decades it was believed that Jamaica would become independent as part of a nation larger in geographical scale than the boundaries of Jamaica itself. An independent West Indies Federation was to include nine other British territories in the Caribbean as well (see Chapter VI). Thus, a few non-Jamaican West Indians also moved into elite roles in Jamaica as part of the transition to independence. Now that Jamaica has reached independence on its own, we can expect such roles to be further "Jamaicanized" rather than "West Indianized." This may be accomplished in part, however, by some non-Jamaican West Indians opting to become Jamaican citizens under the new Constitution.

⁸ The 1943 percentages are estimates based on data given in the *Eighth Census of Jamaica and its Dependencies, 1943,* Kingston, Jamaica: The Government Printer, 1945, Table 10, p. 6. Unfortunately, comparable data for the entire population in 1960 were not available at the time of writing.

⁹ Also, membership in the two major parties became more acceptable to many educated people since the PNP deëmphasized its early socialism and since the demogogic rule of the charismatic leader of the JLP gave ground to a more bureaucratic and democratic party organization. See C. Paul Bradley, "Mass Parties in Jamaica:

Structure and Organization," *Social and Economic Studies,* 9 (December, 1960), pp. 375–416.

[10] *Eighth Census of Jamaica and its Dependencies, 1943, op. cit.,* Table 70, p. 127; and *West Indies Population Census, 1960* (provisional), Bulletin No. 20 (Jamaica), Kingston, Jamaica: Department of Statistics, 1962, Table 6, p. 70, and Table 7, p. 86.

[11] An intergenerational measure was used, if possible, which was based upon the relationship between an elite's occupation and his father's occupation. If the father's occupation was not given, a measure of career mobility was used based upon the relationship between an elite's first reported job and his present job. Where possible, both measures were examined in order to increase the validity of the measure. The occupational rating scale used is given in Appendix I.

[12] *Eighth Census of Jamaica and its Dependencies, 1943, op. cit.,* Table 21, p. 22; and *West Indies Population Census, 1960* (provisional), Bulletin No. 18 (Jamaica), Kingston, Jamaica: Department of Statistics, 1962, Table 1, p. 1. For a more detailed discussion of the data given in Tables 1 and 2, see Emily Roberta Smith (Reed), "Self-Government and the Political Elite in Jamaica, 1939 and 1954," unpublished M.A. thesis, Northwestern University, Evanston, Ill., 1957.

[13] Leonard Broom, "The Social Differentiation of Jamaica," *American Sociological Review,* 19 (April, 1954), p. 125.

[14] David Granick, *The European Executive,* New York: Doubleday, 1962.

[15] Since the University of the West Indies (UWI) was a coöperative service including not only Jamaica but each of the former territories of the West Indies Federation and British Guiana and British Honduras as well, "West Indianization" rather than "Jamaicanization" gives the appropriate frame of reference in this example. As of 1957, only 38 per cent of the entire University staff and even less, 26 per cent, of the University teaching staff were West Indians. Only in the nonteaching, administrative roles did West Indians outnumber non–West Indians; the former occupied 71 per cent of these positions, according to a mimeographed University report.

[16] A summary of the qualifications of MHR's in *The Handbook of Jamaica for 1958* (p. 40) says that an MHR had to reside in the parish that contained the constituency in which he stood for election; however, the relevant clause in the Constitution (p. 60 of *The Handbook*) states only that residence in the island of Jamaica was necessary.

[17] For example, see Wendell Bell, Richard J. Hill, and Charles R. Wright, *Public Leadership,* San Francisco: Chandler Publishing Co., 1961, Chapter Three, "Male Dominance in Public Leadership," pp. 34–55.

[18] *West Indies Population Census, 1960* (provisional), Bulletin No. 14 (Jamaica), Kingston, Jamaica: Department of Statistics, 1962, Table 4, p. 27.

[19] There appears to be a discrepancy between the data given here showing the percentage of lawyers who were Jewish in 1958 as 3 per cent and data given by Broom for 1951 which showed 7.1 per cent of the lawyers as being Jews. It is likely that the apparent discrepancy is accounted for in part by the differences in the methods used to sample the lawyers at the two time periods. For 1951, Broom selected a sample from a list of all barristers and solicitors in residence and in practice given in the *Handbook of Jamaica,* and then used informants to determine ethnicity. For 1958, I tried to select only those barristers and solicitors who were among the more powerful or prominent ones, and used *Who's Who* information to determine religion. Also, another difference is that I classified elites by their major activity. Thus, I did not classify all solicitors as solicitors but called some of them economic elites, since

their major activity was in the economic sphere. In my data, Jews were overrepresented among people who were qualified solicitors whose major activity was not practicing law but was engaging in commercial activities. *Cf.* Broom, *op. cit.,* p. 124.

[20] James T. Duke has completed a study of students at UWI, "Equalitarianism Among Emergent Elites in a New Nation," unpublished Ph.D. dissertation, University of California, Los Angeles, 1963.

[21] Personal communication.

[22] For a discussion of the social participation approach to the study of influence, see Bell, Hill and Wright, *op. cit.*

[23] The complete questionnaire is given in Appendix III.

[24] The validity of this list of top influentials was tested by going over the list with a few key informants who were themselves among the top 72 influentials. With two or three exceptions, there was general agreement that this list was an accurate ranking. Also, during the winter of 1961–1962, another list of reputational leaders was compiled relying solely on interviewing and working with the entire list of influentials when a respondent was doing the ranking. If one makes allowances for deaths between 1958 and 1962 and for the rise of a few new influentials in 1962 who were not on the scene in 1958, the lists are quite similar. See Charles C. Moskos, Jr., "The Sociology of Political Independence: A Study of Influence, Social Structure, and Ideology in the British West Indies," unpublished Ph.D. dissertation, University of California, Los Angeles, 1963.

[25] Moskos, *ibid.*

[26] Broom, *op. cit.,* p. 125.

[27] Broom, *ibid.,* pp. 123–124.

NOTES TO CHAPTER IV: WHAT KIND OF SOCIAL STRUCTURE SHOULD JAMAICA HAVE?

[1] Wendell Bell and Ivar Oxaal, *Decisions of Nationhood: Political and Social Development in the British Caribbean,* Denver, Col.: Social Science Foundation, University of Denver, 1964. For a study of how seven of the big decisions were made in the new nation of Trinidad and Tobago, see Ivar Oxaal, "West Indian Intellectuals in Power: A Study in the Sociology of Knowledge and Power," unpublished Ph.D. dissertation, University of California, Los Angeles, 1963.

[2] For a methodological discussion of this index and a review of findings, see James A. Mau, "Scale Analyses of Status Perceptions and Status Attitudes in Jamaica and the United States," unpublished M.A. Report, University of California, Los Angeles, 1960; James A. Mau, Richard J. Hill, and Wendell Bell, "Scale Analyses of Status Perception and Status Attitude in Jamaica and the United States," *Pacific Sociological Review,* 4 (Spring, 1961), pp. 33–40; Ivar P. Oxaal, *Social Stratification and Personnel Turnover in the Hospital,* Columbus, Ohio: Engineering Experiment Station, The Ohio State University, 1960; Melvin Seeman, "Social Mobility and Administrative Behavior," *American Sociological Review,* 23 (December, 1958), pp. 633–642; Melvin Seeman, *Social Status and Leadership: The Case of the School Executive,* Columbus, Ohio: Bureau of Educational Research and Service, The Ohio State University, 1960; Melvin Seeman with the assistance of Richard T. Morris, *A Status Factor Approach to Leadership,* Columbus, Ohio: Personnel Research Board, The Ohio State University, multilithed, no date; Melvin Seeman and John W. Evans, "Stratification and Hospital Care: I. The Performance of the Medical Interne,"

American Sociological Review, 26 (February, 1961), pp. 67–80; Fred B. Silberstein and Melvin Seeman, "Social Mobility and Prejudice," *American Journal of Sociology,* 65 (November, 1959), pp. 258–264.

[3] Mau, *ibid.*

[4] Louis Guttman, "A Basis for Scaling Quantitative Data," *American Sociological Review,* 9 (April, 1944), pp. 139–150; Guttman, "The Cornell Technique for Scale and Intensity Analysis," *Educational and Psychological Measurements,* 7 (Summer, 1947), pp. 247–280; and Chapters 2 and 3 in S. A. Stouffer *et al., Measurement and Prediction,* Princeton, N.J.: Princeton University Press, 1950, pp. 46–90.

[5] The minimum marginal reproducibility was erroneously reported as .52 in Mau, Hill, and Bell, *op. cit.*

[6] For the purpose of comparing subgroups later on in this paper, the distribution on the Index of Equalitarianism was divided arbitrarily at about the median. Thus, scale types one through five were combined and leaders having these responses were designated "nonequalitarians," as shown in Table 13. It should be kept in mind, however, that these scale types include the strongly antiequalitarians as well as the more moderate persons. Scale types six through eight are combined and leaders having these responses were designated "equalitarians." From Table 13, this dichotomization results in 54.1 per cent of the Jamaican leaders being classified as equalitarians and 45.9 per cent being classified as nonequalitarians.

[7] In a study in progress, Duke, using this same Index of Equalitarianism, finds students at the University of the West Indies in 1961 more favorable toward economic and social equality than Jamaican leaders in 1958. James T. Duke, "Equalitarianism Among Emergent Elites in a New Nation," unpublished Ph.D. dissertation, University of California, Los Angeles, 1963.

[8] See Chapter VII.

[9] Of course, the increased participation of women in leadership roles is itself a part of the trend toward equality. We often forget that women are still the largest "minority" group in most every country and that sex as an ascriptive barrier to equal access to social institutions and social roles is far from eliminated. For example, see Wendell Bell, Richard J. Hill, and Charles R. Wright, *Public Leadership,* Chapter III, "Male Dominance in Public Affairs," San Francisco: Chandler Publishing Co., 1961.

[10] Stefan Nowak, "Egalitarian Attitudes of Warsaw Students," *American Sociological Review,* 25 (April, 1960), pp. 219–231.

[11] Of course, this is not to say that a correlation between education and attitudes toward equality, such as that shown by these data, would exist everywhere, especially outside the area of dominance of Western civilization.

[12] Among the problems confronting bold governmental actions designed to increase economic and social equality were the facts that the electorate approached a 50–50 split between the two major parties and that both parties depended on support from all social classes, although somewhat differentially. The 50–50 split promoted compromise programs within both parties, because in such a close political situation neither party could afford, or so the leaders thought, to do without all the support that it could get. Middle-of-the-road policies, compromises of ideology, and inconsistent action resulted. This would be less necessary if the labor unions all supported one party and the economic dominants supported another party.

[13] Reinhard Bendix, "National Citizenship of the Lower Classes: A Comparative Perspective," unpublished paper.

[14] For a discussion of educational policies in Jamaica, see Duke, *op. cit.* Also of

relevance is the discussion of educational reform in England by David V. Glass, "Education," in Morris Ginsberg (editor), *Law and Opinion in England in the 20th Century,* London: Stevens & Sons, Ltd., 1959, pp. 319–346.

[15] Gunnar Myrdal, *Economic Theory and Underdeveloped Regions,* London: Gerald Duckworth & Co., Ltd., 1957, p. 121. Emphasis provided.

NOTES TO CHAPTER V: SHOULD JAMAICA HAVE A DEMOCRATIC POLITICAL SYSTEM?

[1] This chapter is a revised version of a paper read at the annual meetings of the American Sociological Association, New York, N.Y., August 29–31, 1960, under the title, "Political Cynicism Among Elites in a New Nation."

[2] Of course, another major justification for independence was that it would bring an end to economic exploitation resulting from colonial imperialism, and would permit economic advancement and an increase in economic benefits to the general population. Thus, political developments resulting in self-government were viewed not only as being consistent with democratic theory, but also as conferring new and proper economic rights on the indigenous population. The economic justification for political independence and its implications for conceptions of rights and duties of the lower classes are the subjects of detailed research by Andrew P. Phillips, "The Development of a Modern Labor Force in Antigua," unpublished Ph.D. dissertation, University of California, Los Angeles, 1963.

[3] Charles R. Nixon and Dwaine Marvick, "Active Campaign Workers: A Study of Self-Recruited Elites," paper read at the annual meetings of the American Political Science Association, September, 1956; Dwaine Marvick, "Active Campaign Workers: The Power Structures of Rival Parties," unpublished paper, University of California, Los Angeles, mimeographed; and Dwaine Marvick, "The Middlemen of Politics," paper read at the annual meetings of the American Political Science Association, Washington, D.C., September, 1962. In Marvick's most recent paper he refines the interpretation of the Index of Political Cynicism and emphasizes that it may primarily measure a belief in the "efficacy of manipulative strategies."

[4] Nixon and Marvick, *ibid.*

[5] For another measure of political cynicism, see Robert E. Agger, Marshall N. Goldstein, and Stanley A. Pearl, "Political Cynicism: Measurement and Meaning," *The Journal of Politics,* 23 (August, 1961), pp. 477–506. Agger *et al.* do not attempt to measure the attitudes of elites toward the electorate, but instead focus on the general population's attitudes toward politicians and politics.

[6] Not all elites who were solicitors were classified as legal elites in Table 20. This was because some solicitors were primarily engaged in some activity other than law, such as economic-commercial activity, and they were thus classified, as before.

[7] In Jamaica the situation may have been less complex than in some other new nations, particularly in Africa, where the existence of a traditional tribal leadership added still another dimension.

[8] This follows from the discussion of increasing total power given in Chapter II. Thus, it is quite correct to distinguish between changing *relative* power on the one hand, that is the changing *proportion* of total power that any individual or group has, and changing *absolute* power on the other, that is the changing *amounts* of power that an individual or group has. When this distinction is made, it appears that the established former elites in Jamaica definitely lost relative power during the transition

to independence, but many of the same elites increased in actual amount of power; that is, such elites had a smaller proportion of a much bigger totality.

[9] Although Agger, Goldstein, and Pearl, *op. cit.*, define political cynicism somewhat differently and although their sample is altogether different, some of their findings suggest that the relationship between powerlessness and cynicism may be quite general. They report that persons who feel politically impotent are considerably more politically cynical by their measure than persons who feel politically potent. Also, persons with more political discussion with friends and party activists are less cynical than persons with less such discussion. They report that the relationship between cynicism and amount of political activity depends upon political party preference. Also, Marvick, "Active Campaign Workers . . . ," *op. cit.*, reports a relationship between power and political cynicism, but political party preference is a specifying variable. Among the Democrats cynicism was positively correlated with power, and among the Republicans cynicism was negatively correlated with power. In Jamaica, cynicism is negatively correlated with influence within each of the major political parties.

[10] See James A. Mau, "Social Change and Belief in Progress: A Study of Images of the Future in Jamaica," unpublished Ph.D. dissertation, University of California, Los Angeles, 1963.

[11] Reinhard Bendix, "The Lower Classes and the 'Democratic Revolution,'" *Industrial Relations,* 1 (October, 1961), p. 91. Of course, the ideas underlying some of the political developments in Jamaica can be traced back much further than the developments of the eigtheenth century. Strands of the modern democratic state lead back to Graeco-Roman civilization and to the origins of Christianity. For example, see A. D. Lindsay, *The Modern Democratic State,* New York: Oxford University Press, a Galaxy book, 1962.

[12] Bendix, *ibid.,* p. 92.

[13] From Disraeli's novel *Sybil* as quoted in Bendix, *ibid.,* p. 109.

[14] The strong *positive* relationship between cynicism about the electorate and amount of education among Jamaican *elites* found here can be contrasted with the strong *negative* relationship between cynicism about politicians and politics and amount of education among a sample of the *general population* in Oregon reported by Agger, Goldstein, and Pearl, *op. cit.* Since the measures of cynicism and the samples are quite different, one can't say whether these findings are really contradictory or not.

[15] Strictly speaking, this does not apply necessarily to the nominated persons, but such persons were increasingly dependent upon the politicians for appointment, thus indirectly are increasingly dependent upon the electorate.

[16] For an excellent analysis of some of these apparently unreasonable responses among Jamaican small farmers, see David Edwards, *Report on an Economic Study of Small Farming in Jamaica,* Glasgow: The University Press, 1961.

[17] There were a few exceptions to this. For example, Catholic religious leaders "understandably" opposed the adoption of birth control measures even though such measures appeared to be useful in achieving progress.

[18] In my opinion this raises a most important moral issue for social scientists: the responsibility we have for the consequences of our scientific work, pure or applied. Although a great deal has been written on this subject, we are now confronted by new situations, greater challenges, more general acceptance of our work, and the possibility that we may soon be in positions of responsibility that exceed the most

visionary predictions of a few years ago. Perhaps nowhere is this so apparent than in the emergent nations. In them, the social scientist feels that someone is always listening in on him, and that someone may really act on what he says. Political scientists have helped to write constitutions, economists have helped to write plans for development and defined the rules for thinking about economic growth, and sociologists have devised the most effective ways of getting people to adopt new practices as desired by government or business. The canons of science are inadequate guides for the social scientist who engages in such activities. What we urgently need is more discussion of the social role of the social scientist and a formulation of a set of ethics that would define the *proper* behavior for the social scientist in relation to his various existing and emergent "clienteles."

[19] Gunnar Myrdal, *Economic Theory and Underdeveloped Regions,* London: Gerald Duckworth & Co., Ltd., 1957. For an interpretation of the industrial revolution in England which documents the rising benefits and increasing material well-being of the working classes, and therefore which supports the circular theory of economic growth, see Dorothy George, *England in Transition,* Penguin Books, 1962.

[20] By 1962 this difference between the two parties, however, had been all but eliminated. The PNP had become more pragmatic, to the disillusionment of many of its followers, and the JLP had become more explicit and rationalistic in formulating its image of future progress in Jamaica, and thereby became more acceptable to Jamaican intellectuals and other educated persons among the middle classes.

[21] James S. Coleman, "The Political Systems of the Developing Areas," in Gabriel A. Almond and James S. Coleman (editors), *The Politics of the Developing Areas,* Princeton, N.J.: Princeton University Press, 1960, pp. 532–576.

NOTES TO CHAPTER VI: SHOULD JAMAICA BE POLITICALLY INDEPENDENT?

[1] James S. Coleman, *Nigeria, Background to Nationalism,* Berkeley and Los Angeles: University of California Press, 1958, p. 412.

[2] *Ibid.,* p. 425.

[3] For a more detailed discussion of this, see Wendell Bell, "Attitudes of Jamaican Elites Toward the West Indies Federation," *Annals of the New York Academy of Sciences,* 83 (January, 1960), pp. 862–79. Also, Charles C. Moskos, Jr. has done a more thorough analysis of the rise of nationalism in the West Indies, and his data show that the territorial scale of nationalist attitudes among elites was determined in part by elites' cultural orientations. See Moskos, "The Sociology of Political Independence: A Study of Influence, Social Structure, and Ideology in the British West Indies," unpublished Ph.D. dissertation, University of California, Los Angeles, 1963.

[4] Frank Hill, "JLP, PNP Bulwarks of Two-party System," *Jamaica: Its People and Institutions,* Kingston, Jamaica: Gleaner Independence Supplement—3, July 28, 1962, p. 20.

[5] The causes that I specify are *individual* characteristics. That is, they refer to attributes of individuals and they explain, it is hypothesized, the rise of nationalism as manifested in individual nationalist attitudes. Thus, in this study, I'm searching for an explanation of variations in nationalist–antinationalist attitudes between individuals within a single country. Such variables can be aggregated, of course, in several ways to permit comparisons of levels or averages by countries. However, if one were primarily

concerned with the *aggregate* or *unit* level, that is with why nationalism arose in one country at a certain time and not in another country, for example, then one might formulate some other set of causal variables than the ones specified here, variables that more distinctly reflect the unit or contextual level of analysis. In a sense, this is what Karl W. Deutsch has done in his discussion of nationalism, which is largely cast in an intercountry context with some aggregation of people as the basic unit of analysis. Thus, he specifies such variables as the *rate* of assimilation, the *rate* of mobilization, *similarity* of communications habits, etc. The two approaches should prove mutually correcting, and in the long run, of course, mutually compatible. See Deutsch, *Nationalism and Social Communication,* New York: John Wiley, 1953.

[6] For the organization and discussion of historical materials by types of nationalism —humanitarian, Jacobin, traditional, liberal, and integral—I am indebted to Carleton J. H. Hayes, and I have simply paraphrased him in several places. See Hayes, *The Historical Evolution of Modern Nationalism,* New York: Macmillan, 1950.

[7] Hayes, *ibid.,* p. 51.

[8] Hans Kohn, *American Nationalism,* New York: Macmillan, 1957, p. 8.

[9] *Loc. cit.,* italics supplied.

[10] Kohn, *ibid.*

[11] Hayes, *op. cit.,* pp. 134–135.

[12] Hayes, *ibid.,* p. 159.

[13] Hayes, *ibid.,* p. 163.

[14] Hayes, *ibid.*

[15] Of course, civil and political rights may be abrogated with no beneficial effect upon economic progress whatsoever, as I pointed out in Chapter V. Also, the maintenance of civil, political, economic, social, and cultural rights can contribute to, rather than detract from, national power by increasing the commitment of the people to the nation, by heightening the motivation of people to achieve, by adding to the development of human resources, and by making the distribution of talent and skills throughout the social system approach the optimum. Thus the relationship between "freedom" and "power" is not entirely clear. Interestingly, the campaign slogan of the JLP in Jamaica was "Freedom" and that of the PNP, "Power," although the relative emphasis on these two goals by the different parties is not thereby adequately expressed.

[16] Since education is one of the factors that affects equalitarian attitudes, it should be stated that the relationship between equalitarianism and nationalist attitudes holds up even with amount of education controlled.

[17] The percentages of elites who had nationalist attitudes by political cynicism were practically identical with such percentages by equalitarianism.

[18] Moskos, *op. cit.,* in his larger and more detailed study of the meaning of West Indian nationalism has elaborated and refined these hypotheses. One of his major contributions is the formulation of different types of nationalists.

NOTES TO CHAPTER VII: WHAT SHOULD JAMAICA'S GLOBAL ALIGNMENTS BE?

[1] Data are from the 1958 mail questionnaire survey. See Appendices II and III.

[2] Since a respondent may give more than one reason, the total of the percentages may exceed 100 per cent. But each reason given by the respondents was classified just once.

[3] The Chaguaramas issue was even more of a problem for Trinidad–U.S. relations than for Jamaica–U.S. relations. See Ivar Oxaal, "West Indian Intellectuals in Power: A Study in the Sociology of Knowledge and Power," unpublished Ph.D. dissertation, University of California, Los Angeles, 1963.

[4] Gordon K. Lewis, "The U.S. and the Americas: How Not to Make Friends," *Sunday Gleaner* (Kingston), May 25, 1958, p. 10.

[5] Encyclopaedia Britannica, Inc., *Book of the Year,* 1959, p. 418.

[6] *Daily Gleaner,* October 7, 1958. Jamaica received relatively little in the way of grants and loans from the United States. During the 1957 fiscal year the United States gave the entire West Indies Federation only $1,290,000 compared with $316,-257,000 for Korea, $99,243,000 for Taiwan, $18,466,000 for Japan, $17,039,000 for Brazil, $8,873,000 for Hungary, and $4,503,000 for Haiti, to mention but a few examples. See U.S. Department of Commerce, Office of Business Economics, *Foreign Grants and Credits by the United States Government,* June, 1958, Quarter.

[7] It should be borne in mind that the "least favorable" attitudes for any subgroup which are discussed here are *relative* to the attitudes of other subgroups, and that in no case does the percentage of elite respondents favoring the United States fall below 53 per cent. Thus, the majority of persons in every subgroup still felt that the United States has been morally right more often than the USSR.

[8] The differential character of the PNP when compared with the JLP may account for this difference. The PNP was more likely than the JLP to appeal to the younger person, the highly educated person, and the salaried professional rather than the businessman. Such persons were likely to be friendly to but critical of many policies of the United States. Also, the ideology of the PNP reflected at that time "progressivism," which will be discussed below. This is not to suggest that the PNP was Communistic. It was not. In Jamaica there were very few known Communists, although they were not persecuted. Generally, they exercised their rights like other citizens without fear or prejudice. Nevertheless, in 1952 the PNP removed from its ranks a leftist group that had achieved considerable power in the party.

[9] Where the number of cases permitted, education was introduced as a test variable between each of the other independent variables and attitudes toward the United States. In all cases except one, the relationships remained about the same. In the case of income, it was found that among poorly educated respondents high incomes resulted in more favorable attitudes toward the United States, but among the better educated respondents high incomes resulted in less favorable attitudes.

[10] Lyle W. Shannon (editor), *Underdeveloped Areas,* New York, 1957, p. 11.

[11] *The Jamaica Weekly Gleaner,* Friday, March 1, 1963, pp. 3–4.

[12] See Charles C. Moskos, Jr., and Wendell Bell, "Emergent Caribbean Nations Face the Outside World," *Social Problems,* forthcoming.

NOTES TO CHAPTER VIII: CONCLUSION

[1] Moskos presents data that show the distribution of commitment to Enlightenment values among Jamaican and other West Indian leaders, and he shows how such values entered into the development of West Indian nationalism. Charles C. Moskos, Jr., "The Sociology of Political Independence: A Study of Influence, Social Structure, and Ideology in the British West Indies," unpublished Ph.D. dissertation, University of California, Los Angeles, 1963.

NOTES TO APPENDIX II

[1] *Who's Who, Jamaica, 1957,* Kingston, Jamaica: The Gleaner Co., Ltd., n.d.

[2] *Who's Who, Jamaica, 1957, ibid.,* p. 5.

[3] See Appendix III for a copy of the questionnaire and the covering and follow-up letters.

[4] As stated in Chapter III, each person was classified by only one elite position. In the case of government elites, their government position was used as the basis for classification and their other elite positions were not considered. Among other things, this accounts for the lack of labor leaders, since several of the elected political leaders are also labor leaders, but are classified as political and not as labor leaders in Table A1. For the other types of elites, the major position was used as a basis for this classification if the elite in question held more than one elite position.

Index

INDEX

227